JOURNEY THROUGH A SEASON

JOURNEY THROUGH A SEASON

IAN HALL

The Breedon Books
Publishing Company
Derby

First published in Great Britain by
The Breedon Books Publishing Company Limited
Breedon House, 44 Friar Gate, Derby, DE1 1DA.
1997

By the same author (with John Found)
Cricket at Scarborough: A social history of the club and its festival
(Breedon Books).

ISBN 1 85983 109 5

Printed and bound by Butler & Tanner Ltd., Selwood Printing Works, Caxton
Road, Frome, Somerset.

Colour separations by RPS Ltd, Leicester.

Jackets printed by Lawrence-Allen, Weston-super-Mare, Avon.

Contents

Acknowledgements
The team at BBC Radio Derby Sport.
The team at the Baseball Ground.

This book is dedicated to
Derby County travellers.

'In winter football is a useful
and charming exercise. It is a
leather ball about as big as
one's head, filled with wind.
This kick'd about from one to
t'other end in the streets, by
him that can get it, and that is
all the art of it.'

Francois Misson, *Memoirs of
Travels in England* (1697).

Introduction

SEASON 1996-97 was Derby County's first in the Premiership. The last time the Rams were in the top flight of English football was in 1990-91, when they were relegated from the old First Division of the Football League. That was when Robert Maxwell, having been credited earlier with rescuing it from disaster, almost sent the club into oblivion and many people thought that the Baseball Ground 'roar' would be silenced. Now it is silent — forever.

The last-ever season at the Baseball Ground was always going to be an historic milestone. When the final curtain fell on more than 100 years of football — played on a pitch labelled many things in its time — memories remain. Some are bitter; some are sweet; a few are sad; but all are treasured. The unique atmosphere of the Baseball Ground, with its special magic on floodlit cup nights, has thrilled us all. That is now in the past. A new ground is where Derby County's future lies.

After the Hillsborough tragedy of 1989, the recommendations of the Taylor Report led to changes in football ground architecture which has altered the face of English football. Watching football is now a different experience and a new football culture is developing.

There is no doubt that today's modern stadiums have enhanced the image of the game and even Old Trafford, the 'Theatre of Dreams', has close rivals in Anfield, Highbury and Villa Park. All are superb places to visit. The pitches, too, are immaculate, far, far, far removed from the notorious Baseball Ground mud of old.

This book is not about the Baseball Ground, although, of course, it gets an honourable mention. It is more about journeys to Goodison Park, Stamford Bridge, Elland Road, St James' Park and all the other splendid stadiums of the post-Taylor era. It is about following the Rams away from home, as they played a season in the Premiership, for the first time.

This book is also a journey in time. The Leppings Lane End

terraces at Hillsborough, on which 96 Liverpool supporters died in 1989, is where I stood as a boy, to support Sheffield Wednesday. Later, boyhood dreams came true and I was fortunate to play on all the grounds that the Rams visited in 1996–97, apart from The Dell at Southampton. So when, at the start of the season, the opportunity arose to revisit many of the grounds that I hadn't seen for more than 30 years and witness, at first hand, the changes that have taken place, it was an experience not to be missed.

Naturally, this book contains anecdotes and personal memories. I make no apology for such indulgences. The great American sportswriter A.J. Leibling once wrote: "The world isn't going backwards, if you can stay young enough to remember what it was *really* like when you were really young."

A number of broader issues in football are discussed, as they arose during the season. Some football people have words to say as well. Most of all, though, this book is a story about survival in what has become the big money making business of the 1990s — Premiership football. It's about Derby County's battle to survive — and how they succeeded.

Ian Hall
Cromford
May 1997

Glory, Glory, Hallelujah

White Hart Lane
Wednesday, 21st August 1996

FOR the BBC Radio Derby commentary team, the journey down the motorway was uneventful. At the Little Chef at Brickett's Wood, we stopped for our customary pre-match meal: Olympic breakfast, several rounds of toast, plus tea or coffee. It's a far cry from the boiled fish, or boiled chicken, that was the staple pre-match meal for Derby County footballers when Harry Storer was manager. Then, I was just a junior professional and still wet behind the ears. Harry, on the other hand, was a tough, uncompromising, larger-than-life character, who often called a spade a shovel. Many tales were told about Harry Storer — and some were actually believed!

Harry Storer had played both cricket for Derbyshire and football for Derby County, during the 1920s and 1930s and he almost achieved the very rare distinction of double international status for England. He was good enough to win two caps for his country at football and Will Taylor, who was secretary of Derbyshire County Cricket Club for a total of 51 years and 149 days (1907–59), said that he was the best batsman the county ever had. Harry's father, Harry senior, had also played for Derbyshire and Derby County and his uncle, William Storer, had done the same. Furthermore, Uncle William made six appearances for England at cricket and toured Australia. To say that Harry Storer came from a sporting family is rather an understatement.

If Storer didn't manage to play cricket for England, at least he was a member of the Derbyshire team that won the County Championship in 1936 and, if you ever had a few hours to spare, he'd tell you about it! Amazingly, he managed Coventry City from 1931 onwards, which meant he was manager of a Football League club while still a county cricketer — and he was not slow to tell you about that either. Harry, you see, could talk the hind legs off a donkey and on any subject you cared to mention.

Around 1960, Harry Storer became friendly with Brian Clough. It was at a time when Clough was harbouring ideas of becoming a manager, when his playing days were over. Clough sometimes used to visit Storer at the team's hotel when Derby County were playing in the North-East. That, in itself, didn't concern us much, as even then, Clough had the reputation of being a 'one-off'. What did annoy us, though, was seeing Storer entertaining Clough at the directors' table. Clough, remember, was still a player in an era when every player was expected to know his place. That place certainly wasn't at the directors' table, it was at the other end of the dining room — with us.

Those visits confirmed our opinion that Clough B. was getting far too big for his boots. What is certain is that if Cloughie's boots were too big then, he certainly grew into them later, and some of his methods, especially when dealing with players, seemed to have their origins in those conversations with Harry Storer in the late 1950s and early '60s.

Hard, but fair, was Storer's motto. Sometimes the fairness was difficult to recognise, especially when you were dropped from the team. "I don't pick teams to lose," he would say, dismissively, when you plucked up enough courage to go to see him about it. "If you are good *enough*, I can't leave you out." With an emphasis on the word 'enough', there is still no answer to that. Courage, mental as well physical, was the first quality Storer looked for in a player. He didn't believe in too much technical analysis. "Yes, yes," he would bark impatiently, "but is he brave? Can he *play*?" Courage was also needed to get passed Bill.

Bill was Harry's dog. He used to lie at the bottom of the three steps that led down into the manager's office — and always on Friday mornings. Bill was a sort of husky, used by Belgian trawlermen as guard dogs because of their ferocity, or so Storer told us. "Have your leg off with one bite," said the senior pros and we believed them.

After all his years in the game, Storer was wise in the ways of football and footballers. He hardly ever pinned the teamsheet up on a Friday morning. That was a job delegated to chief scout Sammy Crooks. Storer, meanwhile, waited in his office — with Bill. We always knew when the teamsheet was about to be posted, because we could hear Sammy approaching. Sammy had been a flying right winger who played for England between the two world wars more times than Stanley Matthews, indeed more times than anybody except for the Arsenal captain, Eddie Hapgood. A slight, will o' the wisp figure, Sammy never lost his enthusiasm for football. He was 65 years old, going on ten, and still light as a feather on his feet. He used to wear little metal 'segs' in the toes and heels of his shoes, to protect them from wear, and you could hear them rattle on the concrete floor of the corridor that led to the Baseball Ground dressing-rooms, long before the all-purpose carpet of modern times was installed. Tip-tap, tip-tap, tip-tap. It sounded more like Sammy

Davis jnr than Sammy Crooks, but the sound signalled the death knell for somebody, especially if we'd lost the previous week.

What Storer well knew, of course, was that a player who had been dropped from the side would have steam coming out of his ears as he raced up the corridor to the office. That's were Bill came in. He was always there, in the office, waiting. Lying in his usual place, at the bottom of the three steps. He was there to upset the rhythm, change the pace, affect the concentration and, by the time you'd got past Bill, you had usually forgotten what you were there for in the first place. It was generally accepted that Storer knew far too much for junior professionals and most senior ones too — and what a defender Bill would have been!

Storer ran a very tight ship. Perhaps it was the effects of the war. Even trainer Ralph Hann used to eat the same pre-match meal as the players, just in case he had to play in an emergency. Ralph had put on about four stones in weight since his playing days, so quite what he could have done in an emergency is hard to imagine. On the other hand, it might have been Harry's way of saving a few bob. He was always on the lookout for employees spending unnecessary cash.

We travelled quite a lot by train then, especially to grounds which were near to main-line stations. The 6.33pm out of St Pancras on a Saturday night was frequently used, which meant we had dinner on the train. After dinner, Storer would examine the bill with a fine tooth comb and frighten the dining-car attendants to death. Any player who added lime to a glass of lager, had to pay for his own lime. "What 'ave we 'ere?" he would roar down the dining-car and we'd all shuffle our feet and pretend it wasn't us. Harry Storer didn't approve of 'sissy' drinks. He didn't believe in tips, either.

Nowadays, teams seldom travel by train. For this occasion, the first away match in the 1996-97 Premiership, the Rams had travelled the day before. As we made our way by hired car through the streets of north London, the Derby County players of this day were probably having a pre-match nap.

Colin Gibson, BBC Radio Derby's sports producer, likes to arrive at football grounds early. Usually, very early. Graham Richards, who has commentated on the Rams for nearly 20 years and more than 800 matches, is sufficiently familiar with this part of London not to have to give us the benefit of his skills with the A–Z street map. How he understands it, I don't know, but it has saved our bacon on many occasions on the way to relatively obscure destinations like The Valley, Griffin Park and Plough Lane. This time, though, there was no problem. We were bound for a far more imposing stadium. We were on our way to White Hart Lane, home of the mighty Tottenham Hotspur.

The last time I saw White Hart Lane was on Saturday, 27th October 1962. The following day, I got married. During the summer, Tim Ward had taken over from Harry Storer as the new manager of Derby County, and Tim didn't waste much time. Shortly after I had completed the cricket season with Derbyshire, he transferred me to Mansfield Town. The manager of the Stags was a former Rams legend, Raich Carter, who insisted that I got fit, quickly. So, it was a reserve team match at White Hart Lane on Saturday, a noon wedding on Sunday and back for training on Wednesday. Fit? Like a butcher's dog. There were no frills in 1962. Now, 34 years later, thankfully, we could take things more at our ease.

Three hours before kick-off, at 7.45pm, people were gathering around the stadium. Stewards in bright orange jackets had assembled in little groups to receive instructions. Police horses, with huge blinkers to protect their eyes, snorted impatiently, waiting. Programme sellers had already arranged their pitches, the owners of hot dog stalls were hard at work chopping onions, Londoners' voices sounded everywhere. The sounds and smells around White Hart Lane, as around all football grounds, never change. So, too, all the hustle and bustle, the sense of anticipation, the excitement, which is as much part of the occasion as the match itself. Some people deprive themselves of such pleasures. What great joys the 'new' football audience is missing, its privileged guests encased in glass executive boxes, whisked to and from the ground by silky limousines. They, poor souls, are deprived of the aromas that pervade the senses of ordinary supporters, on their way 't' match'. Such pungent odours are part and parcel of the special atmosphere of football, or are they really pongs and stenches? On such a balmy, late summer evening, the air around White Hart Lane hung heavy with the special smells of curries currying, sausages sizzling, onions frying — and horses.

The main gates at White Hart Lane are at the end of a short road leading to the cramped car-park, which is in front of the glass-fronted main entrance and reception area. We enquired about press and car-park passes. It was made clear to us that there was no car-park pass. It was equally clear that no amount of negotiating would secure one. It was not surprising. Tottenham is nearly as bad as Arsenal for having so few car-parking spaces. Despite that, it didn't prevent either club developing its stadium on existing sites, but that is a discussion for later. At about 4.15pm, the chief parking officer, sweating gently, allowed us to park temporarily, in order to unload the equipment.

The problem of car-parking at football grounds is a fairly recent phenomenon, but it is becoming an increasingly important issue. Not long ago, the Arsenal vice-chairman, David Dein, was reported to have made a trip to America to inspect stadiums there. He was asked by the president of one of the big American football teams, how many parking spaces there were at Highbury. "About 75," said Dein, embarrassed. "Jeez," said his American counterpart, misunderstanding completely, "we've only got 60 [thousand]."

Most American stadiums have been built on the edge of town. Ours are the product of a different culture. Historically, the Victorian age and urban growth shaped our football development and the result is that the majority of our grounds are fitted snugly in the middle of the communities that have grown up around them. Side streets around the ground have been as much a part of the football environment as the pitch itself and it is in that honeycomb of narrow streets that home supporters have their own spots for parking, along with tried and tested short cuts. In those side streets and alleyways, football has been discussed, argued and opinioned for more than a century, as special ways of getting to and from the match have evolved. All this has long been a part of English football culture. Perhaps the new stadiums with their concrete concourses and fast food outlets — a McDonalds is actually built into the new Kop at Anfield — will provide modern alternative meeting places to discuss and argue about the game, compared to the street corner pub, newsagent and local 'chippy'. The 'People's Game' is fast changing and no-one denies it. It needs to change. Traditional ties are loosening and football is preparing to enter the 21st century, but change for its own sake can be a dangerous pastime and it does no harm to pay due regard to A. J. Leibling's words of caution about the lessons history can teach us: "There is still a kick in style, and tradition carries a nasty wallop."

Once the press passes were acquired, the arrangements followed the usual pattern. Our equipment was taken inside, Colin began the task of preparing for the programme and Graham and I disappeared, to explore the neighbourhood. Many years ago, Graham taught at a school in this vicinity and on the premiss that he knew the area well, we took the car to find the Lea Valley Canal. Ten minutes later we were hurriedly reversing out of a one-way street, to the sounds of heavy rap music and the snarls of scurvy hounds. A period of trial and error followed, before we eventually arrived at the canal, hard by a scrapyard which looked like the set for a series of *Steptoe and Son*. Salubrious it wasn't, but the drinks in the pub were cool. So, too, were some of the characters who were lounging on the canal bank side, fishing. They didn't look at all interested in football. The scene could have been a million miles away from White Hart Lane. In fact, it was less than a mile and a half.

As we made our way back, the side streets were filling up rapidly. Luckily, we found a spot near to the ground. It was also fairly close to a 'No Entry' sign and as we parked the car we were hailed by a local resident, dressed in flowing robes and a turban. "The 'Old Bill' sometimes tows cars away from 'ere, me old ducks," was the warning message. This time, we risked it.

To get a proper look at White Hart Lane, Graham and I walked around three sides of the ground. As a youngster in Sheffield, walking to a match at Hillsborough, or occasionally Bramall Lane, I used to think that a perfect place to live would be a few doors from a football ground. The problem of setting off so early to the match would be eliminated and, more important, my legs wouldn't ache. Later, when I realised how much litter is deposited after a football match and witnessed some of the damage caused to property by the hooligan element in the 1970s, I lost that urge to live next door to a football ground. Even so, as a junior at Wolves, I did taste the flavour by lodging at Eddie Clamp's mum's house, just a few doors from Molineux. She was one of the club's landladies in the days when Stan Cullis was the 'Master of Molineux' and Wolves won the League championship three times in nine years. Only once in that period did they finish outside the top three positions and, along with Manchester United, had the most productive youth policy in the country. Being late for training was not advisable in the Cullis era and lodging close to the ground had its advantages.

A player's first sight of the opposition ground, as the team coach approaches through thickening traffic, used to be the high floodlight pylons. That always brought a tingle to the spine, especially when the streets were crowded before a big match and police outriders provided an escort. Eric Kitchen, the Rams' regular coach driver, revelled in that situation. In modern times, a police escort is standard procedure and many grounds have floodlights sited along the roofs of massive stands. Floodlight pylons are less available as landmarks, even to those hardy souls who have seen a match played on every ground in England. They are members of the 92-Club.

Members of the 92-Club, are an elite group. My word, haven't they seen some changes? The club has a few honorary members, two of which have Derby County connections. Alan Durban is one, having played on all 92 League grounds. Jim Smith is the other. Smith has managed a team on all 92 grounds, in a career that has included being in charge of Colchester, Blackburn, Birmingham, Oxford, QPR, Newcastle, Portsmouth and Derby County, but even he is new to the Premiership and some of that competition's new-look grounds.

Since the Taylor Report, most grounds of the leading clubs have altered, in some cases almost beyond recognition. In any case, as a player, you only see them from the inside, which is a limited view. The outside is far more interesting. What impressed me most, as we wandered around outside White Hart Lane, was the friendliness of the people. Admittedly, it was more than an hour to kick-off and they were mostly Spurs fans, but the feeling of tension which so intimidated people in the hooligan days, was no longer apparent. I wonder how far the sale of replica shirts has contributed to that improved feeling? So many supporters, young, old, male, female, tall, short, round, thin, were wearing the Tottenham strip. It must be quite difficult to be aggressive towards someone dressed like you. As queues formed outside the turnstiles and the noise levels increased, even the police horses began to respond, stamping their huge feathered feet, massively powerful and impressive. By now, the burger bars were trading briskly and a buzz was in the air. A big match atmosphere and the Rams, back in the big time.

At the main car-park it was all action. The chief parking officer had moved into top gear. A heavily-built chap, with a sandy moustache and a perspiring brow, his eyes were sharp and everywhere. He was inspecting the comings and goings and was on guard for artful dodgers. He was assisted by several minions wearing earrings. Their main task was to park the vehicles of accredited people, who drew up outside the main reception area. When patrons swept in who were recognised, the chief parking officer was all sweetness and light. Less recognisable individuals were treated with suspicion, until credentials had been established.

Very occasionally, someone arrived who the chief parking officer considered merited his full attention. Such people were usually elderly, female and, most probably, rich. He parked their cars himself. Later, after the match, we discovered that the really high fliers had their own private parking sanctum, a barn-type garage at the side of the main entrance. The cars in there were extremely impressive indeed. They looked very, very expensive. One belonged to Alan Sugar. It was big.

The match ended in a 1-1 draw. The Rams equalised in injury time, through a Christian Dailly header and, just possibly, deserved to win. One sensed that many players, if not exactly in awe of White Hart Lane, were not familiar enough with such surroundings to feel really comfortable. Like guests at a wedding, they didn't really like imposing themselves too much. It was my first view of Aljosa Asanovic, other than on television, and he looked a class act. Whether he can sustain his commitment throughout an English winter remains to be seen, but that is true of all the foreign players that have flooded into our game.

Many of them have come from playing in leagues, rather like the Scottish League, that do not have the level of intensity, week in week out, which is such a feature of the professional game in England. Many a speedy horse runs in the Epsom Derby in June, but the question the professionals always ask is, "Will it stay the distance?" We shall see.

In the post- match analysis and in the newspaper reports of the match, one thing did surprise me. There was no criticism of the goal conceded by the Rams in the first half. A twice-taken free-kick on the edge of the penalty-area was struck by Teddy Sheringham to the side of the human wall. The shot went just inside the post, to Russell Hoult's left hand.

The object of having a human wall is to protect one side of the goal, so that the goalkeeper takes care of the other. Was Hoult worried about the chip over the top of the wall and over-positioned, or did he move early, a little the wrong way? Modern footballs do fly quickly and they do swing about. From the edge of the penalty-area, there is little time to react, but Sheringham's shot didn't go into the top corner, it went in halfway up the post. In my opinion, if the ball goes in the goalkeeper's side of the goal, at that height, he is partly to blame. No-one mentioned it.

After the match, the Rams were in buoyant mood. The first few matches in the Premiership are fraught with danger, as Bolton Wanderers found to their cost last season. After drawing with Leeds on the opening day of the season, the Rams have now played two games, are undefeated and with points in the bag. The talk in the corridors and the car-park afterwards was that of a team gaining in confidence. Not to be beaten in the first away match at White Hart Lane could be be a crucial step on the survival ladder. In north London, on a warm August evening, the Rams have earned respect. That, for every player, is most important.

In very simple terms, professional footballers seek two things. First, to see their name on the team sheet. Second, respect. Respect from the opposition; respect from team mates; respect from the manager and coaching staff; respect from supporters; from the media; from the football world and the sporting world at large. The pitch can be a lonely place.

What does bind a team together is the collective fear of humil-iation; of being publicly exposed by the opposition; of losing res-pect. Such a fear goes a long way to explaining why lower division sides, with the adrenalin pumping madly, occasionally play above themselves and upset their betters in cup competitions. They are desperate not to be made to look foolish and so lose respect. How else could York City win at Old Trafford last season, the only team to do so? At the other extreme, a poor performance sits so heavily in the pit of the stomach on a Saturday night, while defeat makes a poor performance worse.

After this match at White Hart Lane, the Rams management and players were happy. They were well aware that the Tottenham result would have been noted around the Premiership — and respected.

Team: Hoult; Parker (sub Flynn), Stimac, Rowett, Laursen, Dailly, D.Powell, Asanovic, C.Powell, Sturridge (sub Simpson), Gabbiadini (sub Willems).
Scorer: Dailly
Attendance: 28,219.

To The Manor Born

Villa Park — Saturday, 24th August 1996

THREE days after the Tottenham match, the Rams went to Villa Park to play Aston Villa. It took Sir Thomas Holte 17 years to build Aston Hall, where he resided as Lord of the Manor in the 17th century and it was on land once owned by Sir Thomas that Villa Park was built. Great stadiums deserve great players and it is satisfying to record that Edson Arantes do Nascimento once played at Villa Park. Edson Arantes do Nascimento is better known as Pele.

Pele was playing for Santos on a club tour of England in the 1960s and a few of us thought it would be a simple matter to go to see him in action. After all, Aston Villa versus Santos was only a friendly and we reckoned that if we got to the ground about an hour before the start, we would easily find a good spot on the terraces. How wrong we were. North Birmingham was thronged with people. Queues stretched around the ground, six deep. Seldom in a team sport can so many people have been so determined to see just one man play. By the time we had paid our money and struggled through the turnstiles, it was half-time.

I watched the second half from a position halfway up the Holte End terrace, but only by hanging on to the wrong side of a crash barrier, to avoid falling off a step. The floodlights had failed on one of the pylons and the semi-darkness at that end of the pitch added to the aura. More than 60,000 attended that night and Pele didn't disappoint them. Not that he did much, really. In fact, he did very little, but he imposed such a magnetic presence on proceedings that I'm sure an indelible impression was left on all who attended. Even today, you can sometimes hear, when football talk is in the air, a whisper by one person to another of the night they saw Pele play. They could be referring to an earlier match on that Santos tour in 1962, when from a penalty at the Spion Kop End at Hillsborough, Pele mesmerised Ron Springett with a samba shuffle, before dispatching the ball into the roof of the net, long before John Aldridge came on the scene. Usually, though, those whispers are about the night when Pele played at Villa Park and, at least for part of that night, I was there.

Why was Pele the greatest of all footballers? Hugh McIlvanney recognised that greatness transcends technical skill:

'The history of the game brims with great performances and unforgettable talents. But none of the others — not even the imperial Alfredo di Stefano, or the electrifying George Best — could pervade the field with quite the divine sense of superiority that radiated naturally from Pele at the height of his powers. His relationship with the ball was different from that achieved by anyone else. Other great footballers concentrated on mastering the ball and using it like a tool. For him it often seemed to be a living ally, dancing between and around his sprinting feet as if it chose to be there.' *World Cup Magazine* (Spring 1990).

At Villa Park, Pele gave us glimpses of the exquisite control that McIlvanney describes, along with blistering acceleration off the mark and sheer physical power. It was enough. No-one who attended Villa Park could have been left in any doubt. In McIlvanney's words, Pele had a special magic and '…a catalogue of his capacities cannot convey anything like the true impact of Pele in his prime. Permeating all these gifts, and heightening their effect, there was the magic of his spirit, the way he was able to blend ferocious competitiveness with real joy in the beauties of football.'

Pele himself put things more simply, which is what genius is mostly about: "I was born for soccer, just as Mozart was born for music."

Some people have been lucky enough to hear Terry Hennessey talk about playing for Wales against Brazil in the Maracana Stadium in Rio de Janeiro. His job was to mark Pele. If you do engage Hennessey in such a conversation, you had better not be going anywhere in a hurry, for the Welshman is effusive on the topic.

"He had the ball, coming towards me, just over the halfway line. He knocked it passed me and I thought, 'Who's he passed that to?' Then, he accelerated and I realised he had passed the bloody thing to himself. I ask you? Amazing."

Needless to say, after I saw Pele play at Villa Park in 1965, I always believed what Hennessey had to say about him — even allowing for celtic enthusiasm.

Some years before Pele entranced us, I played in a Youth International trial match at Villa Park. The England team that was subsequently selected included Bobby Moore. He was our captain, naturally. We played matches in Northern Ireland, Switzerland and Austria, but little was I to know then what an impact Moore was to have on football and how his most respected opponent was to become — Pele! There's that word respect, again. Me? I was just glad to have been around at what was rather a special time. This time our visit was, again, somewhat special. It was to see the Rams in the Premiership. Is there any wonder that Villa Park is one of my favourite grounds?

One of the great skills of ground development is to link the old with the new. That is particularly important at grounds steeped in football history like Villa Park and the job has been well done. The Trinity Road (Main) Stand has mock red Victorian brickwork, which fronts the entrance and the steps that lead up to it, and it has been restored superbly. On picture postcards, it could be the entrance to a stately home, or a grand mansion, and it retains an imposing and dignified presence. Yet, despite having the most aris- tocratic approach of any ground in England, Villa Park retains a homely feel. What is apparent is that, despite the general rush to modernise as quickly as possible, due to the Taylor Report, here at Villa Park, the past has been recognised and acknowledged.

On the city side of the ground, the enormous Holte End, named after Sir Thomas, used to be the largest end terrace in football. It now seats 13,462 spectators in two tiers and towers away to the right of the Trinity Road Stand, from which its own frontage has been copied. Opinions about the merits of the Holte End construction have been varied among Villa traditionalists since completion in 1994. Some don't like the pastiche, but others claim that, given time and when the interior is fitted out properly and completely, the Holte End could eventually be seen to be one of the best examples of football ground architecture in the country.

Behind the scenes in the Trinity Road Stand, the initial perception of comfortable living is confirmed. Deep pile carpets in the corridors and the press room give a continuing impression of grandeur. The wooden panelled walls are lined with photographs, illustrating great exploits of the past. They also contain photographs of modern times: of the team that finished runners-up in 1993 in the first-ever Premier League and fourth in the Premiership last season. Such photographs sit proudly alongside the ones which record Aston Villa's European Cup winning team of 1982. Seven times winners of the old Football League Division One, seven times winners of the FA Cup and five times winners of the League Cup — the most recent being last season — Aston Villa's great history tends to overshadow modern achievements. That is a pity. If the

Premiership title stranglehold of Manchester United is to be broken and the likes of Liverpool, Newcastle United and Arsenal are to be challenged, Aston Villa has the potential power to do so. The club should be the standard bearer for the Midlands, in the challenge to London and the North-west, but regrettably, the feeling must be that Aston Villa is falling just short of potential.

An hour or so before the time for kick-off, the arrival of some of the Villa players was spectacular. They have access to a special car-park, which enables them to reach the dressing-room without having to run the gauntlet of fans and autograph hunters. It's quite a good idea. Players do need their minds on the game beforehand, but the arrangement means that the public is able to view the arrivals through an iron fence. Perhaps 400 people were gathered, young and old alike, faces pressed to the rails with scarves and shirts in claret and blue presenting a kaleidoscope of colour. It was rather like being at a zoo, or, more accurately, a zoo at Donnington Park, as the layout provides a great opportunity for some of the Villa extroverts to go through their paces. In they zoomed: black BMWs, white Porches, club Rovers, tyres screeching, radios blaring full blast. Were these players, or directors? Was the display confidence, or was it nerves? Perhaps it is a good job that Paul Gascoigne doesn't play for Aston Villa.

Once the match started, it quickly became apparent that the Rams were a pale shadow of the team that had showed so much promise at Tottenham. Villa won 2-0 and totally dominated the game. The Rams could have few complaints and, at times, the team looked tired, dispirited and disorganised. The idea of playing Aljosa Asanovic up front with Ron Willems, seemed to be strange tactics indeed. After the fluent performance from the midfield trio of Christian Dailly, Darryl Powell and Asanovic at White Hart Lane, the changes which brought Sean Flynn into midfield, failed miserably. Flynn is a wholehearted player and can be useful at times, but not if he becomes the playmaker of the team. Too much of anything can be harmful and too much of the ball at Flynn's feet is the recipe for going nowhere, which is where the Rams went in the first half.

An injury to Gary Rowett, after seven minutes, didn't help. Villa scored their first goal shortly afterwards and it's arguable that had Rowett been on the field, he would have covered the danger. That was one of the points that Jim Smith made afterwards, but the manager was clutching at straws. It was also possible that Russell Hoult should have been quicker off his line to claim the through ball, but the writing was on the wall by the meandering way in which the Rams played. On a warm summer afternoon, too many players were lethargic and the match had a dozy feel to it.

Perhaps it wasn't entirely the players' fault, perhaps it was us. The positioning of the press box and commentary position at Villa Park is not good. Situated at the back of the Main Stand, the view is excellent, but is too high, too far back and too remote. The effect is to make the game appear slow. At White Hart Lane, the commentary position is too low down to be ideal, but we were much more in contact with the action, the atmosphere and the pace. Those large, round-faced, pompous individuals, who always sit in the stand, or in a corporate box downing gins and tonic, should be made to sit at pitch side occasionally. They might realise then how fast and violent the game actually is. They might be less inclined to bellow, "Too slow!" at the first opportunity. Then again, they might not.

A disputed penalty at the start of the second half — an alleged push by Jacob Laursen on former Rams player, Tommy Johnson — put paid to any chance of recovery and long before the end, the Rams looked woebegone. More worryingly, they looked sorry for themselves. Villa did do just enough to win, but on this evidence, will be hard put to equal last season's successes. They still look a 'nearly' team to me.

The journey up the A38 is one of the shorter ones of the season and gives minimum time for reflection, but at least the *Sports Argus* was acquired on the way. It takes a week to absorb the country's second-best Saturday night sports paper — the *Manchester Evening*

News Pink 'Un' takes the palm — but the growth of instant communications has meant the first ritual reading of the results on a Saturday night has lost its importance. The decline of the Saturday night sports paper is, in my opinion, one of the nation's great cultural losses.

Team: Hoult; Parker, Stimac, Rowett (sub Van der Laan, sub Gabbiadini), Laursen, Dailly, Flynn, D.Powell, C.Powell, Willems (sub Simpson), Asanovic.

Attendance 34,646

Thursday, 29th August 1996: Jimmy Gordon died today, aged 80. He was trainer-coach during the Brian Clough/Peter Taylor regime at the Baseball Ground, joining the Rams from Blackburn Rovers shortly after Clough took charge. He had been a player with Newcastle United (144 appearances) before World War Two and for Middlesbrough (253 appearances) afterwards. His career ended a couple of years before Clough and Taylor made their Middlesbrough debuts as players.

Gordon was a quiet, but no-nonsense man. He followed Clough and Taylor to Nottingham Forest, where he shared in two European Cup wins and another League championship success. In typical Clough style, Gordon was deputed to lead out the Forest side at Wembley before the 1980 League Cup Final, as Clough and Taylor wandered around the track to their seats on the bench. Forest lost 1-0, to Wolverhampton Wanderers. Gordon retired that year.

Following the match at Villa Park, the Rams had an 11-day break, because of the Moldova v England World Cup qualifying game. It was Glen Hoddle's first match as England manager, after taking over from Terry Venables. England won 3-0.

Wednesday, 4th September: Derby County v Manchester United.

"We're coming out of a strange period, because of the international break," said Jim Smith, before the match. "It's new for me and is part of our learning process at this level. It's a massive game, because United are the biggest club of them all. Ever since the fixtures came out, the fans have been waiting for this one."

Result: Derby County 1 Manchester United 1.

"We're on the right lines," — Jim Smith, afterwards.

"I wouldn't tip them for relegation. I think they look a competent side and full of confidence." — Alex Ferguson, Manchester United manager.

I missed the Manchester United match, being at Taunton to cover Derbyshire's vital County Championship match against Somerset. The cricket match was also drawn, which proved to be a crucial setback in Derbyshire's bid for a second championship title, the first being in 1936. Still you can't have everything. Sixty years ago, though, our two major professional clubs nearly did. Derby County finished runners-up as Sunderland won the Football League title in that cricket championship-winning year. Just imagine, the town of Derby being right at the top of the national sporting scene. The previous year, Derbyshire had finished second and the Rams fourth. They must have been great days.

The House That Jack Built

Ewood Park — Monday, 9th September 1996

THE trip to Ewood Park, to play a troubled Blackburn Rovers, was undertaken with growing confidence. Following the poor performance against Aston Villa, the Rams' improvement to earn a 1-1 draw against Manchester United, in front of a packed crowd at a heaving Baseball Ground, had newspapers trumpeting the headlines 'Rams match United in Thriller' and 'United Shocked'.

It was a good time to play Blackburn. Three weeks before the start of the season, Rovers had been rocked by the transfer of England striker Alan Shearer to Newcastle United, for a world record fee of £15 million. Things had not been helped, either, by the strange departure in the summer of Kenny Dalglish. His obscure post of Director of Football had for a long time been a mystery to most people and, perhaps, to Dalglish himself. His leaving finally left manager Ray Harford to swim, or sink, by himself and Rovers had made a poor start to the season. With Rovers having scored no goals in two home matches, both lost, Derby County were looking forward to setting some old scores with Blackburn.

Four years before, at a less imposing Ewood Park, the Rams were leading 2-0 after 20 minutes of the First Division Play-off semi-final, against a Rovers side that had finished sixth in the table, some three places and four points behind the Rams. Arthur Cox's expensively assembled team looked to be heading for a Wembley Play-off Final. Then, as destiny beckoned, the defence collapsed. Dreadful errors cost Derby County dear and the match was lost 4–2. Despite Derby winning the second leg at the Baseball Ground by 2-1, it was Rovers who went to Wembley, to beat Leicester City 1-0 and leave Rams owner, Lionel Pickering, counting the cost.

Once in the Premiership, Rovers set about staying there. The following season, with the help of owner Jack Walker's millions, Kenny Dalglish built a side which finished runners-up in 1993-94 and won the Premiership title in 1994-95, helped by a good supply of goals from the SAS strike force of Shearer and Chris Sutton. At the same time, Ewood Park was transformed into a state of the art stadium. Only 18 months later, however, there are signs that parts of the house that Jack built, is beginning to fall down.

The match was played on Monday, 9th September, with an 8.00pm kick-off, for the benefit of Sky television. It didn't prevent a good following of Rams supporters making the trip to Lancashire to visit the home of arguably the first major professional club in English football. From the Main Stand and in the eerie silence of a deserted Ewood Park, we broadcast the Monday evening *Sportscene Talk-in* programme, with many fans contributing by mobile phone as they made their way to the match. Quite a number forecast a 2-1 score line.

It was 1885 before professional football was legalised in this country and it wasn't until 1888 that the Football League was

The main gates to White Hart Lane, where the Rams began their first-ever journey through a Premiership season.

Approaching the 'new' Blackburn Rovers, scene of the Rams' first away win – indeed their first victory of any kind – in the Premiership.

Next-door neighbours. Old housing and new stadium cheek-by-jowl at Blackburn.

Behind the goal at Ewood Park. Apart from a few stewards assembling to the left of the goal, we were the first to arrive for the Rams' midweek fixture.

The new 'Kop' at Hillsborough. It bears precious little resemblance to the ground where I first watched football.

'Goodnight, Wednesdayite' – Dreams coming true?

Anfield's Shankly Gates.

The Hillsborough Memorial at Anfield, always bedecked with flowers.

'Living close to Anfield.' The Main Stand as you enter from the Shankly Gates.

'Over the garden wall…' Consideration is everything at Anfield.

They get everywhere — McDonald's at Anfield.

Football in the Community office at Upton Park.

Upton Park's Bobby Moore Stand.

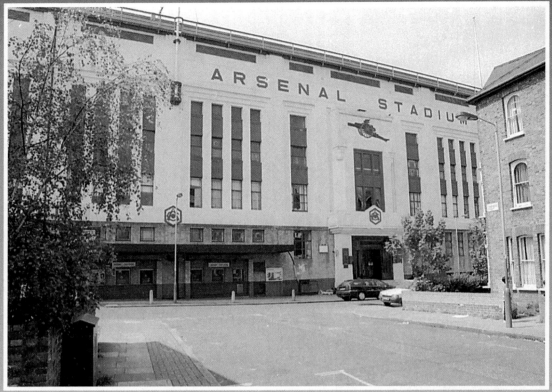

The magnificent façade of Highbury.

Highbury entrance set between prime residential property.

Little details are important. Arsenal's crèche in the shadow of Highbury.

'Return to Arsenal, please.' The London Underground station re-named in honour of arguably the most famous football club in the world.

Outside the Fulwell End at Roker Park. All the houses are painted red and white.

The Roker Bus from where match-day tickets and press passes are distributed.

The Fulwell End at Roker Park, filling up nicely for the match between Sunderland and Derby County, champions and runners-up respectively in the previous season's First Division. Sixty-three years earlier, over 75,000 saw the sides meet at Roker in a famous FA Cup-tie.

Graham Richards discusses conditions at the Priestfield Stadium with Gillingham's groundsman.

Life in the lower divisions. The Main Stand and Executive Club at Gillingham.

Stamford Bridge or a building site? Building work under way as the Rams visit.

The Rams' team coach arrives at Stamford Bridge.

**Outside the main gates at
Stamford Bridge.**

**Chelsea's massive
East Stand joins the
Matthew Harding
Stand at Stamford
Bridge.**

formed. Until then, the major competition was the Football Association Challenge Cup, which was first contested in 1872 by amateur teams, the most successful of which came from universities, old boys' associations and the army. As professional players began to emerge in the Lancashire cotton towns, many coming down from Scotland, Blackburn Rovers became a powerful force. In 1882, they became the first team from the north to appear in the FA Cup Final, losing 1-0 to Old Etonians at Kennington Oval cricket ground, but they were back again in 1884 and won the trophy for three successive seasons 1884–86, the last triumph in a replayed Final at the County Ground, Derby. They won the FA Cup again in 1890 and Ewood Park, their home since 1881, staged international matches against Wales in 1885 and Scotland in 1887.

Incidentally, I wonder how many Rams fans making their way home from the Baseball Ground past the Arboretum realised that there, on Arboretum Field in 1888, Blackburn Rovers, the cream of English football, came an FA Cup cropper, bowing out to a team called Derby Junction who went on to reach the semi-final, where they were beaten by West Bromwich Albion.

They say that 'what goes round, comes round' and it is a remarkable story how the modern development of Blackburn Rovers and of Ewood Park, so closely mirrors the occurrences of more than 90 years ago. Then, in 1905, Laurence Cotton, the aptly named textile baron, was appointed chairman of the club. He, like Jack Walker, set about building a new team and a new ground and spent £12,000 on players and £33,000 on the ground in the period between 1905–14. They were huge sums of money for that time, but the investment brought success. Two League championships were won in 1912 and 1914 and Ewood Park's capacity rose to a massive 70,866. Cotton died in 1921 and as the Lancashire cotton industry declined, so did the comparative fortunes of Blackburn Rovers. Gradually, they were overtaken at the top of the English football tree, by other clubs in areas of larger population. Is the historical analogy about to take place, despite the Walker millions?

If Laurence Cotton financed Blackburn Rovers with profits raised from cotton, Jack Walker used the benefits of steel. A lifelong fan of Rovers, Walker used his fortune — reputedly over £330 million made from the sale of his family business to British Steel — to revitalise Blackburn Rovers, much in the way Cotton had done all those years before. Like then, money was ploughed into the team and the ground was rebuilt. The 'new' Ewood Park cost around £25 million, but to many eyes, the end product is somewhat sterile. Perhaps it is because the stark, straight lines of the stadium make it appear so exposed and isolated, the houses and land around having been cleared for the development. The whole area could easily be mistaken for being part of a light industrial estate. It is undeniable that the club now possesses imposing stands and fine facilities, but the cosiness of the former Ewood Park, with club offices operating from the houses across Nuttall Street, has been destroyed, along with Nuttall Street itself. The modern ground, like steel, lacks warmth. Mother's home baking, replaced by sliced bread. How sad that a club like Blackburn Rovers, having such rich early traditions, should now play, even on the same site, in a stadium that has absolutely no feeling for the past. Ewood Park is such a cold monument to Walkersteel.

The match was undistinguished. Too much poor passing, too little form and shape. Not that it mattered much to Sky. At half-time, the press room television monitors were spewing out great volumes of eulogising verbiage, delivered by Alan Parry and Richard Keys. It was as though the game was comparable with, say, Real Madrid v Eintracht Frankfurt (1960), England v West Germany (1966), or Brazil v Italy (1970). Most of the assembled journalists were staring intently at the screen. A pity they don't stare as intently at the match. If they did, they might be able to make up their own minds, rather than having to rely on what managers tell them afterwards. Instead, the consensus view prevailed, aided and abetted by Sky.

The coverage given to football matches by the media is becoming increasingly like varnish on a piece of wood. Hard, glossy and uniform. Had this match been played in the humbler surrounds of Roots Hall, or Griffin Park, without the addition of a television audience, the standard of play would have been reported in far less favourable column inches of newsprint than did the match at Ewood Park. There is no doubt that modern Premiership stadiums, together with Sky's sycophantic presentation, do sometimes enhance 'the product', as football is increasingly being called. This was one such time.

The Rams were not bothered about that. In recording a first victory in the Premiership, Derby County were entitled to feel happy. It was their fifth attempt and despite the promise of previous games, there is no substitute for tangible reward. The 2-1 victory, thanks to a fine late goal by substitute Sean Flynn, brought sighs of relief all round and a massive boost to confidence, both on and off the field.

In defence, Igor Stimac was outstanding. What a thoroughbred player he looks when he is in this form. Even so, the Rams have conceded too many goals and have been unable to keep a clean sheet in one half of play often enough. At least they did in the second half at Ewood Park, to bring the total to two clean sheets in ten halves of play. Before the season started, everyone was aware that goals would be scarce in the Premiership, but that has made it more important for the Rams to play to their strengths, which are in defence. As yet, they haven't been solid enough in that department. Good defence requires concentration and discipline, not only from defenders, but from forwards and midfield players too. So far this season, the Rams have been lacking in those qualities too often.

It's a truism that most spectators look at football from an attacking point of view. Problems in that area are easier to identify than those in defence and, in any case, spectators go to football matches for a bit of excitement, among other things. Attacking equals excitement and entertainment for most supporters, defending means worry. It's not by accident, though, that Brian Clough's teams were based on sound defence. His defenders were usually players with excellent footballing skills, like Roy McFarland, Colin Todd, Dave Mackay, Ron Webster, David Nish — and Igor Stimac. It's the same in cricket, batting takes the eye before bowling. It's the wrong way round. Carts before horses don't progress too far. The Rams need to keep the back door locked more firmly, if Premiership football is to be enjoyed for more than one season.

If winning brings smiles to people's faces, the opposite is true of losing. In the press conference after the match, the Blackburn manager, Ray Harford, was long of face and miserable. The rumour mongers were soon busy querying the security of his job. Harford tried hard to be optimistic, but he is steeped in football logic, not in PR image making and the whole silly session was depressing and downright embarrassing.

Why should a decent man have to justify himself to jackals, because someone in a grey suit at Premiership headquarters deems it necessary to put on a public face in the interests of so-called press relations? Press conferences immediately after the match should be abolished, immediately. A previous Blackburn manager used to say, "Write what you see." He was correct. Perhaps Harford needs a few lessons from Alan Parry and Richard Keys on talking things up. On second thoughts, definitely not.

Jim Smith was not fooled and gave his verdict: "There are things we have to do better in order to get results consistently. The ball was given away too often in unforced positions."

Team: Hoult; Rowett, Stimac, Carbon, Laursen, Dailly, D.Powell, Asanovic (sub Flynn), C.Powell, Sturridge, Willems (sub Gabbiadini).
Scorers: Willems, Flynn.
Attendance 19,214.

Friday, 13th September 1996: An interesting news item

circulated: Paul McGrath is poised to join Coventry City, after being told he can leave Aston Villa.

Saturday, 14th September 1996: Derby County 1 Sunderland 0 A battle. Richard Ord was sent off by referee David Elleray in the 65th minute. Asanovic's disputed penalty (84 minutes) won the match. Gary Rowett summed up the season so far: "Our start is beginning to look respectable. After winning at Blackburn on Monday, it was good to add another three points, because two victories takes us forward. We've done better from six games than we thought." A realistic view from a player who has looked at home in the Premiership and is still improving. Is Craig Short nearly £2 million a better player than Rowett? I think not. A good example of football prices not reflecting proper football value.

"We're working harder than ever before on the training ground. We have to do that to keep our heads above water." — Jim Smith.

Chalets On The East Side

Kenilworth Road (Coca-Cola Cup, Second Round, First Leg) — Tuesday, 17th September 1996

AFTER the splendour of White Hart Lane, Villa Park and Ewood Park, it was back to basics at Kenilworth Road. The problem with living in a rarefied atmosphere is that people forget. In thinking of where you're going, it is easy to lose sight of where you have come from, and the cramped stadium at Kenilworth Road was a sharp reminder of how life is in the lower leagues. If that wasn't a big enough shock to the system, the Rams display against Luton Town most certainly was. Lacking in motivation, incentive and, crucially, professionalism, they slumped to a 1-0 defeat. They were fortunate it wasn't more. The Hatters were far the more impressive side, played better football, and missed enough chances to put the tie out of reach. Is this a warning? Never mind, with the second leg to come at the Baseball Ground, the feeling after the match was that the Rams would still go through to the next round. How easily are such warnings brushed aside, like a troublesome fly from the arm. Sometimes the fly turns out to be a wasp, with a nasty sting.

The commentary position at Luton hadn't altered since both the Rams and the Hatters left the Endsleigh Insurance League Division One last season. Derby County went up, Luton Town went down. Only 4,459 people bothered to attend this match, but, as usual, we were obliged to have to sit behind a huge pillar, which meant that the goal and much of the penalty-area to our right was totally obscured from view, unless we contorted around like electric eels. The possibility of changing seats was nil. Despite 'vacancies in all parts of the house', as the notices in London's theatreland announce, officialdom at this theatre of living art decreed that once numbered seats for the press box had been issued, presumably in tablets of stone, only nuclear war or bubonic plague could change the status quo. Thus, with an enlightened attitude such as this, certain football clubs lurch towards the new millennium.

Opposite the Main Stand at Kenilworth Road, used to be a standing area covered by a roof, called the Bobbers Stand. It was so called, because it used to be a 'bob' in old money (one shilling = 5p) to stand there. It was built by supporters in 1933, to incorporate a café, a games room and a room where supporters could wash and change if they came to the match straight from work. The Quaker influence was strong in the Kenilworth Road part of Luton and, because the Bobbers Stand was equipped with the only two licensed bars in the area, it served as a sort of early community centre. 'Football in the Community' a long time ago? The Bobbers Stand is no longer in existence. It was converted to seats in 1977 and pulled down in 1985. In its place was constructed a line of sponsors' boxes, which could be easily be mistaken for a row of beach huts on the promenade at Great Yarmouth, or a new line in double-glazing chalets. Thus, the whole of one side of the ground, which once was a well used community facility, has, since 1985, become a private viewing area for 210 spectators.

To accompany the chalets, came the plastic pitch. The plastic pitch at Loftus Road, was one of Terry Venables' contributions for the advancement of English football. Luton soon trailed Queen's Park Rangers down the green plastic road, Preston and Oldham followed suit. Most professionals disliked them. Liverpool, particularly, hated them. "If you have artificial pitches," said Kenny Dalglish "you produce artificial footballers." What you surely produced, on a windy day, was blow football. Eventually, common sense prevailed and the Venables vision for the future of football disappeared, although Luton were not finished with innovation, yet. In the same year as the plastic pitch and the chalets appeared, the club banned visiting supporters from the Kenilworth Road ground. A good job they didn't ban the Rams travelling faithful on this occasion, or the atmosphere would have been funereal.

Luton full-back, Julian James, scored the vital goal in the 26th minute, with a deflected shot which gave Russell Hoult no chance. Ashley Ward began this match, but was anonymous. He wasn't the only one and midway through the first half we checked to see whether all the Rams players had got off the coach.

Jim Smith put a brave face on it. He was grateful for a second chance. Lennie Lawrence was his usual quotable self. "If Derby play well, next week, they should win. If we play well and they are not firing on all cylinders, we have a chance. We need to keep this standard up against Blackpool on Saturday."

Rams followers were not concerned with Blackpool. The next trip was a short one, to play Sheffield Wednesday, at Hillsborough, on Saturday. They were probably of the same opinion as us: that a Tuesday night in Luton in September, could have been worse. It could have been in January!

Later in the week, Jim Smith was still unhappy and ruminating about the display at Kenilworth Road. When players perform like that, it nags away in the professional mind. "The only performance last season as poor as this, was at Watford. It was so unprofessional, defenders running with the ball and being caught in possession. I was very disappointed. It looked like a team thinking it's in the Premiership, playing somebody from a lower division," he told the *Derby Evening Telegraph*.

Team: Hoult; Laursen, C.Powell, Parker, Stimac, Rowett, Dailly, Van der Laan (sub Carsley), Asanovic, Ward, Simpson (sub Cooper). *Attendance: 4,459.*

Thursday, 19th September: It was announced that Igor Stimac and Aljosa Asanovic had signed new four-year deals for Derby County. There had been national newspaper speculation about possible transfer bids for the Croatians, particularly in view of Asanovic's early form in the Premiership. Four years? Despite the Bosman ruling, it seems a long time. "A week is a long time in politics," said Harold Wilson when he was Prime Minister, but football is even more volatile than politics and as Wilson always claimed to be a Huddersfield Town supporter, he should know.

Meanwhile Jason Kavanagh turned down a possible move to Gillingham, which re-emphasised the problem of reducing the staff. Too many players nowadays are given contracts which are too long. How often do we see young players denied the chance to make progress, because the system gets clogged up with too many experienced players playing in the reserve team? Long contracts for star players is acceptable, but shorter contracts for more players would result in greater flexibility, although it would need better judgment by clubs and greater self-confidence by players to make it work. It won't happen. Anxiety casts a long shadow and fear stalks the game, as never before.

It's salutary to recall that before the abolition of the maximum wage, in 1963, only one-year contracts were allowed. That's why the 'retained list' was such an important item towards the end of the season. Despite high salaries and long contracts, I'm constantly told there is great pressure on players nowadays. Well, £20 per week and a one-year contract could be a problem, too — and, don't forget, the number of names on the teamsheet is still the same.

Saturday, 21st September: Martin Taylor is loaned to Crewe Alexandra.

Goodnight, Wednesdayite

Hillsborough — Saturday, 21st September 1996

JIM Smith was born in Sheffield in 1940, but despite beginning his football career with Sheffield United, the Derby County manager is actually a Wednesdayite. It meant that when the Rams went to play against Sheffield Wednesday at Hillsborough in September, it was inevitable that Smith's memories of the football heroes of his childhood, would be rekindled. I knew how he must have felt. Having lived my early life in Sheffield, I, too, am a 'Wednesdayite'.

Of course, football is about many things. Excitement, thrills, glamour, money, ups, downs and the indefinable ingredient that makes it the most popular game in the world. Yet there can be no denying that, for older supporters, much of football is about memories, whereas for youngsters, it's all about dreams. This chapter is a little about both.

I was born at Sutton Scarsdale, near Chesterfield, just a few months earlier than Jim Smith. My parents are both Sheffielders and it was there where I grew up during World War Two and after, living with my mother and her parents at Crosspool, while my father served in the Royal Navy as a wireless operator, mainly on aircraft carriers. Science has demonstrated that long-term memory can be more vivid than short-term memory. Long-term memory can recall incidents of long ago and as Crosspool is the highest part of Sheffield, the sight of the fires that lit up the sky and burned in the city, after intensive German bombing raids, is still etched in the recesses of my mind. So, too, is the memory of the iron table under which we sheltered in the living room and the blinds that were drawn down over the windows as soon as air-raid sirens shrilled. So, too, the dark hole which was the entrance to the air-raid shelter, built in the grounds of Lydgate Lane Infant School, there to sit for hours, with our backs to the cold stone wall, blankets draped over our feet. War, eventually, gave way to peace and my thoughts, and, inevitably, the thoughts of small boys throughout the country, turned to what we in all innocence, considered to be more important matters. Matters that involved a ball.

Our family lived in Headland Road, which is a dead end. Dead, because at the end is a large cemetery, which is still there. At that time, the cemetery had two, huge, iron gates which, very conveniently, formed one of the goals, when two pairs of short trousers played against each other at football. It was usually Wednesday versus United, or sometimes, England versus Mars. Either way, it was always up and down the road and my opponent was always Michael Blake. He was a year or so older than me and lived opposite. Naturally, there was a lot of dribbling in our contests, the only passing occurred when we played one-twos off the kerbstones. We necessarily had to learn the rudiments of what coaches grandly call 'the wall pass', at a very early age.

GOODNIGHT, WEDNESDAYITE

The goals at the other end of the pitch were rather less impressive than the cemetery gates. They were a couple of bricks, 'borrowed' from the yard, where the marble headstone slabs for the graves in the cemetery were carved and stored. The only interruption to our games came when a tall, gaunt, man, dressed in a sombre uniform and wearing a cap with a metal badge on it, opened the cemetery gates. We knew that was a signal.

Headland Road slopes slightly and when the hearse appeared at the other end, about 100 yards away, we had just enough time to remove the bricks, before retreating to the footpath. There, we stood to attention as the funeral procession passed by. My grandma told us always to remove our caps, but sometimes we forgot. Matters of life and death, even so very close, did not sit too heavily on the shoulders of an impatient seven-year-old boy and his pal.

Despite being a Derby County season ticket holder for more than 30 years, my father is still, at heart, a Wednesdayite. So was his father and, no doubt, his father before him. It's in the blood. Blue and white stripes ran strongly in that side of the family, so you can imagine the consternation when Grace, my father's sister, married a Sheffield United supporter, a dreaded 'Unitedite'. Not only that, but they lived with my grandma and grandad Hall, in the early years of their marriage. Saturday nights could be a little lively, once the results were known and the match reports in the *Green 'Un* had been absorbed.

Grandad Hall was a long-time season ticket holder at Hillsborough and besides going to all the first-team matches, he went to most of the reserve matches as well. In those days, all clubs had staffs of more than 40 professionals and reserve-team matches alternated with first-team games on Saturday afternoons. I think grandad Hall only went to Sheffield United's ground at Bramall Lane on a handful of occasions throughout his lifetime and that would be when Wednesday were playing. He wasn't quite as rabid as some Wednesdayites, who, I was gravely informed, never ate bacon, because the red and white stripes reminded them of United's colours!

Nevertheless, United were not looked upon with any particular affection, unless, of course, they were being beaten by Wednesday.

I suppose in my most impressionable years, football was essentially about three things. Playing in the street, reading *Stanley Matthews Football Annual* under the bedclothes by torchlight and going to football at Hillsborough. It was always a thrill to trek through the streets of Walkley with Grandad Hall, as we made our way to Hillsborough for reserve-team matches and me being lifted over the turnstile to get into the Main Stand. It was apparent that Grandad had an arrangement with a particular turnstile operator, who lived near to where he painted the trams in the tramsheds in Crookes. I knew there would be a good chance of going to the match the following day when, on a Friday night, Grandad would announce, "Billy's on t'gate." It was always a good enough reason to go round on Fridays.

Sometimes, we used to go round for tea on Sundays. Very occasionally we had tinned salmon, which was a real treat after the war, with brown bread. Grandad had a special way of slicing Hovis. He used to butter the loaf first and then slice it towards him with the most delicate of slices, using an action that would surely have taken his thumb off, had he not been quite so skilled with the knife. Oddly enough, he never used to carve the Sunday joint. My grandma, a very Victorian lady, used to do that, after furiously sharpening the blade as though she was the tester-in-chief for the whole of the Sheffield steel industry. She used to say that young children should only speak, when spoken too. Secretly, I reckoned she was a Wednesdayite.

In the early post-war years, I graduated to standing on the Leppings Lane End terraces at Hillsborough, with my father and Uncle Fred, who, although a Unitedite, did go to watch Wednesday and they used to meet Uncle Len, Uncle Bernard and, occasionally, Uncle Will — who was a Unitedite — just to the right of the goal, about eight steps back. Small boys were always allowed to push though to the front, to get a better view. "Make way for t'lad," was the cry, as like rabbits down a tunnel, youngsters would burrow through. Occasionally, older ones tried to burrow through too. Then the ranks would close as tightly as the doors at Attercliffe Palais on a Saturday night. "Nay, tha should 'a been 'ere sooner, lad," and then, for those unfortunates, it was a matter of standing on tiptoe to get brief glimpses of the action.

Sometimes, when there was a particularly big crowd and spectators were tightly packed, boys used to be 'rolled', which means that they were rolled like logs down a Rocky Mountain river, over the heads of the crowd down to the front. I was never rolled, because we always arrived early, but the sight of boys being rolled from the top to the bottom of the massive Spion Kop, opposite Leppings Lane End, was spectacular stuff indeed. Spectators who were not feeling very well were also rolled. I used to wonder how many of those adults, who finished up sitting with the first-aid men at the bottom of the Spion Kop, were genuine cases. If they weren't when they started, they were probably genuine enough cases by the time they got to the bottom.

The only other person to be allowed in front of the fence at the Spion Kop End was the man who put up the half-time scores. He sat in the corner, near the corner-flag. At the Leppings Lane End, there was a splendid long wooden control room on top of the roof, with a double row of spaces under the letters of the alphabet, where the half-time and, later, the full-time score were posted, but at the Kop End, there was simply a low board about the size of the advertising boards that encircle our modern grounds. When the man at the Kop End was informed of the scores by the main box, he used to make a little journey round the track, to post the numbers. The numbers were on plates, like on village cricket ground scoreboards and people used to try to see which numbers the man was carrying, especially if United's score still hadn't been posted under the appropriate letter. Sometimes he would have a little game and tease the crowd by pretending to show one number and then, after a delay, putting the other one up, to gasps of disbelief. It was all part of the half-time entertainment and, as always, the brass band played on. The match ball, itself, was sometimes left sitting in lonely isolation near the centre circle, where the referee had left it after he had blown the half-time whistle. It was in no danger. The pitch, then, was sacrosanct. To go on to the pitch in those days, you had to have earned the right. Even the brass band used to stand right at the edge of the pitch. They did have the right. They were performers. They were good enough. Of course, all young Wednesdayites like Jim Smith and me, dreamed of going on the pitch. One day ...one day ...as we walked slowly back home, with the adults discussing the match in animated fashion and the youngsters being seen and not heard. One day ...

I saw some great players in action at Hillsborough. In the period after the war, massive crowds attended football matches and we were taught very early to keep our hands high when leaving the ground in the crush and to keep away from the side walls as we were carried along by the crowd, through the main gates and out into Leppings Lane. Tom Finney, Wilf Mannion, Neil Franklin, Len Shackleton and John Charles were figures who seemed to step straight from the pages of *Charles Buchan's Football Monthly* or the *FA Book for Boys*. Later, I saw Vasas of Hungary, play under brilliant floodlights which could be seen for miles around and Sandor Koscis of Hungary, star for Barcelona. The Spanish team had a Uruguayan winger called Villeverde, who, like Tom Finney, played on the left and dribbled with his right, or was it the right and dribbled with his left? Later, I saw Derek Hogg of Leicester City do the same and, later still, Chris Waddle. I also saw Johnny Haynes and Bobby Charlton sweep long passes around the pitch for England School-boys, and Tommy Taylor, Eddie Colman and Duncan Edwards play for the Busby Babes. Was Duncan Edwards the best player of all? He might well have been.

Despite the great players in the opposition, my main concern was with Wednesday. In those years, they became known as the yo-yo team, due to the frequency with which they gained promotion to

Division One and the rapidity with which they were relegated back to Division Two. Every season seemed to be fraught with anxiety, but, there was always something happening. In the mind's eye I see Wednesday's Scottish goalkeeper, Dave McIntosh, spectacularly prone to error, stretching like elastic to make a wonderful flying save and then, within a blink of an eye, let a high centre drop limply from his fingertips. Infuriating for the crowd, but manna for the photographers. Full-back Hughie Swift, of the telescopic left leg and sliding tackle; inside-forward Redfern Froggatt, a master of the crossfield pass and low shot; Jackie Sewell, a British record signing at the time, came from Notts County. He played for England against the magical Magyars from Hungary in the 6–3 drubbing at Wembley in Coronation Year. We caught a glimpse of Eddie Kilshaw, a dribbling right winger, signed from Bury. He thrilled us all, briefly. His career was tragically terminated by a broken leg after only 20 matches. He might have become the new Stanley Matthews. Many people thought so. Later still, came 'golden boy' Albert Quixall, all short shorts and ballet lessons and, together with Alan Ball, the best passer of a moving ball I've seen; Alan Finney, a flying winger, was a regular in the first team at 17 years of age and scorched the right wing touchlines; Denis Woodhead, an equally fast left winger, with a tremendous left-foot shot, who peppered the Spion Kop and sometimes the goal net.

Woodhead was transferred to Derby County, via Chesterfield, to combine with Tommy Powell on the opposite flank when the Rams won the Third Division North championship in 1956-57. Centre-forward Ray Straw scored 37 League goals in that season and many were headers, converting centres which came from either wing. Woodhead had a quick wit and made trainer Ralph Hann's life a misery with his apparently carefree attitude. In February 1959, 'Woody' was transferred to Southport and Ralph though his worries were over. Not likely. Woodhead failed a medical and returned to the Baseball Ground the following week. Friday morning, as we were getting dressed after training, the home team dressing-room door was flung open and a pair of boots landed in the middle of the floor. As everyone wondered what was happening, the door opened again — slowly — and 'Woody's' grinning face appeared. Ralph nearly had a heart attack. Woodhead did have a serious side and always had time for young players. He had a word for me when I played my first-ever Central League match for the Rams' Reserves at Burnley. "Whatever you do," he said, "Try to play at your pace, not at someone else's pace." It was good advice. I heard Bryan Robson say recently that Juninho does that and all the great players have done so. Dennis Woodhead became commercial manager for Sheffield Wednesday at Hillsborough for several years. I bet he was a good one, too.

Despite all the stars, the larger- than-life hero of all Wednesdayites at the beginning of the 1950s, was a tall, awkward, raw-boned, ginger-haired centre-forward, whose name was Derek Dooley. His career was as brief as a comet, but it was as spectacular. In 63 appearances, the 6ft 2ins Dooley scored 64 goals, including 46 in 30 League matches in 1951-52, as Wednesday again gained promotion to the First Division. Then, tragedy struck. Dooley broke a leg in a collision with Preston goalkeeper George Thompson, at Deepdale. Gangrene set in. The leg was amputated. The football world mourned. Wednesdayites were devastated. It's strange how small the world can be. One of the doctors on duty at Preston General Hospital, when Derek Dooley lost a leg, later became our family doctor.

The Dooley story is well documented and those who saw him play have their own recollections. Mine are of a huge man ploughing down the middle of the pitch, with defenders hanging on to all sides like passengers on the side of a Sheffield tram at rush hour. Then, a definitive finish, with a right-foot blow sending the ball hurtling past the visiting goalkeeper, to bulge the net. It was like Desperate Dan dispatching someone through a brick wall in the *Beano*, or was it the *Dandy*? Dooley scored five goals in one half, against Notts County. Leon Leuty was reckoned to be a top-class centre-half, but he couldn't handle Dooley on that day.

GOODNIGHT, WEDNESDAYITE

The amazing thing about Derek Dooley was that he wasn't a footballer at all. He hardly headed the ball, he couldn't kick with his left foot, his dribbling skill was non-existent and his control was poor. He had a knack, though. That knack was scoring goals and the atmosphere at Hillsborough when he was doing so, was fantastic. Clear memories resurface of days of pouring rain, with steam rising off 60,000 people on the terraces, as the crowd sang the old Guy Mitchell hit tune *Truly Fair*. The sound rolled around around the stadium: "Dooley, Dooley, fair; Dooley Dooley fair. How we love our Dooley fair." We all sang. He was our hero. Whatever else football needs, it needs heroes. Over 50,000 attended his testimonial match.

Sadly, Hillsborough will be tainted forever with the disaster of 15th April 1989. Ninety-six Liverpool fans died on that day and whenever people go to the ground, they are reminded of that fact. Yet the ground itself is not to blame. Human error caused the disaster, but Hillsborough is a word that can no longer be heard without certain connotations being attached — rather like Munich. For someone who spent so many happy hours at Hillsborough, that is particularly sad. On the other hand, perhaps, it is only right and proper.

In the first minute of this match, Marco Gabbiadini had a glorious chance to put the Rams ahead. Towards the end, Christian Dailly had another. Neither succeeded. Gabbiadini's header hit the bar at point-blank range, after a superb centre from Chris Powell. Dailly slid a low shot at the goalkeeper from around the penalty spot. The result was a goalless draw. A drab match played in drab, drizzly conditions, only remarkable for the number of yellow cards waved around by referee Graham Barber. He took seven names and left members of the press spluttering with false indignation afterwards, about the injustice of it all. Interestingly, the players were not so alarmed and felt the referee had handled things quite well, if rather too eager to book technical offences.

Jim Smith was upbeat afterwards: "We didn't believe enough in the first half. They seemed to be happy drawing at Hillsborough. It was much better in the second half and I was pleased with the performance." Being the Rams' seventh match in the Premiership, it is still early days, but this Sheffield Wednesday team looked very ordinary and the bookmakers' view that, despite their excellent start, they will struggle looks justified. Smith's point about 'belief' is also important. The Rams still look like the new boys on the block.

The Spion Kop at Hillsborough is still an imposing sight. Before the roof was put on, it used to have an irregular profile against the skyline and you could see as far as the houses on the hills in the distance. Almost 18,000 fans could stand there and get thoroughly wet when it rained. Now, the Kop is square in outline and seats 11,210 spectators. Enclosing the sides has meant that the acoustics are about the best in all of England and the volume of sound that used to roll down from the standing masses, now echoes around and out from the Kop and contributes impressively to the atmosphere. Not too many people realise that the pitch itself slopes down towards the Kop, mainly from the halfway line — a drop of 2ft 6ins over the entire length — and, like Liverpool at Anfield, Wednesday try to kick towards the Kop End in the second half, as it is still the favourite vantage point for the majority of Wednesdayites. No-one had pointed that out to Igor Stimac. He won the toss and gave Wednesday that supposed advantage.

Before the match started, we walked around the ground. For many years after the war, Hillsborough was where one of the FA Cup semi-finals was played, virtually every season. In the years when Sheffield Wednesday were alternating between divisions, the policy decision whether to use money to strengthen the team, or develop the ground, was fiercely debated. The secretary-manager at the time, was a far-seeing administrator called Eric Taylor, who took the view that players would come and go, but the ground was permanent. During Taylor's 16-year reign, Hillsborough established its reputation as one of the best grounds in the country, although Wednesday never finished higher than 14th in the old Division One. Once the North Stand was built in 1961, with one of the first cantilever roofs covering just under 10,000 spectators, it was certain that Hillsborough would be a venue for some of the group matches in the 1966 World Cup. The young Franz Beckenbauer was to make a great impact there.

1966 was also the year of Gerry Young's mistake at Wembley and Sheffield Wednesday were beaten 3-2 by Everton in the FA Cup Final. The following year, Wednesday were drawn at home in the fourth round, against Mansfield Town, the club I'd joined from Derby County. The attendance was 49,049. We lost 4-0. Unforgettable. In the club shop at Hillsborough, which is situated behind the North Stand off Middlewood Road, among the mass of Wednesday merchandise is displayed a nightshirt. It is in white, with blue trim. On the front a young owl, with one eye closed and a night cap on its head, is dreaming …dreaming. Underneath, the caption reads: 'Goodnight, Wednesdayite'. For one small boy, dreams did come true.

Team: Hoult; Laursen, C.Powell, Rowett, Stimac, Parker, Dailly, Carsley, D.Powell, Sturridge (sub Simpson), Gabbiadini (sub Ward). *Attendance: 23,934*

While the Rams were drawing against Sheffield Wednesday at Hillsborough, Derbyshire were beating Durham to finish second in cricket's County Championship table. It was a triumph of leadership by the Aussie pairing of captain Dean Jones and coach Les Stillman. They helped to cajole and inspire talented players to produce something near to their potential, not just occasionally, but over a five-month period. Talent is not usually a problem — all players at professional level can do things. Making use of talent at the right time, is. That is called ability. Ability is always essential, but good leadership helps.

Wednesday, 25th September 1996 (Coca-Cola Cup, Second Round, Second Leg).
The Rams' worst fears came true. 1-0 down after the dreadful showing at Kenilworth Road, they played better at the Baseball

Ground, but still went out of the competition. It shows the fine margins in professional sport, especially when one side is keen to win and the other doesn't concentrate. A lot of supporters were disappointed. They know a Premiership title is beyond the team at present, but in the Coca-Cola Cup — or even the FA Cup — who knows? For the Rams' highly-paid players to be outplayed in one leg of the competition was bad enough, but to be second best in both was inexcusable. "In the two legs, they did well and I have to say, we did not deserve to reach the third round." — Smith. He must have been a non-plussed as anyone, but the whole affair left a little niggle in the back of the mind. Have some players begun to believe their own publicity? If so, the Rams are doomed.

Result: Derby County 2 Luton Town 2. In the next round, Luton are away to Wimbledon.

Saturday, 28th September 1996: Derby County 0 Wimbledon 2

Wimbledon were impressive. Strong, disciplined, pace up front, quick and agile at the back and with a lot more skill than people had given them credit for. They won, comfortably.

"That's the least change we've had out of any side this season." — Dean Sturridge.

"We were a lot stronger than Derby. They say we're a long-ball side, but you saw what they were throwing at us." — Vinnie Jones.

"We took the goals very well and, although there was some pressure from Derby, it was mostly long balls, which we dealt with." — Joe Kinnear.

"That was our worst League performance of the season. If we'd defended properly, we'd have got a 0-0 draw out of it, but their goals were as bad as I've seen from a defensive point of view." — Jim Smith.

"I think they're the best side we've met this season." — Lee Carsley.

Quite so.

Wednesday, 2nd October: Derby County 0 Aston Villa 3
(Midland Youth Cup)
If Derby County are to compete successfully in the Premiership, the club will have to produce some of its own players, to offset the spiralling costs of transfers and wages. Dean Sturridge and Lee Carsley are home-grown products, but one of the criticisms of the later Arthur Cox years was that only Paul Williams emerged to become either a first-team player, or a valuable asset in the transfer market. Derby County's record in the premier youth competition, the FA Youth Cup, which has spawned talent like Steve McManaman, Robbie Fowler, David Beckham, Nickie Butt, Sol Campbell and Paul Merson, is abysmal.

Thursday, 4th October : Derby County are reported to be interested in 26-year-old Portuguese striker Paulo Alvez, who plays for Sporting Lisbon.

Saturday, 6th October: "We know now that we can compete and believe there is better to come. I don't believe there is anything to fear. The players have shown they can compete, play on the same park as international stars and have a chance. We've found it's like playing the best four of five teams from Division One, every week." — Steve McClaren, Rams' first-team coach.

Wednesday, 9th October: England 2 Poland 1
The Rams are reported to be chasing the signature of Paul McGrath from Aston Villa, who wants first-team football. "I'm not giving Paul any guarantees," said Jim Smith, "but I've offered him a place on Saturday. Paul would add strength and experience to what is essentially a youthful team."

The fee was £100,000, rising to £200,000 if Derby County avoided relegation. A 35-year-old with dodgy knees, who, apparently, has hardly trained for years, seemed a strange move, especially as the Rams are well covered in central defence. On the other hand, the fee was not excessive. McGrath had played 29 Premiership matches for an Aston Villa side that had finished fourth last season and, most important, McGrath still has the desire to play. When Ron Atkinson was manager at Villa, he described McGrath as 'the best defender in Europe', which wasn't too long ago and there is no substitute for class.

Thursday, 10th October: Paul McGrath signs for Derby County.

Friday, 11th October: Robbie Van der Laan goes to Wolves on loan.

Saturday, 12th October: Faustino Asprilla fails to return to Newcastle from Colombia and misses the match at the Baseball Ground.

Derby County 0 Newcastle United 1.

McGrath had an excellent debut. He was partly at fault with the Newcastle goal scored, inevitably, by Alan Shearer, but the cross should have been cut out earlier. Shearer did miss two good chances and scored with a half-chance. There is much talk of lack of goals at the moment, but had Ashley Ward had two and a half chances, he might well have scored as many as Shearer. Defending, as distinct from 'the defence', is also a worry. Two successive home 0-0 results have been lost by inadequate defending. Interesting in the light of the McGrath signing, Jim Smith was the man who signed Les Ferdinand (now of Newcastle United) for Queen's Park Rangers — from Hayes of the Isthmian League. Tonight, the Rams stand 13th in the Premiership.

Monday, 14th October: Marco Gabbiadini joins Birmingham City on loan.

Down By The Trent

City Ground — Saturday, 19th October 1996

A TRIP to Nottingham Forest has been, at certain times, a mixed blessing for the press. Officious stewards and lack of a decent press room has brought about a feeling that the media, although tolerated, is not particularly welcome. This time, things had improved.

We did the match commentary standing up. We had been allocated one half of the BBC Radio 5 commentary box, with Pat Murphy, who was covering the match for national radio, in the other half. The arrangement wasn't ideal, on either side. In fact, there was only just enough space for Graham Richards and me to stand side by side during the match, with Colin Gibson making the best of things behind and us shuffling around when Colin needed to be on the main microphone. Graham has been known to get a little excited during matches, especially against Forest, so plenty of jostling took place. It was a bit like a crowded penalty-area. At least the front window opened. There is nothing worse than having to do commentaries from behind glass, because any atmosphere is dissipated, although the effects microphone does pick up crowd noise for the airwaves.

The result was 1-1, but the truth was that Forest looked a poor side and the Rams didn't really capitalise on their undoubted superiority. There was rather too much square passing for the sake of it and little creativity around the penalty-area, and had Dean Saunders, having scored the opening goal in 72 seconds, taken any one of three excellent chances which followed, the Rams might have been left with nothing. In the end, it needed a controlled side-foot shot from ten yards, by Christian Dailly, to salvage a point.

It was salutary that after all the over sophistication of the previous 58 minutes, the goal eventually came from an orthodox centre, a knock down by Ron Willems and a nudge sideways from Aljosa Asanovic. Simple, really. The Rams did play better in the second half, with Asanovic taking a much more central role, but one thing is certain. If the Rams do not stay in the Premiership, they will look back at matches like this, with regret.

Dailly knew the importance of the game to Rams fans, especially those who live and work on the borders of Derbyshire and Nottinghamshire, in places like Heanor, Ilkeston and Sandiacre. "It was important for us and I know how supporters felt. So many friends and neighbours spent weeks telling me we had to do well against Forest."

Although football is reported in terms of towns and cities where clubs are centred, much support for the Rams comes from the surrounding countryside. Derby County is as much a county club, as a town team and draws its support from the whole of Derbyshire in areas as far apart as Buxton and Chesterfield in the north and Burton (yes, I know it's in Staffordshire) in the south. People who live on the borders have to put up with the rivalry of fans who support clubs like Manchester United, Manchester City, Sheffield United and Sheffield Wednesday, as well as Nottingham Forest. It's a bit like defending territory and those on the fringes have a harder time, sometimes, than those who live at the centre.

Afterwards, most of the questions to the Forest manager, in the new Forest press room, were about the possible 'take over' of Forest by various consortiums. How anyone expected Frank Clark to bring some sense to those obscure dealings is hard to imagine, but the inane questions so often posed in after-match press conferences are symptomatic of the lack of knowledge and interest about what is happening on the field. So much is about tittle-tattle and gossip, which should be left to the midweek news columns. Saturday should be about the match. No wonder Kenny Dalglish was never popular with pressmen who require managers to do the job for them by supplying them with explanations and quotes. Joe Royle is in no doubt that the standard of journalism has declined. "There are very few real journalists now," he opinioned in the *Sunday Times* (16 November 1996). "Just a lot of quote collectors and back stabbers."

Before the obligatory and desultory press conference, football reporters used to have to earn their corn. Nowadays, the instant quote, the action replay and the insatiable detail about the politics surrounding the game, has produced a race of journalists who are illiterate about the game itself. The lack of appreciation that Dailly's first-half through pass to Ron Willems was hit too hard, was a prime example. Poor Willems. He was instantly blamed, for being too slow. The fact is that even Linford Christie would not have caught the straightforward pass that could have won Derby County the match, but from the cosy confines of the press box, ignorance slipped lightly off the lap-top computer.

Later, the dangers of television editing were revealed in *Match of the Day*. Commentator John Motson conveniently omitted to mention that the 'referee's assistant' had his flag raised a long time before Saunders 'missed' what would have been an easy chance from a few yards out. Or did Motson fail to realise that the referee waved play on? The same clip was repeated on Sky television the following week, as Forest's predicament in the Premiership table was highlighted as being simply the consequence of missing chances. Oh yes? Most of us have heard that kind of talk before. Was this a case of 'doctoring' the television evidence to fit the 'missed chance theory'? The more I see of television recordings of matches where I have been present, the more it confirms that the two experiences are completely different. Once the cameraman, the commentator, the editor, the producer, the experts in the studio and the presenter have finished with them, football matches are reduced to showbusiness packages, full of gloss and glitter and with the raw edges smoothed over. What is left is a sanitised product for armchair consumption. Harsh realities are ignored. Truth is distorted. What is true is that three of the five senses are eliminated when football is seen on television. You need to be at the match to 'smell' and 'taste' football — and only then can you really make up your own mind.

If the grounds of Everton and Liverpool on Merseyside are but a mile or so across Stanley Park, the grounds of Nottingham Forest and Notts County are much less distance across the River Trent. The floodlights of each ground are plainly visible from the commentary box at the front of the pavilion at Trent Bridge Cricket Ground, which itself is less than 100 yards from the City Ground. Nowhere in Britain is there such a concentration of professional sport than in this small area of West Bridgford and, inevitably, the histories of all three clubs are intertwined. Both Nottingham Forest and Notts County used Trent Bridge Cricket Ground to play some early matches before they arrived at their present grounds, Notts County being residents there when they became one of the founder members of the Football League in 1888. It's significant that Nottingham, along with Sheffield, was the centre for cricket in the north of England in the early part of the 19th century and if Sheffield Club is recognised as the oldest football club to be established, Notts County is the oldest League club, being formed in 1862, a year before the Football Association itself and, although not founder members, Forest can lay claim to being the third oldest club in the League. They even donated a set of red shirts to Arsenal, to enable that most famous of clubs to begin life as Royal Arsenal at Plumstead Common in 1887.

The allocation of European Championship group matches to the

City Ground during Euro 96, is an indication of how much improvement has been undertaken in recent years, yet Forest's ground has not outgrown its humbler origins. Perhaps one reason is that the Main Stand lacks the imposing entrance of many other grounds in the Premiership. There is a lot of open space as you approach it and a number of single-storey buildings look as though they are there only on a temporary basis. Some of them are. Forest have plans to develop their shop area to catch the present tide of commercial opportunity in the leisure wear market.

If the Main Stand is not impressive, the view from the entrance to the Trent End Stand is positively scenic. The River Trent flows but a few yards from the rear of the stand and in spring, when the swans and the oarsmen share the same stretch of water as pleasure craft and fishermen, the walk over Trent Bridge to get to the match is more agreeable than the approach to any Premiership ground in the country. Perhaps the proximity to Trent Bridge Cricket Ground, not much more than 100 yards away, adds to the feeling that going to the City Ground is something of a rural experience.

Team: Hoult; Laursen (sub Carsley), C.Powell, Rowett, McGrath, Stimac, Dailly, Asanovic, D.Powell, Ward (sub Carbon), Willems (sub Simpson).
Scorer: Dailly
Attendance: 27,771.

Questions about 'Derbies'

What constitutes a 'derby' match? Before the season started Everton and Liverpool had met in 154 'derbies', all in the top division. Everton had won 52, Liverpool 56 and no-one would argue against the label of 'derby'. Neither is the Birmingham 'derby' between Aston Villa and Birmingham City (P98:Villa 39: City 32) in dispute. Clubs with the same city name are obvious 'derbies'. Manchester

United v Manchester City (P124: United 48: City 32); Bristol Rovers v Bristol City (P78: City 30: Rovers 23); Sheffield Wednesday v Sheffield United (P98: Wednesday 31: United 37); Nottingham Forest v Notts County (P86: Forest 35: County 28), but what about the rest? Generally accepted would be Arsenal v Tottenham Hotspur (P118: Arsenal 47: Spurs 44 — all in the top division); the East Anglian 'derby', Ipswich Town v Norwich City (P60: Town 31: City 20); the North-East 'derby', Newcastle United v Sunderland (P118: United 42: Sunderland 39); and the Potteries 'derby', Stoke City v Port Vale (P36: City 14: Vale 12).

The issue then becomes more clouded. Are these all 'derbies'? Southampton v Portsmouth? Newcastle v Middlesbrough? Middlesbrough v Sunderland? Any London club against any other London club? Watford v Luton Town? Barnsley v Rotherham United v Doncaster Rovers v Sheffield United/Wednesday? Burnley v Blackburn Rovers? Preston North End v Blackpool? Stockport County v Manchester United/City v Bury? Nottingham Forest v Derby County? I think not.

Despite all attempts to manufacture it, to call a match between Derby County and Nottingham Forest a local 'derby' just doesn't sound right, any more than does a match between Derby County and Leicester City. There is local rivalry, of course, which has intensified in recent years, but that doesn't make it a proper 'derby'. On the other hand, what does?

Monday, 21st October. Igor Stimac is suspended for three matches. Not good news.

Wednesday, 21st October. John Gregory appointed manager of Wycombe Wanderers. In his prime, Gregory is another former player who would have been a valuable addition to this Rams midfield. He was such a competent passer of the ball.

This Is Anfield

Anfield — Sunday, 27th October 1996

A S YOU GO down the players' tunnel to play against Liverpool, a sign on the wall above your head reads, 'This is Anfield'. You cannot miss it and it is there for a reason. It is a threat and a promise. It is saying that life is not going to be easy in the next 90 minutes and unless you are on your best mettle, you will be swept aside. It is no place for the timid, tentative and fainthearted. Many good teams have sunk without trace at Anfield. This is the biggest test yet for the Rams.

Going to Anfield is like being on a pilgrimage. The match was played on a Sunday and the M6 motorway was a continuous stream of cars and coaches heading towards Merseyside. Many of the coaches carried Rams followers, but most were carrying supporters wearing red. From all parts of the country they came. Wivenhoe in Essex, from Sussex, Hertfordshire and Birmingham, coaches packed with supporters, many, presumably, 'going home'. The cars bore registration numbers of infinite variety and, inevitably, there were roadworks. We began to get anxious about our time of arrival at Anfield.

A 4pm kick-off — for the benefit of Sky's television audience — contributed to a strange feeling as Graham Richards and I headed north — Colin Gibson was away in Florida, in Disneyland! No matter how much the schedule is affected by international matches, television requirements and so on, Saturday is the proper day for football. It's habit. Ingrained. Over a lifetime. Floodlight matches are for mid-week. Anything else is unnatural. Playing football at other times, seems oddly false.

If Sunday wasn't the real day for it, at least it was a real football day. Grey, overcast, a hint of drizzle in the air and heavier rain forecast for later. The papers are reporting a proposal to start the season a week earlier next year. That will mean the Charity Shield at Wembley taking place in July, probably in a heatwave. The authorities blame the increase in international matches and the need to release players to prepare for them. It seems to me that preparation is becoming an end in itself. It's growing like Topsy. The results of our national teams, at both football and cricket seem not to have improved in proportion to the increased amount of time spent 'preparing'. Only a few weeks ago, Poland played the pants off England at Wembley, after rounding up players from all parts of Europe and having only a couple of days of preparation. England prepared for nine days and were then, according to television summariser, Trevor Francis, 'surprised' by the way the Poles played in the first 20 minutes. How much preparation time do they need before they are not 'surprised'? A fortnight? Three weeks? Six months? I suppose the army of assistants that have grown up around the England team need something to do. Meanwhile, our Saturdays are taken away, no football matches at Easter and we are obliged to drive up the M6 on Sunday afternoons.

Sir Alf Ramsey wouldn't have stood for it. He was single-minded to the point of obstinacy. On one occasion, a very famous football manager, rang him at his home on the Sunday before an international match, which was scheduled for the following Wednesday. The manager thought he would be helping Ramsey by informing him, at an early stage, that a key defender had been injured and would not be able to play for England. So he rang Ramsey at home. The famous manager had hardly begun his message, when Ramsey interrupted him. "Do you know what day it is?" enquired the England boss, brusquely. "Sunday," was the reply. "Quite!" said Ramsey — and put down the telephone.

Just over 100 years ago, Liverpool had only one senior football club in the city — and that club was Everton. More surprisingly, Everton played at Anfield Road. It was only because of a row between Everton and the landlord of the Anfield Road ground, John Houlding, over the raising of the rent from £100 to £200, that Everton eventually moved away. Ironically, Houlding was Everton's main sponsor, but that didn't prevent him investing £500 to form his own club. His club became Liverpool Football Club. He wanted to take the name Everton with him but the FA decreed that name 'belonged' to the majority of members who had stayed behind.

It's no wonder, therefore, that Liverpool's manager of the 1960s and early 1970s, the legendary Bill Shankly, used to use Everton as a stick to whip up enthusiasm among Liverpool fans. "If Everton were playing at the bottom of my garden," said 'Shanks', "I would draw the curtains." The Reds' supporters loved it. Not that they have ever needed much whipping-up as far as Everton are concerned. The rivalry is fierce, intense, but usually laced with good humour. Shankly again: "There's only one place to be in Liverpool?"

"Where's that, Bill?"

"Looking down the table at Everton."

The Shanklyisms are numerous: "There are only two teams in Liverpool. Liverpool and Liverpool Reserves." It was in Shankly's time that the sign in the tunnel appeared.

Shankly loved to regale listeners with a favourite story of how HRH Princess Margaret was being introduced to the teams before the 1966 FA Cup Final, when Everton beat Sheffield Wednesday 3-2:

HRH: "But, Mr Labone, where actually is Everton?"

Brian Labone: "In Liverpool, ma'm."

HRH: "Of course. Of course. We had your first team here, last year."

Everton supporters, though, always remember that when their club won its first championship in 1891, it did so while playing at Anfield Road, where Everton played for eight years. Evertonians also claim that while Liverpool supporters' blood may be red, their blood is royal blue.

When Everton moved, they didn't move far. In fact, they moved just across Stanley Park, a matter of a few hundred yards, to Mere Green and on that site Goodison Park was developed — 'the first major football ground in England,' according to Simon Inglis in *The Football Grounds of England and Wales*.

The consequence of those manouverings 100 years ago is that within a very small area of Liverpool are two wonderful stadiums, housing two formidable teams. As kick-off time drew nearer, the Rams management and players would become increasingly aware that they were going into to a real hotbed of football. To play at Anfield is a great thrill. Jim Smith was upbeat, but he had a cautionary word for Igor Stimac: "This is not just an outing. We're going there with a sense of purpose. I hope Igor has a good game and he is sensible. Six bookings in nine games shows a lack of thought."

We parked in Stanley Park at about 2.30pm. Already the streets around the ground were a hive of activity. A real buzz was in the air. It was a reminder of when big crowds were commonplace and getting to matches early was essential. Police horses were everywhere, especially at the entrance to the narrow car-park that runs behind the Main Stand, which backs on to the terraced houses. The entrance to that car-park is through the Shankly Gates and as we approached along Anfield Road, we passed a sizeable crowd inspecting the memorial to those people who died in the Hillsborough disaster of 1989. The memorial is in marble and set into the wall alongside the Shankly Gates. It contains the names of 96 people. A copy of the Shankly Gates is in the memorial garden in Hillsborough Park, Sheffield. In lettering above the wrought iron Shankly Gates at Anfield are the words, 'You'll Never Walk Alone'.

The press box at Anfield is situated just behind the directors' box, about ten yards inside the Kop half of the pitch. It is a marvellous view, one of the best in the Premiership, despite the seats being cramped and space being limited. A full hour before kick-off, the ground was filling up and a crowd around 40,000 looked a likely attendance. Away to the right, on the famous Anfield Kop, supporters were beginning to take their accustomed seats. Even when it was a huge standing terrace, regular supporters had their own special places and there was a form of hierarchal system at work, so that strangers could not interrupt the pecking order. People used to be packed on the Kop like sardines, surging to and fro with the sway, especially in the 1960s when Shankly was the 'Pied Piper', Liverpool the centre of Beatlemania and everyone was a comedian. Many tales about life on the Kop are probably apocryphal, but the noise was real enough. Many of the more humorous football chants originated on the 'old' Kop at Anfield, while the Kopites probably had a special one for 22nd August 1964. That was the date of the first-ever *Match of the Day*, broadcast on BBC2 to a television audience of less than 75,000. Arsenal were the visitors and Liverpool won 3-2.

Opposite the Main Stand towers the huge Centenary Stand. The upper tier was completed in 1992, but it would have been finished much earlier, had it not been for the Mason sisters. Back in 1981, they owned the only house on Kemlyn Road that had not been previously bought over the years by the mighty Liverpool Football Club, number 26. They refused to sell and on many occasions were subjected to less than savoury harassment by Liverpool fans, who felt that the club's 'progress' was being denied. Perhaps they were Everton fans, but it took until 1990 and the threat of legal action, before Nora and Joan agreed to vacate their home. They then accepted an out-of-court settlement and moved to 'an undisclosed address', hopefully to live in peace and quiet. A blow for the 'little people'? Maybe, but it was an expensive delay for Liverpool.

As rain began to descend on Anfield, the sky darkened and the Rams' hopes of salvaging a point receded in the gloom. In eight previous visits, various Derby County teams hadn't scored even a single goal and this first-half performance gave little indication that things were about to change. It would be illuminating to know how many English teams, setting out to play for a draw, actually achieve that desired result. The continental teams seem to be much better at that sort of thing than we are. Perhaps the different tempo of the game in this country and the atmosphere in which matches are played has an effect. In the event, the Rams 'master plan' fell apart when Russell Hoult made a hash of a low shot from Liverpool's latest recruit, Patrik Berger, and Robbie Fowler snapped in the rebound. It wasn't the first time the ball bounced back off Hoult in this match and on one such occasion in the first half, Steve Mc-Manaman hit a post. When Fowler headed a second, a couple of minutes later, there were visions of a real hiding for Derby County. Fortunately, Liverpool didn't press home their advantage in the next ten minutes and the Rams recovered somewhat. Certain Liverpool teams of earlier years, those with a more ruthless streak, would not have been so generous. Two minutes from the end, Ashley Ward made the score 2-1, but the result flattered the Rams and everyone knew it.

It was Ward's first goal in the Premiership for the Rams and reward for a wholehearted display in a lone role at the front. If he can build on this display, the problems in attack will be reduced. Ward has had a difficult time since he came to Derby. It takes most people a period of time to settle into a different routine, when they change jobs, houses and move to different parts of the country. Yet those very people are rather quicker to be critical of players, if they don't settle immediately. Ward is one of the few Derby County players who has played in the Premiership before and the Rams are short of that sort of experience. This Anfield experience ought to stand Ward in good stead and his goal against Liverpool could be the start of better things to come. Significantly, Ward's goal was the first scored by the Rams at Anfield since 1977, when Kevin Hector found the back of Liverpool's net. The Rams still lost 3-1 and the latest result contributes to ten consecutive defeats against Liverpool at Anfield, a dismal record indeed. Nevertheless, it was a pleasure to return there. It is one of the most impressive grounds in English football.

Afterwards, I sensed Jim Smith was quite relieved to get away with an odd-goal defeat, despite making brave noises about 'taking the game to Liverpool more'. In reality, a margin of 3-0 would have been more appropriate, although it seemed to me that the Liverpool defence was not as secure as many people believed and that their new 'star' Dominic Matteo has plenty to do to justify being in the England squad. Later in the week, Jim Smith talked about Liverpool being the best side the Rams had played: "We've met Manchester United and Newcastle, but I think Liverpool are the best team we've faced so far." My preference would be for Wimbledon — on the day.

Team: Hoult; Laursen, C. Powell, Rowett, McGrath, Stimac, Dailly (sub Simpson), Asanovic, D. Powell (sub Carsley), Ward, Willems (sub Flynn).
Scorer: Ward
Attendance: 39,515

Football Idols (part 1)

On the weekend before the Liverpool match, Chelsea Football Club suffered a grievous blow, when vice-chairman Matthew Harding was killed in a helicopter crash. The aircraft was carrying a party back to London following Chelsea's Coca Cola Cup match at

Bolton and there were no survivors. The national press carried massive coverage of the death of Harding, who had been instrumental in providing financial backing for Chelsea's ground improvement schemes. He had also had some well publicised fall-outs with the spiky Chelsea chairman, Ken Bates, which provided the newspapers with plenty of material. Harding was an extremely popular figure around the King's Road.

The following is an extract from an article I wrote for the *Burton Mail*, published the week after the Rams played at Anfield:

> Forgive me if this sounds callous and maybe I am out of step, but I cannot, in all honesty, understand the eulogising of Matthew Harding. Harding's death was, obviously, a tragedy, as is anyone's at the age of 42. Undoubtedly, the family suffered considerable grief and sympathy is extended to them. Of course, Chelsea Football Club have, unexpectedly, lost a vice-chairman and a benefactor, but after that, I fail to see why so much publicity has been given to the death of someone who, a couple of years ago, most people had never heard of and who had no impact on the game beyond, the boundaries of Stamford Bridge.
>
> Over the years, I've stood on many grounds and observed a minute's silence to the memory of football people. In recent times, Billy Wright and Bobby Moore, were two icons of the game that merited observation of such a tribute at football grounds throughout the land. I've also stood on grounds when a similar tribute has been paid to someone who had a special significance for the home, or visiting, club. That, at Stamford Bridge, would have been appropriate for Matthew Harding.
>
> What we had instead was the national press indulging in a orgy of dripping sentimentality and spectators on grounds throughout the Premiership observing the ritual. Standing along with almost 40,000 people, observing a

minute's silence in memory of an obscure vice-chairman of a London club, before the Liverpool versus Derby County match at Anfield — where they know a bit about football tragedy after Heysel and Hillsborough — was an odd experience. It seems to me that making a martyr of Matthew Harding illustrates the confused and muddled state of thinking that football has managed to get itself into. Beware, football is beginning to worship false idols.

Football Idols (part 2)

On Monday, 28th October 1996, a memorial to Steve Bloomer was unveiled. His grandson, Steve Richards, a former journalist, conducted the ceremony and the memorial stands in the Lock-up Yard, in The Cornmarket, to remind passers-by that the legendary Bloomer scored 332 goals for the Rams in 525 appearances, between 1891 and 1913. To raise money for the marble memorial, some of Bloomer's England caps were auctioned. One of the buyers was Michael Knighton, who made an audacious bid to buy Manchester United for £10 million in the late 1980s and who is now chairman of Carlisle United. Great players including Tom Finney, Nat Lofthouse, Wilf Mannion, Johnny Morris, Arthur Rowley and Roy McFarland attended the ceremony, followed by a reception at the Assembly Rooms. Many former Rams players, along with Lionel Pickering and Jim Smith, also attended a poignant occasion.

Tuesday, 29th October 1996: The Rams released 32 year-old Paul Parker. The former England defender joined Derby in August on a free transfer from Manchester United, in order to provide Premiership experience. He was on a monthly contract and played four Premiership and two League Cup matches for the club, but the signing of Paul McGrath meant he was surplus to requirements.

Wednesday, 30th October 1996: Reports linking Jim Smith with the vacant manager's position at Blackburn Rovers were denied. "The report is absolute nonsense," said Smith. "My ambitions are with Derby and I am not thinking of moving."

Good.

November promise

Two valuable home victories at the start of the month saw the Rams begin November in fine style. After the encouraging start to the season, the 1-1 draw against Nottingham Forest in October, plus defeats against Newcastle United (1-0) and Liverpool (2-1), left the Rams vulnerable and supporters edgy. With three home matches and an away fixture in the month, against teams likely to finish in the bottom half of the table, it was vital for the Rams to take points all round. Following a competent victory over a limited Leicester City (2-0), a fortunate win against troubled Middlesbrough, on Sunday, 17th November, proved to be a very useful result.

Pastures New

Sunday, 17th November, the day of the Middlesbrough match, was significant for another reason. Lionel Pickering performed the ceremony of laying the foundation stone for the new stadium at Pride Park. On a bitterly cold and rainy day, more than 1,000 people turned up to see the event at 1.15pm, before moving off to the Baseball Ground to see Fabrizio Ravanelli and Juninho *et al*. The player they didn't see was the other Brazilian, Emerson. He was back home in Brazil and, apparently, about to cause Middlesbrough a few problems in locating him. Agents trying to engineer a transfer to Barcelona were rumoured to be behind Emerson's sudden discontent with Teesside in winter — "What did he expect, bloody palm trees?" asked Brian Clough — from where another Brazilian, Branco, had been released, his contract being paid up to the tune of many tens of thousands of pounds. The whole Middlesbrough cosmopolitan gravy train seemed to be going off the rails. Since the importation of foreigners began in the previous January, Middlesbrough had sunk down the Premiership like a stone and five wins in 32 matches was not doing a lot for international relations. Talking of relations, Emerson's newly-acquired wife was also playing a leading role in the drama, as Bryan Robson, the Middlesbrough manager, struggled bravely to come to terms with what the media had thought was a good idea at the time. Meanwhile, the youngish Middlesbrough chairman, Steve Gibson, was threatening all sorts of retribution against his wayward travelling star. Not that it mattered much to the Rams. Emerson was suspended anyway and his delayed arrival from Rio de Janeiro and Copacobana Beach was purely of passing interest. He eventually watched the match from the stand. Result: Derby County 2 Middlesbrough 1. The Rams were lucky.

Blowing Bubbles

Upton Park (Boleyn Ground) — Saturday, 23rd November 1996.

WEST Ham United 1 Derby County 1. The London press said it was a dour match. How on earth did they arrive at that opinion? The game flowed from end to end. There were patches of decent football. Some chances were created and missed. It wasn't a classic, but there were some good individual performances. For example, Aljosa Asanovic's display was outstanding and worth the admission money on its own. It was Asanovic's best so far and was from a deeper position, which meant the whole team was forced to play shorter than in the previous home match against Middlesbrough. Dean Sturridge did well, especially in the second half, and the goal he scored should help his confidence, while anyone who does not get pleasure from watching Paul McGrath play, is seriously in need of a break from football. I knew McGrath was a good player, but I didn't realise he was as good as this. No. It was a better match than the London scribes told their world. Their world tends to move in small circles.

Of course, what constitutes a 'good' match, depends on what you are looking for. What was lacking at Upton Park was the controversial incident, which makes for a 'story'. Unfortunately, for many journalists, it wasn't there and so it was the football match itself that they had to concentrate on. Not surprisingly, the defensive expertise of McGrath, Dean Yates and Gary Rowett, received scant mention and the continued excellence of Chris Powell was completely ignored.

Actually, the Rams did well to get back into the match after Russell Hoult threw away a goal in the 16th minute — literally. "Don't throw the ball straight down the field," the coaches tell junior goalkeepers. "Throw it towards the wings." Hoult didn't remember. Darryl Powell was caught straining to reach the ball as it sped away from his outstretched foot some 40 yards out. Ian Bishop intercepted, moved forward before Powell could recover and struck a beauty. Hammers one up. Bishop doesn't score many, but he'll remember this one. Jim Smith's face must have been a picture as the shot bulged the Rams' net, right in front of the travelling supporters. No wonder managers get excited. Such happenings could lead to heart attacks on the spot.

If the Rams did well to recover, so did Hoult. Good temperament is an essential requirement for a goalkeeper. It's not all about talent, this football game, and goalkeeping is essentially about mistakes, not saves. Not too long ago, when managers wore overcoats and sat in the stand, the best ones used to check on something they called 'character', before spending other people's money on transfer fees. That meant that they built teams that didn't fold in adversity and acquired players that had a consistent level of performance, somewhere near to potential. Goalkeeping, more than anything, is about that and it will be interesting to discover whether Hoult has it. There are further encouraging signs that with just over a third of the season gone, the Rams are beginning to show the kind of resilience of spirit — and character — that can overcome greater talent.

Graham Richards always describes Upton Park — or the Boleyn Ground, as he prefers to call it — as London's answer to the Baseball

Ground. The Boleyn part of the name drives from a house that stood next to the ground until the 1950s, which at one time was used as a Catholic school. The house was built in 1544, had two turrets and was called locally, Boleyn Castle, after Henry VIII's second wife, Anne Boleyn. Many grounds are named after the road, street, or district in which they stand, which is why Upton Park has become the more fashionable name. In that respect, 'The Baseball Ground' is a neat and unusual exception to the district rule, being named after a specific game that was played there. Following that precedent, shouldn't the Rams' new stadium be called, simply: 'The Football Ground'?

Graham's description of Upton Park is accurate, particularly as it used to be, so tight and intimidating. It was so tight that the goal nets used to hang down so close to the goal-line, you felt that the goalkeeper was in danger of being entangled in them. Now, like on many Premiership grounds, the goal nets extend well back and the whole goal is like a big rectangular cage, with a lot of space into which the ball travels before it hits the net. A goal always looks more spectacular like that. Photographers must like it as they get more time to catch the explosive shot — like Bishop's.

Upton Park was intimidating when I played there in a League Cup tie in October 1965. At the end of that season, three West Ham United players won World Cup medals. Unsurprisingly, we lost 4-0. Later that evening, in the same way as Jack Charlton did after that same World Cup triumph, I went on to the Astor Club in the West End. Sulkie's, as it was known, was a regular sportsmen's haunt in the 1960s, for teams playing in London, but if 'Big' Jack went to celebrate, we went to drown our sorrows. Shortly after midnight, I rang home. The voice that answered was not that of my wife, Angela, but that of my mother and, to the sounds of cabaret in the foreground and the clink of gambling tables in the background, she gave me the news that our eldest son, David, had been born at about the same time as Peter Brabrook rattled in the fourth. Such is life.

Latterly, Upton Park has moved with the times. The Bobby

Moore Stand, completed in 1994, dominates the skyline at the Barking Road end of the ground. Behind the goal at the other end is the Centenary Stand, which opened the following year. They are the modern versions of the Osmaston and Normanton Stands, which were built at the Baseball Ground over 60 years ago. I wonder if they will last as long? At the time they were built, the Osmaston and Normanton stands must have been every bit as impressive as the giant structures of today. They certainly remain the most potent symbols of Baseball Ground history and, because they enclose and capture the sound so effectively, have been instrumental in the creation of the unique Baseball Ground atmosphere that so worries and sometimes intimidates visiting teams.

As always before duties commenced, a wander round the stadium was called for, with a visit to the Bobby Moore Stand, obligatory. In the foyer of the stand is a reception desk from where executive members and box holders can be transported by lift to their plush banqueting accommodation. There, they are hosted by former West Ham heroes like Geoff Hurst. Downstairs, alongside the reception desk, is a bronze bust of Bobby Moore himself, with a portrait on the wall behind. You feel that he is casting an eye on all who enter.

Just outside the ground, less ostentatious, but, perhaps, more significant, is another and more homely recognition of Moore. Tucked into the wall of the road that runs behind the East Stand and at right angles to the Bobby Moore Stand, there is a small, superbly run serving hatch, from which huge rolls and large hamburgers can be purchased, to include free salad off the dishes on the counter. The little room behind is scrupulously clean and spic and span, while the girls that serve there are bright and cheerful. Photographs of West Ham heroes adorn the wall at the rear and side of the cabin and form a picture gallery of the Hammers' history. In pride of place, right in the centre, is a signed photograph of Bobby Moore OBE. He was, indisputably, one of football's all-time greats and a favourite son of West Ham United. Bobby Moore died of cancer in 1993. He was aged 51.

There is never any doubting the strong feeling of community around Upton Park, particularly represented in the East Stand. In front of it used to be the notorious 'Chicken Run', where the East End's finest always congregated to make the opposition winger's life a misery. So tight to the pitch was the narrow paddock and so tight was the crowd, packed together on the terrace, that the 'Chicken Run' often swayed and surged like a live thing taking part in the match itself; and I suppose that, in a way, it was. Certainly, there was no shortage of advice and many wingers tended to play in a style that today's coaching parlance would call, 'narrow'. Now, spectators in the 'Chicken Run' are seated and the general complaint from supporters at Upton Park is that the ground has lost a lot of the atmosphere of former days and which made it unique. Amazingly, the same is said about Highbury and Old Trafford. Will Derby County's new stadium retain the acoustic qualities which have been dissipated at these other Premiership venues? We shall see. Certainly, the famous Hammer's song, *I'm Forever Blowing Bubbles*, was strangely muted on this day. After the euphoria of the laying of the foundation stone of the new stadium at Pride Park dies down, one hopes that the construction will allow for a similar atmosphere to be created to that which made the Baseball Ground famous. If so, supporters of Derby County will have less to grumble about, than the patrons around E13.

What the patrons around E13 had most to grumble about on this ideal football day in November, was the quality of football they were seeing from their team. Although the Hammers did, at times, try to play in the traditional West Ham style — keeping the ball moving through midfield, with plenty of mobility off the ball — they were not good enough at it. Having Iain Dowie at centre-forward meant that the high ball up the middle was always a temptation to which they subscribed too often. The result was a falling between two styles of play and the Hammers rarely looked like scoring. The present playing style is symptomatic of the club generally. West Ham United is a club that seems to have lost its way.

Harry Redknapp, the Hammer's manager and former player, can sometimes look as doleful as a chastised spaniel. He probably wore a similar expression when he plied his trade as a nervous winger in front of the 'Chicken Run'. Whatever the reason, his face was longer than ever after the match and no wonder. The fact is that for a club that has produced so many of its own players, West Ham United have gone too far in speculating in foreign lands. There are 11 foreigners on the club's books, the highest number in the Premiership, many with unpronounceable names. Some managers think that Scandinavian players are more likely to settle in our game than southern and eastern Europeans, or South Americans, but it seems that Redknapp does not subscribe to that view. Like a man at the check-out at an Asda store, Redknapp has impulsively bought an assorted bag of exotic 'all-sorts'. He may regret it. On the evidence of this match, Hugo Porfirio, Stan Lazaridis, Slaven Bilic and Ludek Miklosko are not likely to get the Hammers' fans singing 'bubbles' too often. Whether Illie Dumitrescu, Florin Raducioiu, Paulo Futre, Steve Mautone and Mark Reiper can do so is even more unlikely. They didn't even play.

Significantly, the mood around the ground and the talk among Hammers supporters, even before the match started, was of bewilderment about the direction in which the club is going and that West Ham United has taken a wrong turning. A club that once prided itself on being intrinsically identified with its supporters has, for the moment, lost its identity. It is likely that the problem began with the ill-founded Hammers Bond scheme, which was launched in the early 1990s, to finance ground development and in that messy affair, it was shown that the West Ham United board of directors had lost touch with the club's supporters.

Whether a bond scheme — an up-front payment which guarantees a seat for a certain period of time — is a desirable means of raising money from supporters is debatable. In East London it patently was not (and the Hammers Bond scheme guaranteed a seat for only one season, not several as at Highbury and Elland Road).

In 1991, the West Ham club sent out a consultative questionnaire to its supporters asking for their opinions about the scheme. Seventy per cent of respondents expressed an interest. Were their views heeded? Apparently not. When the club eventually announced that the Hammers Bond could be purchased, less than five per cent were bought. The affair caused much heartache, bitterness and recrimination. Pitch sit-ins and boycotts against the scheme were organised and unofficial supporters' groups were formed. In the meantime, terrace ticket prices went up 80 per cent and the Hammers were relegated. The image of the 'family club' disappeared, quickly. Whether it can be rebuilt remains to be seen, but an unsuccessful foreign legion playing in claret and blue seems a strange way of trying to do it. Alf Garnett would have a few words to say.

Team: Hoult; Laursen (sub Carsley), C.Powell, Yates, McGrath, Rowett, Flynn, D.Powell, Asanovic, Sturridge, Ward.
Scorer: Sturridge.
Attendance: 24,576

P.S. The nickname 'The Hammers' is not because they come from West Ham. It's because workers in the shipyards used hammers and London's East End Docks is where the club was formed in 1895. Thames Ironworks was the largest shipyard in the area and the owner, Arnold Hills, was the man who formed the club which bore that name. He withdrew his support when professional players were signed in 1898, but Thames Ironworks reformed in 1900, as West Ham United. They moved to the Boleyn Ground in 1904 and are sometimes still referred to as 'The Irons'. 'Appy 'Ammers, though? Not at the moment.

Marble Halls

Highbury — Saturday, 7th December 1996.

FRIDAY 6th November 1996: The Rams go to Highbury tomorrow in ninth place in the Premiership table, with 21 points from 15 games. Back in August when the season started, most people thought that such a position would have been out of the question. Now, a few are whispering about the possibility of qualifying for Europe. Why not? The Rams have shown themselves to be hard to beat and the players are confident in their ability to cope with this standard of football, but Arsenal, we fear, will be a different proposition to Coventry City, last week's visitors to the Baseball Ground, who were beaten 2-1. Arsenal lead the Premiership by three points and under their new French manager, Arsene Wenger, appear to have added midfield flair and greater goalscoring potential to their defensive reliability. Jim Smith is already talking about altering the Rams' formation to counter the threat from the Gunners. His problem is that he has four excellent central defenders, Igor Stimac, Paul McGrath, Dean Yates and Gary Rowett, to fit into three central defensive positions in the 3-5-2 system that the Rams play. What will he do? We shall see. Meanwhile, we're all looking forward to visiting one of the really great stadiums in the football world.

Saturday, 7th December 1996: This was the day the Rams came of age in the Premiership. Any lingering doubts that Derby County do not really deserve to be in the top flight, were banished by their best performance of the season, so far. Arsenal were second best to a Rams side full of composure and a determination to be taken seriously. The impression Derby County made on the London press was considerable; the fright given to the Arsenal faithful was enormous; the confidence given to Rams supporters for the rest of the season was almost measurable. The Rams earned new respect around the Premiership, as Arsenal only rescued a point with a spectacular second goal 11 seconds from the end. It was that close. A 2-2 scoreline. It was a memorable occasion.

The day began normally. An early start and The Little Chef at Brickett's Wood. There's nothing like a familiar routine for a difficult fixture. Much of the talk was about who would play. Whether Gary Rowett might be detailed to man mark either Paul Merson, or Patrik Vieira, so allowing Dean Yates to play. In the event, neither happened. Chris Powell returned to the side after a particularly painful bereavement, the death of his new-born baby daughter, otherwise the team was that which beat Coventry City. In that match many people were impressed by the performance of Dean Sturridge. His pace was altogether too much for the Coventry central defenders, Liam Daish, Richard Shaw and former Rams favourite, Paul Williams.

Williams and Sturridge are two players to have come through the Rams youth system, but it has taken a long time. Jim Smith was not complimentary about that aspect of the club's activities in recent years, when he spoke at the shareholders' meeting last week and a heavy defeat in the FA Youth Cup, by Bolton Wanderers, added weight to his opinion. At least the new Rams Academies system, instigated by director Stuart Webb and administered by John Jarman and Barrie Greenwood, to increase coaching for juniors around the county, is a step in the right direction. It does not begin to compare with Liverpool's investment of £8 million to set up their own

Academy, based on the Ajax model in Holland, but as the Chinese proverb says, "Great oaks from little acorns grow." Sometimes.

Back in the 1950s, Manchester United and Wolverhampton Wanderers cornered the market in schoolboy international talent and established strong youth schemes. The results of that policy was that United won the FA Youth Cup in the first five years of its existence between 1953-57. That competition was the breeding ground for players like Duncan Edwards, Eddie Colman, David Pegg, Mark Jones, Billy Whelan, Roger Byrne and Geoff Bent — who all died in the Munich air crash in February 1958 — Albert Scanlon, Denis Violett and Bobby Charlton. They became known as the 'Busby Babes'. Many other players, who did not make the first team, at either club, were sold at a handsome profit. The emphasis on youth development paid many dividends.

Perhaps the wheel has turned full circle. The Bosman ruling on contracts has concentrated some minds on the necessity of tending the grass roots of the game, if football talent is to be nurtured properly. You can never tell where a diamond might be found. If the Rams Academies scheme can unearth a Duncan Edwards — who began as a schoolboy in Dudley, near Wolverhampton — a Roger Byrne, or a Bobby Charlton, it will have paid for itself many times over. Tony Adams and Paul Merson are products of the Arsenal system, Robbie Fowler, Steve McManaman and Dominic Matteo are Liverpool examples and Manchester United still lead the way. Is it not significant that they are our three most successful clubs in the past decade?

One would be hard pressed to name another stadium so completely enclosed by houses as Highbury. Goodison Park and Anfield are similarly surrounded, but not quite as tightly as the ground that Arsenal have occupied since 1913. Parking is at a premium around the ground and, after we had decided to stay in London on Saturday night, the equipment was dropped off at the stadium and Graham and I went to park the car at our overnight lodgings near to the Embankment. That meant we could travel back to the ground, via the London Underground, which enabled us to observe Arsenal supporters on their way to the match and marvel at the change in attire for supporters that has taken place over the past 30 years. In bygone days, a single rosette, a wooden rattle and, perhaps, a scarf would have been all that was required to denote a youngster's allegiance. Few adults would deign to be so seen so obviously supporting their team. Not now. These days, the regalia is endless. Elderly men in red shirts, many apparently displayed over jackets and coats, because of the cold. Women with badges, scarves, hats, gloves. You name it, they had it, all to identify with their heroes. The power of commercialism is frightening. Was football ever just about playing and watching? Perhaps not, but there's no doubt now that the business of football, is business. Everyone's at it. Perhaps, in a more subtle way, it was always so. Such a reminder came when we alighted at London Underground's Arsenal station. The station was formerly called Gillespie Road but in 1932, the club — or rather their legendary manager Herbert Chapman — persuaded London Transport to change the name to Arsenal. The result was that Arsenal's name is incorporated on all the underground maps and literature associated with the underground system — and at no charge! Now that really is marketing. I'll say.

Outside the station, the preparations for a big match were well under way. Street vendors of all descriptions were busy enticing young and old alike with mementos, memorabilia and all the para-phernalia and nick-nackery imaginable. Tee shirt printers were doing a roaring trade in not only promoting pro-Arsenal messages, but anti-Spurs and anti-Chelsea slogans. I noticed several who had been similarly busy at West Ham, with anti-Arsenal slogans. Leopards changing their spots. Several Victorian terraced houses had their huge bay fronted windows open and were acting as mini burger and sandwich bars, others were selling scarves and Arsenal replica shirts. The police horses, too, were moving into position, clanking their massive hooves on the road surface and leaving a hot, steaming trail to bring on the rhubarb crop, as evidence of their progress.

On match day, the streets around Highbury have a life of their own. I wonder how the trend to modern, edge-of-town stadiums will affect the football culture that has grown up around traditional grounds where much of the population has grown up with them. Going to a match involves so much more than the match itself. It is being part of where spectators congregate in groups. Regular meeting places where you can see the same faces. Younger supporters, too, dressed in appropriate colours, always impatient to get in, tugging on the sleeves of parents to hurry them to the turnstiles. Apparently oblivious to the game itself, street sellers ply their trade as officials push past, looking serious. Programme and magazine sellers shout the odds. "Get, yer official programme 'ere," they cry. "One fifty, only." There were days were when you could get the best seat in the Main Stand for that. Not now. The ticket prices, prominently displayed for the next match, against Aston Villa on Boxing Day in three weeks time, tell a much more expensive tale. Even so, most are sold.

The main entrance to Highbury backs on to Avenell Road and entry into the marble foyer of the East Stand is up a flight of half a dozen steps. Around the foot of the steps, and spilling out on to the road, a crowd of several hundred always gathers to catch sight of real, or imagined, celebrities and to watch the visitors' coach arrive. It's noticeable, here, that the ticket touts have begun to filter back to football, not just to cup-ties and internationals, but to ordinary Premiership matches such as this between Arsenal and Derby County. That's a sure sign that football is prospering.

Ernie Hallam, as always, stands outside the main entrance of the home team stadium, as kick-off time approaches. From Torquay to Carlisle and Newcastle to Southampton, Ernie has seen them all. He organises the away trips for Supporters' Club members and still looks as spry as he probably was when he saw the Rams win the FA Cup in 1946, by beating Charlton Athletic 4-1. That was the first Cup Final after World War Two, which means many people remember it as a very, special occasion. The Cup is an evocative and integral part of any football season and once the season reaches into December, the entry of the major clubs into the competition becomes imminent. Dreams of drawing Manchester United at Old Trafford fill the minds of the minnows. Or Arsenal at Highbury.

Bob Wilson appears briefly in the doorway, searching for a face in the crowd. Many years ago, he and I played in the same Chesterfield Boys under-15s team that reached the semi-final of the English Schools FA Shield. We drew 1-1 against Swansea Boys, in front of 18,500 at Saltergate, but lost the replay 2-0, the following week at the Vetch Field, this time before a crowd of just over 18,000. In between, I played for England Boys at Wembley, in front of 95,000. Smaller crowds, bigger prices. It's a different game now.

The Rams team were late arriving. Premiership rules require them to be at the ground and handing in the team sheet an hour before the start. The Rams have been staying at St Albans and we were to learn later from chief executive Keith Loring that the Metropolitan Police escort, having arranged to meet the team coach at a particular traffic island to guide the party to the ground, had gone to the wrong destination. Hence the delay. The club will be fined. More important, some players will be deflected from their pre-match routine. Little things can mean a lot as kick-off time approaches.

It's quite strange how players vary in their preparations before a match. Some players like to be in the dressing-room early, others are always arriving at the last minute. The modern fashion of warming up on the pitch has altered a lot of what used to be well-established pre-match routines. Former Rams goalkeepers Ken Oxford and later, Reg Matthews, always disappeared into the toilet for a quick fag. It must be the nature of the job. Trainer Ralph Hann reckoned he would put a stop to it, but that was only for the benefit of everyone else. He knew it would be more than his life was worth to separate either from the weed at such an important time. Rumour had it that 'the Ox' kept a nub end behind one of the goalposts, just in case he needed a 'pick me up' in the second half.

He sometimes did need a 'pick me up', especially when he knocked himself out on the back post after backing along his line for a high centre. He did that on more than one occasion. Jack Parry usually went in goal. No substitutes, of course. Ken Oxford was one of the bravest goalkeepers I've ever seen. No turning, no flinching, when short-range stuff was in the offing and feet were flying. In later years he worked in the security business, collecting money from banks and the like. On one occasion, he received a commendation from a judge for his bravery in resisting an attempted robbery in Ilkeston. You could depend on 'the Ox'.

If Oxford was the bravest, Matthews was the hardest. Reg always considered he had not performed well in the match, unless he had left his mark on at least one opposing forward. His reputation was such that most forwards kept out of his way, but he was always on the look out for the unsuspecting. As all goalkeepers do, he fancied himself as an outfield player and used to career around in five-a-sides, all knees and elbows. Anyone who came even near him was liable to carry a bruise afterwards. Like 'the Ox', Reg smoked like a chimney, but it didn't affect his athleticism. He was agile and, like a cat, could stretch like elastic to make the flying save that photographers spent hours waiting for as they sat along the line at the side of the goal on a wet November day. Now, photographers use telephoto lenses, so spectators no longer have the pleasure of seeing a big, hairy defender sliding into them, to send hats and tripods flying in all directions.

Reg was capped five times by England in the mid-1950s. He was playing for Coventry City then, who were in the Third Division South at the time. That was an amazing achievement. Also amazing was his pre-match routine, whereby he put his kit on from his boots upwards and woe betide anyone who upset his routine. Taut? Like a violin string. Reg Matthews was the most highly strung player I've ever seen.

The press room at Highbury is luxurious. Wooden panelling, plush carpets and alongside is a special interview room in which the managers give the obligatory after-match press conference. The interview room is like a small courtroom, with three or four rows of theatre seats facing what could be a judge's bench at the front. Graham Richards, who knows a thing or two about such things, was mightily impressed. It was all very formal. Always hovering is the lady press officer, who ushers the managers in and ushers the various sections of the press out, when time is up. The whole business is a ritual. I am amazed why managers put up with the charade of the press conference. I suppose the regulations of the Premiership, drafted by a civil servant, demand it, but it makes for a cosy consensus all round and a lack of individual and incisive match reporting.

Jim Smith is always very patient in such circumstances. After he had departed, Arsene Wenger arrived. He impressed and it was easy to see why he is getting such a good reception in the London media. Once Wenger had said the right things about the match, the press officer, Claire Tomlinson, took charge. "Sundays out," she ordered and a dozen or more hard bitten hacks sheepishly filed out of the room. "Mondays only," was the next instruction and a number of Fleet Street's finest crowded to the front to get a Monday 'exclusive" with Patrick Vieira, who Wenger had brought to the gathering. Thus Vieira was almost guaranteed star billing in the Monday tabloids, regardless of how he had performed in the match. As it happened, he had scored the last-minute equalising goal, although he did little else apart from clatter Sean Flynn from behind in the second half. It was enough for the 'Mondays', however. 'Arsenal owe it all to Viera,' shrieked the headlines, followed by an 'exclusive' interview.

Later that evening, we went to The Gaucho Grill in London's West End. Going to Highbury means doing things in style. The bill was horrendous.

Team: Hoult; Laursen, C.Powell, Rowett, McGrath, Stimac, Flynn (sub Carbon), D.Powell, Asanovic (sub Dailly), Sturridge, Ward.

Scorers: Sturridge, D.Powell.
Attendance: 38,018

Monday, 16th December 1996: Derby County 0 Everton 1
Did Jim Smith make a substitute mistake? Ten minutes from the
end, Asanovic was surprisingly replaced. That released Everton midfielder Joe Parkinson from his man-for-man marking job on Asanovic and he ventured forward for the first time in the match, to hit
the bar with his shot. Nick Barmby netted the rebound. A point
thrown away? Perhaps so.

Harbour Lights

The Dell — Saturday, 21st December 1996

THE last Saturday before Christmas brought a trip to Southampton. It's traditionally a day when attendances are low, due to last-minute Christmas shopping, although the shops are open at night and on Sundays now, so it is hard to imagine why you would have to do your shopping when there is a football match to watch. At The Dell, the attendance wasn't affected. It is always low, despite a sell out crowd.

The Dell is the smallest ground in the Premiership, with a capacity of only 15,352. In a football age dominated by money, the Saints are now looking elsewhere to boost their income. In fact, they are looking to Stoneham, which is an open area on the edge of the city, and a new stadium to seat 30,000. In theory, it would enable Southampton Football Club to double its money every match. That is the theory — but we've heard it all before. Unfortunately, there are a couple of important snags. First, the theory assumes that the stadium will always be full. That rapidly brings into focus the second problem. The club needs to stay in the Premiership to fill it.

There is no doubt that, in the past, the Saints have had their moments. When Lawrie McMenemy was manager in the 1970s, he adopted the policy initiated by Tony Waddington at Stoke City in the 1960s, by recruiting big-name players who were coming towards the end of their careers. Alan Ball, Peter Osgood, Jimmy Gabriel, Peter Shilton and Kevin Keegan joined established Saints like Terry Paine and Mike Channon to make Southampton attractive to watch and hard to play against. They acquired quite a tasty reputation off the field, too.

On a warm May day, some 20 years ago, Bobby Stokes scored a second-half goal, from a pass by Jim McCalliog, for Southampton to pull off one of the major Wembley shocks of all time, by beating Manchester United 1-0 in the 1976 FA Cup Final. The Saints were in the Second Division at the time and Tommy Docherty was the United manager. I wonder what he said about that? Probably, that the goal was offside. It certainly looked like it, but few had sympathy for United that day.

In 1984, Liverpool won the League championship — again — and Southampton were runners-up. The Saints qualified for Europe. They were great days then on the south coast, but this is now and the evidence of recent years is less encouraging. Last season, Southampton escaped relegation by the skin of their teeth on the very last day. A better goal-difference kept them up and sent Manchester City down with 38 points. A couple of years earlier, the Saints survived by a single point. At the start of each season, Southampton are one of the bookmakers' favourites for relegation and even the recruitment of Graeme Souness as manager, has not changed that.

Despite the 3-1 win against the Rams, the bookmakers could be right. Southampton look to be relegation material. On the day, that didn't say much for Derby County, whose own stadium plans have similar reasoning to that being propagated by Southampton. Next week, on Boxing Day, we will hear the same message at Sunderland. They, too, are to move from Roker Park and have already announced a flotation on the Stock Exchange. In his column in the match-day programme, Southampton chairman Guy Askham indulged in some 'business speak', calculated, in his mind, to reassure the doubters:

Dear Supporter,

You may be aware that on December 10 it was announced that the club is to merge with Secure Retirement plc, subject to shareholders' approval.

This will mean that in due course the Club may become a subsidiary of the merged group that will be renamed Southampton Leisure Holdings plc.

This is a very important deal for the Club, its supporters, staff and shareholders.

Secure is bringing to the table cash, assets, access to Stock Market funding and proven business skills. We have great ambitions for this club and this change will play a very important part in achieving them …etc …etc.

Secure Retirement plc is an odd name to be associated with a football club and, although Askham's message sounds very impressive, can all three clubs — Southampton, Sunderland and Derby County — avoid relegation? And if they fail, what happens then? There is talk in the newspapers that Sir David Frost is interested in investing in Southampton Football Club. Frost made his name in a 1960s satirical television show called *That Was the Week that Was*, which is an apt title for being involved in football. Frost did have trials with Nottingham Forest as a youngster, which indicates he might have some regard for the game itself, although less encouraging is that Frost is involved with 'a syndicate'. Having 'a syndicate', or 'a consortium' around a football club is like having Blind Pugh around a dark alley and about to slip you the black spot. Ask Nottingham Forest. At least these days the Rams are in the hands of local people.

The way the Rams played at The Dell, it looked as though they had been slipped several black spots. The travelling supporters must have been dismayed. The real chance to win the match came in the first 20 minutes when, despite the absence of Dean Sturridge, the Southampton defence was all at sea as Rams players ran through from the halfway line. Christian Dailly did score by such a process after eight minutes and the Rams might have been three goals ahead in no time at all. Then, crucial errors by goalkeeper Russell Hoult turned a 1-0 lead into a 2-1 deficit, all in 13 minutes. After that, the Rams simply hammered the ball around the field. Jacob Laursen and Gary Rowett gave the lead and most of the team forgot about the controlled passing, which was such a feature of the visit to Highbury. As against Everton, the Rams were too easily drawn into a game in which the tempo was dictated by the opposition. Jim Smith was not impressed. "Our worst performance of the season," he said. No-one disagreed. For the first time in the Premiership, Derby County were beaten by a team below them in the table and, to make matters worse, Southampton were clearly an inferior outfit. Christmas had not got off to a good start.

It was my first-ever visit to The Dell for a football match. I had wandered down from the cricket ground on Northlands Road, during a break for rain in the Hampshire v Derbyshire match of a year ago, to inspect one of the few grounds I had never played on. The reconstruction of the Milton Road End, that end where the peculiar 'Chocolate Boxes' — three concrete platforms on stilts, the only uncovered upper tiers of terracing on a British ground — used to be, was taking place and it struck me that if the Baseball Ground is cramped, The Dell is even more so.

Like Derby County, Southampton played their early matches on the county cricket club's ground, before moving to their present site in 1898. (The Rams moved to the Baseball Ground from the County Ground in 1895). Like existed between Derby County and Derbyshire, the links between football and cricket have always been close between Southampton and Hampshire. Several players, in years gone by, played for both clubs and of the 12 players who reached the heights of playing for England at both sports, Southampton and Hampshire provide two.

One was the great C.B. Fry, who played in the 1902 FA Cup Final, also held the world long jump record and was once offered the throne of Albania (and who is buried in Repton Churchyard).

The other was Johnny Arnold, a nippy outside-left and right-hand opening batsman, who played once at cricket, against New Zealand in 1931 and once at football, against Scotland in 1933. He was a true one-cap wonder, but what a pair of caps.

Being a dual professional sportsman had its moments. Back in 1961, on 23rd August, I played against Luton Town at the Baseball Ground in front of a crowd of 18,645. Seven days earlier, I had completed my cricket season by playing for Derbyshire against Hampshire at the County Ground. A few days training, a reserve match on the Saturday and into a Second Division match on the Wednesday night. Hectic stuff. There were a few cricketer-footballers around then. Derbyshire had two others in Ian Buxton and Ray Swallow (who also had a few games for Arsenal) and we played together both for Derby County and Derbyshire in several matches in 1959. Ted Hemsley (Worcestershire, Shrewsbury Town and Sheffield United), Jim Standen (Worcestershire and West Ham United), Jimmy Cumbes (Lancashire, Surrey, Warwickshire and Tranmere Rovers, West Bromwich Albion, Aston Villa) were others who combined the two sports. Training for football after close of play, having fielded for three or four hours, was hard work and the benefit of pre-season football training was clearly missed. It usually resulted in a series of niggly thigh and muscle strains around October. Later in the season came the problem of slogging through the Baseball Ground mud, but for a 19-year-old, it didn't matter too much at the time and the joy of a sporting life is hard to beat.

In many ways it is a pity that football has extended into summer and, as the seasons have increasingly overlapped, the opportunity for someone to play both sports as a professional have gone. Could it be done from a physical point of view? I don't see why not, but now the clubs would not allow it and the finances of football, particularly, demand total commitment to the single game. I suppose Phil Neale (Worcestershire and Lincoln City), now the director of cricket at Warwickshire and manager of recent England 'A' team tours, was the last of a dying breed of cricketer-footballers.

No longer will someone like Denis Compton score 3,816 runs and 18 centuries in an English cricket season (1947) and win a League championship medal with Arsenal the following winter. What an inspiration he was to youngsters. Such is genius, if it gets the chance.

Nearly as impressive as Compton's feat was that of Chris Balderstone, who was nowhere near being a genius. He did, however, play for Yorkshire, Leicestershire and twice for England at cricket (1961-83) and he was a skilful midfield player with Huddersfield Town, Carlisle United, when they reached the old First Division, and Doncaster Rovers (1959-75). After that, he played for a while in the Scottish League, for Queen of the South. In all, Balderstone played in more than 300 County Championship cricket matches and made over 500 Football League appearances, scoring 91 League goals. That's not bad, but it's not everything. In the final match of the 1975 season, Derbyshire played Leicestershire at Queen's Park, Chesterfield. Early in the match, Leicestershire took enough bonus points to win the championship title, under the captaincy of Ray Illingworth. At close of play on that first day, Balderstone was batting and was 51 not out at 6.30pm. A fast car then transported him to the Belle Vue ground at Doncaster, where he turned out for Doncaster Rovers in a Football League match on that same Wednesday evening. The following day he completed a century, taking his score to 116 before, not surprisingly, being run out. Was he tired? You bet. He still cannot leave the game alone, though. He is now a Test Match umpire.

Southampton is the longest trip of the season, so Graham Richards and I travelled down on Friday night and stayed overnight in the New Forest. The following morning, we relaxed at a coffee bar alongside the harbour and watched the boats and yachts in the Marina. In the early part of the 19th century, Southampton was recognised as an upper-class seaside resort where those who could afford it went to bathe and 'take the waters'. By the middle of the century, the development of steam power had altered the landscape and, according to A.B. Granville in *The Spas of England and Principal*

Sea Bathing Places (published in 1841), the 'all-devouring railway company, and its still more grasping twin sister, the dock company, swept clean away the bath-buildings and the bathing-shores'. With the decline of the shipping industry, tourism has returned to the area as a main source of wealth and the shoreline is being developed to cater for modern leisure pursuits. It is a shallow substitute. The huge liners that once occupied Southampton Water have been replaced by luxury speedboats and dingys, which floated idly at rest on a cold December day. Seaside towns, out of season, can be sad places.

As we were relaxing, the other member of the BBC Radio Derby commentary team was struggling hard. Having been at a party the night before, Colin Gibson was travelling down by train on the morning of the match, in plenty of time and comfort, or so he thought. Two breakdowns, a cancellation, umpteen different trains and several unscheduled stops along the way, he arrived breathless in the press box at about 2.0pm. He had set off from Derby, once one of the great centres of the railway industry, at 6.45am. Not that the press box at The Dell is very welcoming. It is a long, wooden affair at the back of the Main Stand and is so narrow that squeezing past some portly gentlemen of the 'fourth estate' is difficult. The half-time sandwiches are passed along, so those people nearest the door get first grab. Those at the end are left with scraps. We were at the end. Like Paul McGrath on the pitch, there is no substitute for good positioning.

As at the City Ground, earlier in the season, we were behind glass, but this glass didn't open, while the alternative to perching on high, uncomfortable bar stools was to do the commentary standing up. Like at the City Ground, we did so. At least Colin felt at home. It was rather like standing in the corridor of a railway carriage and because of the low roof of the stand, our view had a Cinemascope effect. If the ball went higher than 10ft at ground level, it was out of our sight. The way the Rams played, it was out of our sight quite a lot.

At least the press room at The Dell is comfortable. Graham Souness spoke well, but still looked fierce. Southampton came into the match on a run of five successive defeats and someone asked Souness if he had experienced that sort of run before. "No," he said.

"You didn't have that sort of run at Liverpool," observed someone else, factually.

"Memories, memories," said Souness, with a wry smile, and closed his part of the press conference.

Jim Smith was less relaxed and blamed Russell Hoult for both goals. "We gave away two soft goals and although there were things going wrong in other places, I blame the goalkeeper for both of them. He should have handled the first one better and caught the cross before the second. Russell didn't thrill us." Hoult played well last season and, overall, looks to be a useful goalkeeper. The hoary old saying that all goalkeepers make mistakes tells us nothing. How many, is the acid test and Hoult has made mistakes that have cost goals in each of the last four away matches, at Liverpool, West Ham United, Arsenal and Southampton. Those mistakes have arguably cost the Rams between five and seven points.

It is interesting to try to estimate how many points a season a goalkeeper can cost a side, before he becomes too much of a liability. How many does David Seaman cost Arsenal? Tim Flowers cost Blackburn Rovers? David James cost Liverpool? Is it five, ten, fifteen? Some goalkeepers are luckier than others and mistakes do not cost goals and points. Hoult is going through a dodgy spell at the moment, but is still in credit. He cannot afford too many more games like Southampton, though.

Peter Shilton was, overall, the best goalkeeper I have seen, although I have a soft spot for Bert Williams of Wolves. He could run 100 yards in nearly even time and was probably the first goalkeeper to develop his own schedule of exercises, a method Shilton copied later. Williams was also spectacular and spectators do appreciate such goalkeepers, who are to football what the high flying trapeze artists are to the circus, like Reg Matthews, another spectacular goalkeeper. Football and the circus have much in common. Brian Clough called a Polish goalkeeper 'a clown' at

Wembley in 1973, but the 'clown' had the last laugh when England failed to qualify for the World Cup finals. Will Poland stand in the way again, I wonder?

Graham's favourite goalkeeper is Gil Merrick of Birmingham City, who played in the two thrashings handed out by Ferenc Puskas' Hungarians in 1953. Merrick was unusual in that he rolled up the sleeves of his woollen jersey to the elbow, in the style of the modern French goalkeepers. Other goalkeeping 'greats' include Pat Jennings, Gordon Banks, Bert Trautmann, David Seaman — and Joe English. Joe English? He played for Nick Smith's team in the *Rover* comic years ago. The *Rover* and its sister comic the *Wizard*, were really short-story magazines and some of the characters like Alf Tupper — the Tough of the Track and Wilson of the Wizard were as popular as Dennis the Menace and Corky the Cat. Joe relied entirely on angles for his goalkeeping expertise. Sometimes he'd be standing on the penalty spot to receive a ball rebounding from the crossbar. Angles, you see. One day the team were 4-0 down at half-time and Joe was in deep trouble. The big stand at the back of the goal threw a shadow across the penalty-area and the flight of the ball from light to shade was making a mess of Joe's calculations. He'd have had a problem with the Normanton End. Perhaps not as much as Joe Corrigan of Manchester City, who pointed out to the referee that there couldn't be penalty at his end, because the groundsman had forgotten to paint in the penalty spot! Goalkeepers? Mad as hatters.

It was Southampton's first win at home in five years without Matt Le Tissier. Chris Powell summed it up best : "It's a long way to travel to play as poorly as that."

Team: Hoult; Laursen (sub Gabbiadini), C.Powell, Rowett, Yates (sub Carsley), Stimac, Flynn, D.Powell, Asanovic (sub Willems), Dailly, Ward.
Scorer: Dailly.
Attendance: 14,901.

Roker Roars

Roker Park — Thursday, 26th December 1996

O N Boxing Day it was time to visit an old friend. It's strange how things happen. The first live, full-length football commentary I ever did was at Roker Park and now we were going back to the famous old ground for the last time. From Southampton in the south, to Sunderland in the north, the miles clock up and the Little Chefs along the way do a roaring trade. All this before and during Christmas. Increasingly, travelling supporters must feel that the Premiership fixture list has been designed by a horse, for a donkey. Soon the debate about a mid-season break will be under way, as it has been for every season that I can remember. In the 'big freeze' of 1962-63, the Rams, for instance, did not play a League match between 22nd December and 23rd February and the weather produced such a natural break that many players and supporters suffered severe withdrawal symptoms. Some grown men were reduced to tears. Whatever else, let's make sure that football remains a winter game and leave summer to cricket and the 'Souper League'!

Like Southampton, the Rams' opponents of a week ago, Sunderland, are moving to a new ground, which will be ready for the start of the 1997-98 season. Roker Park, venue of three England international matches, four World Cup matches in 1966 and home of legendary players like Raich Carter, Len Shackleton and Brian Clough, will be sold. Sunderland first played there in 1898, when Liverpool were the first visitors and the entrance fee was 3d, but the 100th anniversary of playing at Roker Park will be missed by just a year. In many ways it is sad that Sunderland are leaving and I, among many, will miss the place with its massive Fulwell End to the right of where the teams come out (£16 to stand these days), from which the famous 'Roker Roar' is carried on the sea breeze, to strike fear into the hearts of opposing defences. It can be so desperately cold and bleak in winter, defending the Fulwell End with a north-easterly blowing, especially in the second half.

Outside the main entrance at Roker Park stands the 'Roker Bus'. It is painted red and white and is a permanent feature, because it is the Sunderland ticket office. After collecting the press passes, we were, as usual, the first into the press box, which at Roker Park, is excellent. It is long and of two rows width, situated in front of the Main Stand about 10ft off the ground and above the heads of the supporters who still stand on the Main Stand terrace. It offers a superb view of the game and is close enough to the action to get a feel of the passion that has always been present on Wearside.

Roker Park and Blundell Park, Grimsby, are the closest grounds in England to the sea. A visit to Roker Park, therefore, always demands a pre-match stroll along the seafront. On this Boxing Day, the North Sea looked cold and grey as the waves washed over the beach, while the harbour, which once welcomed massive cargo vessels, now stands idle and forlorn, as the decline in the North-East's industrial past hangs heavily in the air. Much warmer was the welcome in the Roker Hotel, where a substantial number of Rams fans mingled with the red and white stripes of Sunderland supporters.

Inevitably, a supporter's view of Christmas is different to that of a player. Since the policy of playing a full Christmas Day fixture list ceased in 1957 — the last-ever Christmas Day match at the Baseball

Ground was the previous year when Scunthorpe were beaten 4-0 in the Third Division North — matches taking place on consecutive days, usually against the same opponents, no longer happen. When they did, some spectacular reversals of results often took place and sparks were inclined to fly, for there was hardly any time for tempers to cool after unsavoury incidents of the previous day. Furthermore, both teams often travelled on the same train after the match for the Boxing Day fixture — the 'away' team staying overnight — and minor injuries were treated 'on the hoof'.

Those Christmas Day matches I remember with great childhood affection, tramping through the streets to Hillsborough, with the Leppings Lane End terrace full of cheerfulness and cigar smoke. If Wednesday won, the mood was even more of eager anticipation, as the aroma of roast turkey, roast pork and apple sauce, wafted through the doors and windows of terraced houses in Walkley and Crookes. Appetites were always hugely stimulated, by the time grandma sharpened the carving knife.

Only five clubs have won the Football League championship more times than Sunderland and, although the last time was long ago, in 1936, 'Rokerites' are still weaned from an early age, on the memories of immortals like Raich Carter, Bob Gurney, Len Shackleton, Charlie 'Cannonball' Fleming, 'Slim' Jim Baxter, Charlie Hurley and Jim Montgomery. They are also regaled with the magical fairy story of how Sunderland, then of the Second Division, beat the mighty Leeds United in the FA Cup Final of 1973. The single, winning goal came from Ian Porterfield and for those lucky enough to see it, if only on television, that fabulous double save by 'Monty' lives forever in the memory — along with Bob Stokoe's pork-pie hat.

Those are unforgettable moments in the past, but these are modern times. Money rules. Like Southampton, Sunderland are being floated on the Stock Exchange and the share issue is already two and a half-times over subscribed. Part of the money raised will be used to finance the new ground at Monkwearmouth, a ground that will seat 40,000 and have all the facilities imaginable. The new ground has caught the imagination of the Sunderland supporters, like a new toy this Christmas. Hopefully, the atmosphere of Roker Park can be recreated there. Hopefully they will still be in the Premiership to enjoy it.

On this occasion, the past was linked neatly with the present in the shape of a special Sunderland guest. Johnny Mapson, who played in goal and is the only living member of the Sunderland FA Cup-winning side of 1937, drew the half-time lottery. Mapson was signed from Reading in 1935, specifically to replace Jimmy Thorpe who died tragically after suffering a head injury against Chelsea. Mapson received a £20 signing-on fee and, never having seen a £20 note, preferred to receive four separate fivers. He went on to make nearly 400 appearances for Sunderland, either side of World War Two. By the manner he ran up the steps to the directors' box after half-time, he looked good for a few more appearances and the crowd gave him a wonderful welcome.

Roker Park on this Boxing Day was full, but the capacity was a meagre 22,512, an attendance a far cry from the 75,118 who cram-med the ground on 8th March 1933, to see an FA Cup replay on a Wednesday afternoon! The visitors then were Derby County, who won the match after extra time. How interesting it is to note that the Rams have been involved in four other ground attendance records: The Den, Millwall (48,672 in 1937), Villa Park (76,588 in 1946), Fratton Park, Portsmouth (51,385 in 1949), and Sincil Bank, Lincoln (23,196 for a League Cup game in 1967, in Brian Clough's first season in charge).

It would have been a real confidence booster after the losses against Everton and Southampton, to have avoided defeat on Wearside. It was not to be. The Rams lost for the third time in suc-cession and on a chillingly cold day, there was little Christmas cheer for the supporters who made the long journey north. Result: Sun-derland 2 Derby County 0.

Aljosa Asanovic was left out of the team for this match. 'Rested' and 'tactical' were the words used by Jim Smith, who claimed that foreign players are not used to the rigours of the English game and that Asanovic would return for the home games against Blackburn Rovers and Sheffield Wednesday. Whatever the merits of that idea, there is little doubt that the Rams' future is heavily dependent on Asanovic, who provides the essential creativity in the team.

My view is simple. Asanovic needs to be in possession of the ball as much as possible and the best place for that to happen is in a deep role in midfield, not in an advanced position behind the two strikers. He may play there for Croatia, but it doesn't suit the Rams. In that advanced position, it is harder to get the ball to him and easier for the opposition to mark him, as Joe Parkinson of Everton did so successfully. Opposing teams are doing their homework. The sight of a dissatisfied Asanovic being substituted at The Dell, did not, at the time, bode well. Let us hope that there is nothing unto-ward in his non-appearance at Roker Park. The manager did point out that Asanovic had recently played two international matches for Croatia, that the pair had discussed the Christmas programme and that Asanovic was in favour of the action. Nevertheless, Asanovic was badly missed against Sunderland and the Rams were well beaten. It was not a welcome Christmas present.

The Sunderland match marked the halfway point of the season: 22 points gained from 19 matches, but only one point from the last four games and successive defeats by teams below the Rams in the table. That's the first time that they have been beaten by teams below and December needs to end with a flourish. An improving Blackburn Rovers need to be beaten on Saturday, otherwise the New Year will have an edgy start. What is clear is that the Rams have to perform in Steve McLaren's words 'better than 90 per cent' every match. In the First Division, it is possible to coast a little and still pick up points, but every match in the Premiership is hard and intense. If the Rams fall below that 90 per cent standard in the Premiership, they lose.

For what is is worth, I am of the opinion that if the Rams attempt to play like they did at Highbury, a style based on controlled and patient passing with Asanovic at the hub, they will survive comfortably. They won't always succeed in playing that well, but it should be the aim to play that way. If they play like they did against Everton, it will be a close run thing. I was less impressed with that performance than was the management. It seemed to me that Everton played 'cup-tie' football and the Rams were seduced into playing the same way. What is certain is that if the Rams battle and scrap like they did at Southampton and Sunderland, but with too much long ball and lack of composure, they will be relegated. 'Battle' and 'scrap' are emotive words loved by journalists, managers, coaches under stress and nervous directors. There is no substitute for class.

As we left Roker Park for the last time, I was again reminded of how so many of our major grounds lie cheek by jowl with houses belonging to working class people. Around the ground at Roker, so many of the terraced houses have doors and window frames painted red, to denote allegiance to the Sunderland club, which their owners support and with which they have grown up. Like a red haze, the colour pervades the senses as you progress towards the stadium, even pylons of the street lights are painted red and the tarmac, which covers many of the pavements around the ground, is red also. Only the approach to Everton's Goodison Park is comparable for colour — and that, of course, is blue.

Roker Park is one of the grounds that sits amidst the people. Down at The Dell in Southampton, the Milton Road corner backs up so close to the ground that the residents can almost reach out to touch the pitch. At Highbury, the entrance to the West Stand is actually between a row of Victorian terraced houses and at Filbert Street, Leicester, there is an entrance to a stand that is so tight between houses, an absent minded person, absorbed in reading the match programme, could easily finish up in someone's front room. How, I wondered, will the new grounds develop their own character? I suppose the vast car-parks surrounding the new stadiums, which are claimed to be an essential component of attending football matches in the 1990s, reflect the new audience attending. I do hope that the architects designing the new stadiums for 'the People's Game', remember that the old audience is used to walking to 'the match'. How else could J.S. Lowry have painted that picture?

Team: Hoult; Laursen, C.Powell, Rowett, McGrath, Stimac (sub Yates), Flynn, Dailly, D.Powell, Sturridge, Ward.
Attendance: 22,512.

Halfway Review

I F ANYONE had offered Jim Smith and Steve McLaren 22 Premiership points at the halfway stage of the campaign, it is likely that they would have taken it. The apprehension among supporters about the first five matches, when the fixture list was first published, was palpable. A return of six points from those five matches, with only one defeat, did much to build confidence within the team, ambition within the club and hope among the supporters. A realisation soon dawned that despite media hype, the Premiership is not entirely full of mercurial strikers, marvellous midfielders and magnificent defenders, all combining to produce irresistible teams and memorable matches. In the first half of the season, there was plenty of ordinary play as well; even dross, at times. "Without the bad," said Danny Blanchflower, Spurs' double-winning captain of 1961, "you can't recognise the good." Blanchflower was full of Irish'isms, a wonderful player and an inspiring leader.

What the Rams have found different from last season, is the intensity of each League match. Every game has been a hard game. In the First Division, win, lose, or draw, some games were less intense than others, especially in some home matches. Not so in the Premiership and, because the Rams are stretched, both for quality and depth in the squad, the season and the task of staying in the Premiership will not get easier. It will, undoubtedly, get harder. Already, opposition teams in the cold of winter are marking Aljosa Asanovic more closely than they did in the warmth of late summer.

HALFWAY REVIEW

In November, Jim Smith won the Premiership 'Manager of the Month Award'. He well deserved it. No one in their right mind could have predicted the exciting upturn in the club's fortunes since he was appointed. The Rams won three and drew one of the four matches played, to reach the dizzy heights of seventh in the table. Some people began to dream of Europe and why not? Onwards and upwards should be the aim, just like the scaffolding and steelwork on Pride Park, where we are told the corporate boxes are selling like hot cakes and the idea of filling in the remaining two corners between the 'horseshoe' and the main stand, in order to increase capacity, is being mooted. Is that being too ambitious?

Vice-chairman Peter Gadsby told the *Derby Evening Telegraph:* "At the moment, Jim Smith and his team are our best salesmen."

Exactly.

December was a less profitable month. Two points gained from five matches. More significantly, the Rams lost for the first time to teams below them in the table. As 1997 dawned, old apprehensions floated to the surface.

A document that has become increasingly popular in the world of grey suits, is the business plan. Such plans are formulated from statistics. Beware. 'There are lies, damned lies and statistics.' Here are a few statistics. Since 1990 in the top division, each team has played 42 matches in four seasons and 38 matches in three seasons. The team that finished fourth from bottom of the table gained an average of 1.07 points per game over 42 matches and 1.06 per game over 38 matches. At that ratio, the Rams need 40 or 41 points to survive this season. That is the business plan. Easy, isn't it?

Despite business plans, the most important place is still the pitch. On the pitch, performance is paramount. The popular idea being peddled at the moment is that the Rams need to 'battle' their way out of any potential trouble. What does that mean? Battle at what? There are two sorts of courage in sport, physical and mental and the Rams are not short of the former. Whether they have sufficient of the latter will determine whether they survive. If they play the composed, passing type of game of which they are capable and impose that style on the opposition sufficiently often, they have the potential to finish halfway up the table. It sounds as easy as the business plan, but it is infinitely more difficult to produce and Jim Smith is already talking about the need to improve the quality in the side.

The best team the Rams have played on their travels, in the first half of the season, has been Liverpool. At Anfield, the Rams were outclassed. Apart from that single occasion, the Rams have looked to be playing at least in the same league as the opposition in the other nine matches played away from the Baseball Ground. It is easy to forget that footballers are not machines and one of the attractions of the game is its endless variety and variability. Despite the attempts of television analysts to convince us otherwise, football is not a form of running chess and it is far from being an exact science. Performances vary, despite good intentions. The perform- ances at Ewood Park, Hillsborough and the City Ground were moderate, the one at Villa Park, insipid. Beside the sea at The Dell and Roker Park, the Rams played poorly. On the other hand, the performance at Highbury was excellent and at Upton Park, the Rams played as well as they did at White Hart Lane, back in August. In that mixture, there is a bit of everything. When asked about a particular half-time talk when he was manager of Millwall, Mick McCarthy replied, "I told them the same as I always do. Sometime it works, sometimes it doesn't. Don't ask me why."

At the Baseball Ground, Wimbledon impressed. They would be my nomination for the best team we saw in 1996. Tight, well org- anised and disciplined, it would be a real fairy story if they could land the title. The last match of 1996 brought Blackburn Rovers to the Baseball Ground for a 0-0 draw. They were the second-best team to visit Derby, being a vastly improved from the sad outfit against which the Rams recorded their single away victory in early September. "Being a caretaker manager is easy," said former player and now caretaker manager, Tony Parkes. "I just open up in the morning and lock–up at night." Maybe, but Rovers have only lost one in ten since Parkes took over with his homespun philosophy. He doesn't want the job, so Rovers have gone to Sampdoria in Italy to recruit a Swede, Sven Goran Erickkson, as manager for next season. "We'll have to get used to Armani suits," said Parkes, wryly fingering his tracksuit in the press conference afterwards. Six of the Rovers' side that won the Premiership under Kenny Dalglish were in action at the Baseball Ground and it showed. If the Rams stay above Blackburn Rovers in the second half of the season, they will have no worries.

1997 opened to freezing conditions. Snow fell between Boxing Day and New Year's Day and matches scheduled to take place at Selhurst Park and Filbert Street were postponed, due to neither club having undersoil heating and the pitches being frozen. One would have thought that the Premiership authorities would have insisted on such undersoil provision, as we approach the 21st century. On New Year's Day, the pitch at the Baseball Ground was in good condition for the fixture against Sheffield Wednesday, but the match did not take place. The Derbyshire Constabulary were of the opinion that the major roads in Derbyshire and South Yorkshire were too bad to allow supporters to travel to the game. Sunderland supporters must have discovered a different route through the area to get to Coventry for the afternoon kick–off at Highfield Road, while 50,000 people attended Old Trafford on the same evening, to watch Manchester United play Aston Villa, many presumably, travelling from the Derbyshire hills in the High Peak. It was all very strange. Less surprisingly, the FA Cup third-round tie at Gillingham, due to be played on the first Saturday in January, was also postponed. No undersoil heating at the Priestfield Stadium.

The new scenario saw the Rams facing three successive away fixtures in the Premiership. Visits to Wimbledon, Chelsea and Leeds to be undertaken, before Liverpool visit the Baseball Ground on 1st February 1997. Such an itinerary is not good footballing sense. When a team is struggling to keep afloat, the last thing needed is a leaden weight of fixtures, arranged in such illogical fashion. Winning is the key to retaining confidence and the Rams need to win very shortly, both for points and confidence. Fortunately, the match at Gillingham should be useful in that respect and the fourth-round draw does gave the Rams a home tie, probably against Aston Villa. Nevertheless, the season is balanced on a knife edge. Defeat at Gillingham will be catastrophic.

Monday, 6th January 1997: It is announced that Howard Wilkinson is to be the Football Association's first technical director. Wilkinson, who made 22 League appearances for Sheffield Wednesday and 116 for Brighton and Hove Albion in the mid-1960s, was signed by Jim Smith, to play for Boston United when Smith was starting out on his managerial career. Smith encouraged Wilkinson to take up coaching, at a time when the serious approach to coaching was in its infancy and Allen Wade was the FA director of coaching. The South Yorkshire and Lincolnshire area was strongly represented in the early coaching scene, forming its own association. Graham Taylor was another to cut his coaching teeth around this time, being a member of the same group of aspiring coaches.

Wednesday, 8th January 1997: The football world is rocked by the news that Kevin Keegan has resigned as manager of Newcastle United. Vast areas of newsprint are devoted to speculating on the reasons for Keegan's departure with implication that certain banks, involved with Newcastle's proposed flotation on the Stock Exchange, have exerted pressure to bring it about. Such a possibility is calculated to send shivers down the spine. If such suggestions are true, it won't be too long before the only stripes that matter in Newcastle will be on the suits of City financiers.

Former Derby County manager, Arthur Cox, now chief scout at Newcastle, and Terry McDermott, Keegan's assistant manager, are in temporary charge of the Magpies. Reports indicate that Keegan had spent £60 million on bringing players to St James' Park, recouping £20 million in outgoing transfers. At least Cox knows how to spend big money. He spent plenty at Derby during his latter years at the club.

The early runners in the field to replace Keegan are Kenny Dalglish, Bobby Robson and John Toshack. The bookmakers make Jim Smith 14-1 to return to one of his former clubs. Smith's reaction to that is that the odds ought to be nearer to 14,000-1 and he isn't going back in any case.

Later in the week, 22 year-old Mario Rahmberg, voted Sweden's 'Rising Star of the Year', joined the Rams on loan until the end of the season. If everything goes well, he could be signed in a three-year deal, for a transfer fee of £700,000. The striker was recommended by Lennart Johansen, President of UEFA, to Rams director Stuart Webb and it will be interesting, if not illuminating, to discover whether the leading administrator in Europe is a good judge of a player. The Rams will certainly welcome competition in the striking department.

Bleak House

Selhurst Park — Saturday, 11th January 1997

I T'S NOT EASY visiting Wimbledon Football Club. South London is a vast, urban sprawl, full of featureless houses and twisting roads, which are crammed with parked cars and traffic lights as the boroughs of Lambeth, Croydon and Merton merge together like treacle sponge pudding. On a cold, misty, grey and dank day, with mud-stained snow scattered over sparsely grassed verges along the roadside, Saturday morning shoppers lugged over full baskets and carriers along filthy streets which were littered with black plastic bags containing a week's rubbish and waste. No wonder London is known as the scruffiest capital city in the whole of Europe. Many of the bags had spewed their contents over the greasy footpaths, adding to the general impression of grubbiness, while stray cats and dogs prowled and scavenged among the litter. I have no doubt that many of the people who inhabit this part of the world are the 'salt of the earth', yet the faces on the streets were careworn and serious. Smiles were few and far between. Perhaps the burden of life lies heavily here. Perhaps, it has every reason for doing so.

Of course, football and Wimbledon must not be confused with tennis and Wimbledon. The Dons are not greatly interested in strawberries and cream and they don't play in Wimbledon either. They play at Selhurst Park, which is the home of Crystal Palace and is in the Borough of Merton. Since leaving their ground at Plough Lane, Wimbledon have become the cuckoo in the Premiership nest and, as cuckoos well know, their presence has not been welcomed wholeheartedly. Like the baddie in town, Wimbledon have performed miracles in surviving on scraps and they have been known, at times, to be a little rough and tough in their methods. It is only comparatively recently, under the influence of current manager Joe Kinnear, that Wimbledon have planed the edges of their abrasive and combative style, to present to the glitzy world of Premiership football a smoother image. In so doing, they have not abandoned their indomitable spirit, founded on an 'us against the world' outlook. It is there where the heartbeat lies, but are the 'Crazy Gang' becoming too sophisticated? Hardly. More likely they are becoming more like Fagin's men in *Oliver Twist*. Stealthier and more cunning and ever ready to pick a pocket or two. Even now, it's best not to laugh at Wimbledon. Playing against Wimbledon is no laughing matter, especially at Selhurst Park, the Bleak House of the Premiership.

Back in September, Wimbledon won 2-0 at the Baseball Ground and gave the Rams a stern lesson in the realities of Premiership life. Well organised and disciplined, they surprised many people with the quality of their football. Wimbledon's performance on that day made them the best side the Rams have met this season — so far. Only one defeat in 16 Premiership matches confirms Wimbledon as serious challengers for the title itself and, as the teams took the field and with two matches in hand, the Dons were in a position to go top of the table.

That the teams took the field at all was credit to the Wimbledon administration. Selhurst Park does not have undersoil heating and without a home fixture since 14th December, Wimbledon were keen to play. To that end, a hot-air balloon was hired from a firm in Glasgow, to thaw out the frozen surface and even as we arrived at 12.30pm, groundstaff were still clearing snow to the sides of the pitch. The pitch itself looked likely to cut up and it promised to be one of the more difficult surfaces the Rams are to play on during the season. With the temperature around freezing and the wind whistling through the draughty stand, the words that fitted the circumstances best, as the match preliminaries got under way, were cold and raw. Wimbledon thrive on rawness.

Although they are only the tenants, Selhurst Park could have been built for Wimbledon. It fits the bony image. It is a distinctly uncomfortable place. The schizophrenic personality of having two clubs sharing the same ground is matched by having a football ground sharing the site with a supermarket. When someone drives into the car-park at the Sainsbury End, it's hard to know whether they are going to purchase match tickets or brussels sprouts.

At the rear of the Main Stand and level with one of the penalty-areas, three or four disused and dilapidated hospitality boxes are used as a press box. The view is poor, especially towards the super-market end, and although there is sufficient space and room, the whole area is tatty and neglected. The newer hospitality boxes are in the stand which has been built behind the goal at the Whitehorse Lane End, which is where Sainsbury's is situated. The boxes have sitting-out areas at the front, rather like at Highbury, but few people were sitting out on this bitterly cold day. They were probably watching racing on the television.

The press room, under the concrete pillars of the Main Stand, is a tip. It's as inhospitable as a market place bus shelter late on a Saturday night, while the piece of paper attached to the press passes was informative and to the point:

UNDER NO CIRCUMSTANCES are members of the press allowed to vacate the Press Box to gain interviews within the stands.

Only one warning will be given to any member of the press who ignores this ruling, a repetition of such behaviour will result in a permanent ban from all Wimbledon home matches.

The only media allowed inside the Stadium to carry out interviews are the authorised television companies.

If the setting was harsh, so, too, was the match. It looked as though the Dons had decided that because the pitch was likely to cut up — and it hadn't been helped by the so-called warm-up — passing along the floor was an indulgence they were not going to bother with. Vinnie Jones, in particular, hoofed the ball in the air at every opportunity and Wimbledon's front two of Marcus Gayle and Efan Ekoku pressured the Rams defence with every twist and turn. The Rams' midfield was non-existent.

It was instructive to see how well drilled Wimbledon are. Whenever the ball was collected just outside their own penalty-area, the Wimbledon midfielders played it long and to the left. With Gayle in a wide position around the halfway line, his speed often took him into a one-against-one situation with one of the Rams three central defenders. Eventually, Dean Yates twisted once too often in trying to block a centre from the left by Gayle and it was clear that one of those dodgy knees was on its way to the treatment table, for some considerable time.

What an unlucky player Yates is. His career has been dogged by knee trouble. I have a suspicion that Yates could have reached the highest class, but for those creaking joints. More important, the Rams have not really got enough tools in the locker to be without players of Yates' quality. Perhaps, after they retire, Yates and Paul McGrath will make a living entering knobbly knees contests.

In the second half, Wimbledon's pressure looked like it would pay off when they scored after 60 minutes, predictably from a corner. The Wimbledon supporters believed the game was won and, to be truthful, so did many others, but the Rams were not finished. As Wimbledon appeared to relax, the Rams took up the quest for an equaliser and forced the Dons on to the back foot. None did better than Darryl Powell in this period. Powell substituted for Yates and his energy did much to revive the Rams after Wimbledon scored. Deservedly, Ron Willems, on as substitute for Ashley Ward, popped up with the equaliser a few minutes from the end, after good work by Dean Sturridge, who nodded back a ball which looked to be going out of play on the by-line. 1-1 was the final scoreline and a valuable point rescued for Derby County. The arch muggers, mugged.

"It was a hard-earned point for us," said Jim Smith. "We could do with winning a few games, especially at home, but it was a fair start to a tough month."

Wimbledon are an amazing club. What are their secrets? Producing home-grown players is one. Five of those who played against the Rams began as Wimbledon trainees. Who are the men behind the scenes who keep the production line going, their names a mystery to most people? Assistant managers like Terry McDermott (Newcastle United) and Brian Kidd (Manchester United) are well known. Others like Pat Rice (Arsenal), Ronnie Moran (Liverpool) and Graham Rix (Chelsea) are recognised, but who is the assistant manager at Wimbledon and who runs the youth team? In the past couple of years, Wimbledon have sold a back line of Warren Barton, John Scales, Keith Curle and Terry Phelan. Now they have produced a central defender in the 5ft 9ins Chris Perry, who is already an outstanding performer, to go with other useful Wimbledon products in central defence, Dean Blackwell and Brian McAllister.

Someone at Wimbledon is also a good judge of other people's players. Five of the team that played against the Rams were bought form lower division clubs. It is arguable that goalscoring midfielder, Robbie Earle, is the best value-for-money transfer of the past few years, having played 294 League games for Port Vale, before Wimbledon 'spotted' him. Personally, I just don't believe the easy line being trotted out — that there are no useful players in the lower divisions of the Football League. Neither, it seems, do Wimbledon. Apparently, Joe Kinnear spent most of the summer touring Europe looking for players. He came back saying that he had as much talent in his 'own back garden' and the only player he was interested in was a Russian and the hassle associated with bringing him to England wasn't worth the effort. In the financial climate of the 1990s, perhaps more football clubs and managers should look less towards Manchester United, Newcastle United and Chelsea and more towards Wimbledon. Afterwards Colin had to work hard to get interviews. Nothing at Wimbledon is easy.

Team: Hoult; Laursen, C.Powell, Yates (sub D.Powell), McGrath, Rowett, Flynn (sub Dailly), Carsley, Asanovic, Sturridge, Ward (sub Willems).
Scorer: Willems
Attendance: 11,467 — for a team that could go top of the Premiership!

Royal Engineers

Priestfield Stadium — Tuesdays, 14th and 21st January 1997

Business boys

On the day before the Rams played Gillingham in the FA Cup, Kenny Dalglish was installed as manager of Newcastle United. Three days after the appointment, chairman Sir John Hall announced details of a share flotation of the club on the Stock Exchange. The flotation is estimated to value Newcastle at £140 million, the second most valuable club in England. Eleven clubs are currently quoted on the Stock Exchange, 14 others are clamouring to join. Can this be football's 'pot of gold' at the end of a rainbow? If the Stock Exchange is football's new financial salvation, why within the bones of football followers is there a deep-seated unease about the relationship of football and big business? Dalglish represents football; Sir John Hall represents big business.

Dalglish, as most people know, grew up as a boy in Glasgow wanting to play football and dreaming of representing Celtic and Scotland. He became a footballer and eventually realised his ambitions. So, too, did legends like Bobby Charlton, George Best and

John Charles, for England, Northern Ireland and Wales respectively, and many others did too, albeit at lower levels. In its simplest form, football is just a game for boys. That those boys grow old, is a simple fact of life. Football is a boy's game. Ask a footballer's wife.

Sir John Hall is a builder of supermarkets. He is a man of business. Business is for adults. It is not what boys dream of doing. That's where the uneasiness, that exists between football and business has its roots. As small boys grow up dreaming of football glory, the game becomes ingrained in their psyche. To hear Bobby Charlton talk about football is to hear the voice and sense the enthusiasm of a small boy. I wonder what Sir John Hall dreamed of, when he was a boy? To hear him talk about football, chills the blood.

Tuesday, 14th January 1997: Priestfield Stadium (part 1)

Derby County made two trips to Gillingham in the third round of the FA Cup. On the original date, the traditional first Saturday in January, the pitch at the Priestfield Stadium was frozen and there was never any chance of the match being played. It was rearranged for ten days later. Many other ties in the round suffered the same fate and the fourth round was drawn with a lot of matches unresolved. What with replays entering the equation as well, matches being switched for television, matches taking place on different midweek nights, frost and snow, police regulations to be observed and the draw itself taking place at some obscure time, is there any wonder that the magic of the FA Cup is being diluted?

Yet, despite all the irritations, a certain magic remains. First played for in 1872, the FA Cup still excites players and public alike and all tickets were long since sold by the time the Rams finally journeyed to Gillingham. In that very first FA Cup Final between amateur teams, The Wanderers beat the Royal Engineers 1-0. Appropriately, Gillingham was — and still is — the home of the Royal Engineers.

The day was clear and sunny, with the temperature a few degrees above freezing. Having set off at 10.00am for a 7.45pm start, we were there early enough to position our equipment on the roof of the Executive Box — now that's really going up in the world. In mid-afternoon, by kind permission of the groundsman, we inspected the pitch at our leisure. There was no sign of the referee. The verdict? Perfect, except for a strip about six or seven yards wide under the shadow of the Gordon Road Stand on the opposite side from the newly-refurbished dressing-rooms. It was a bit slippery there, where the frost had stayed in the turf, but over the whole area the pitch was very flat indeed.

The following is an extract from an article I wrote for the *Burton Mail:*

> Paul Alcock is the referee from Redhill in Surrey, who abandoned the Rams' FA Cup tie at Gillingham last Tuesday. He should be charged with bringing the game into disrepute. All his talk afterwards about the pitch being fit at the start and deteriorating conditions was a load of twaddle. One question and one question alone was need-ed, at the time he abandoned the match: 'Was the pitch fit for play?' Alcock said no. Virtually everyone with pro-fessional experience of playing the game, plus the players on the pitch and a few thousand others in attendance, thought otherwise. Alcock's claim that players of both sides were complaining was not substantiated by any player of either side. As an example of indecisive, post-uring and incompetent decision making, Alcock's performance would be hard to beat. Except, of course, by the simpering, snivelling drivel churned out by most sections of the press, about the difficulty of playing on such a surface. Rubbish.
>
> Two hours after the match finished, the pitch was still able to 'take a stud'. By that time, Alcock had long gone from the stadium, accompanied by a considerable police presence. There was no demonstration. The streets were

empty. Derby County supporters were halfway back up the motorway, counting the cost. Gillingham residents were having their cocoa. It was a complete farce.

There is little doubt that the referee had it in his mind to abandon the match at some stage. He had expressed fears about the pitch when he inspected at 6.30pm and his actions throughout the match, indicated a strong desire to bring about a self-fulfilling prophecy.

The reaction of the professionals was revealing. They wanted to play on, despite a silvery sheen that had developed on the surface, indicating that frost was about, even though the temperature on the car computer never fell below freezing before the game. It didn't fall below freezing afterwards, until we reached Leicester Forest East services on the journey home. Agreed, conditions were not easy, good balance and technique being required, but in the 20 minutes played after half-time, not one player fell over and, by then, all were adapting better than at any stage previously. The proposition that a pitch must be ideal for an entertaining match to take place is false. Mistakes add to the flavour. As soon as Alcock blew his whistle, he shot down the tunnel to his dressing-room like a ferret down a rabbit hole. The score was 0-0 and most spectators in the crowd of just under 10,000 were completely flummoxed. Perhaps petty officialdom is sent solely to try the patience of football followers. The Rams travelling contingent were utterly dismayed.

Before he entered the legal profession, Graham Richards was a PE teacher at a school in Gillingham and before the match, he insisted on taking us on a guided tour. Various lodging places were pointed out and other mysterious habitats were referred to, usually with a nod and a wink. It was a long time since he had visited the area and much was changed, but still there was St Bartholomew's Hospital, where he had first met his wife, Jeanette, who was training to be a nurse. After the match finished, Graham, as usual, went to fetch the car, while we dismantled the equipment. He was gone longer than usual. When he got back, he told us that he had received a message. The message was that Jeanette, who had recently been diagnosed as having cancer and was having treatment in a Nottingham hospital, had only two months to live.

The following night, two other postponements took place. Coventry City's tie against Woking was called off by referee Gerald Ashby an hour before the start, to the amazement of officials on both sides. Ashby said the pitch was playable in both goal-areas and on the wings, but too hard in the centre circle. Four thousand Woking fans paid almost £50,000 for the privilege of a wasted trip, although the referee received half his match fee, plus expenses. The Woking chairman, Phil Ledger, claimed the temperature was exactly the same when Ashby inspected at 5.0pm as it was when he called the match off at 6.45pm. Ledger also remarked that referees were given too much power to call matches off and other opinions needed to be sought.

Further east, an Avon Insurance Combination League match between Norwich City Reserves and West Ham United Reserves was called off by referee Bill Jordan because of fog. The clubs didn't agree with the referee's decision. The Canaries sent out an SOS for qualified officials and at 7.50pm the match kicked-off, as a friendly, in front of 1,300 spectators. A Football League linesman refereed, assisted by a local linesman and one of the original linesmen. The Avon League secretary, Neville Chamberlain, was present and was sufficiently impressed to consider having the match classed as a bona fide league fixture. No thoughts of appeasement here. West Ham Reserves won the match 3-2. Meanwhile, back at the Baseball Ground, young Swedish prospect, Marino Rahmberg, had his first taste of English football, as the Rams Reserves lost 1-0 to Walsall.

Team: Hoult; Laursen, C.Powell, Rowett, McGrath, Carbon, Carsley, Asanovic, D.Powell, Sturridge, Ward.
Attendance: 9.529
Score: 0-0 (abandoned 65 minutes).

Tuesday, 21st January 1997: Priestfield Stadium (part 2)

The following week, it was off to Gillingham again. How is it that the match could be, in effect, replayed in a week, when replays take ten days to arrange? This time the referee was at the ground extremely early, although there was never any doubt that the pitch was perfect. Strangely, because of a stiff easterly, the evening felt much colder, even on top of the executive club hospitality box. A total of 9,042 spectators turned up, a number on a repeat trip from Derby, and the Rams did a good, professional job. They won the match 2-0, both goals coming in the second half.

The first was significant. It came from a corner, the first time the Rams had scored from a corner all season. Ron Willems was the scorer from close range after Robbie Van der Laan had headed down Gary Rowett's corner-kick. Van der Laan? Indeed it was, coming on at half-time in place of Darryl Powell. The Rams looked better for his presence and there is no doubt that the Dutchman's qualities of leadership have been missed, especially in the last month. This is Derby County's first win in eight games and, although without wishing to be disrespectful to Gillingham, it is extremely welcome. Nothing breeds confidence more quickly than winning, it doesn't matter who it is against. Bill Shankly always made sure that he was on the winning side in five-a-sides and Liverpool played a lot of those in training. No wonder Shankly was supremely confident.

The Rams gave a good professional performance in the second half. "I'm delighted for Robbie," said Jim Smith. "He did an excellent job and wanted to prove us all wrong." He did, too. With all due respect, it was nice to be leaving Gillingham behind.

Team: Hoult; Carsley, C.Powell, Laursen, McGrath, Rowett, Flynn, D.Powell (sub Van der Laan), Dailly, Sturridge (sub Simpson), Willems (sub Carbon).
Scorers: Willems, Van der Laan.
Attendance: 9,042.

Just Off The King's Road

Stamford Bridge — Saturday, 18th January 1997

I N EARLY January, under lowering skies in the capital, Derby County were beaten 3-1 by Ruud Gullit's cosmopolitan Chelsea outfit, to bring the gaunt spectre of relegation hauntingly into view. How different to just over a month ago, when we marched confidently out of Highbury, disappointed to have only drawn and permitting ourselves thoughts of European qualification. Survival is now paramount in the minds of Rams followers. Directors, too, must be shuffling uneasily in their seats. Yet at Stamford Bridge, the Rams played better than in several recent performances and were the unlucky victims of some unforgivably poor refereeing by Graham Poll, the controversial Hertfordshire official. Clive 'the Whistle' Thomas, lives on.

A cautious start, then a thrilling free-kick from more than 35 yards, by Aljosa Asanovic, put the Rams into a 25th-minute lead. Hopes were raised. I've never seen a free-kick scored from as far out as that, which perhaps proves you can teach old dogs new tricks, but ten minutes later Chelsea equalised through Dennis Wise. We thought the Rams had done well to keep the scores level in the first half, as Chelsea knocked the ball about rather flashily, then catastrophe, as, on the stroke of half-time, in stepped the referee. Graham Souness had suggested during the previous week that Mr Poll was intent on making a name for himself. Here, from a position at least 30 yards from the incident and not at the best angle, he awarded a penalty as Matt Carbon made a clumsy attempt to head a centre that was passing over his him. The minimal contact Carbon made with Mark Hughes was quite sufficient for Mr Poll to give the decision.

It is just possible that the referee was right. A few tongue-in-cheek Chelsea supporters suggested that. Rob Sheppard, in the *Daily Mail*, was absolutely, so very, very certain, he was. On the other hand, it's possible he was wrong, as Derby County supporters, in different parts of the ground, argued. These are matters of opinion. What is absolute fact is that, from the position he was in when the decision was made, Mr Poll had to be guessing. That is unacceptable refereeing.

What actually happened is that, just like the Rams players, the referee was caught going the wrong way when Gary Rowett carelessly lost possession of the ball, just over the halfway line. Like the Rams midfielders, he was left floundering the wrong side of the action as Chelsea broke very quickly. He was definitely caught in no man's land, about 30 yards away, when Carbon and Hughes came together. He gave the decision, the action stopped and he then caught up with the play, as Chelsea supporters smirked knowingly. They, to every man and woman, know that 'Sparky' Hughes has been around more penalty-areas than Matt Carbon — and Mr Graham Poll — have had hot dinners.

Whatever the rights and wrongs of the case, three things are certain. First, the decision greatly influenced the course of the match. Second, if penalties are to be awarded each time an offence like that is committed, there will be 20 penalties per match. Third, guesswork should not be in the referee's toolbag. Don't talk to me about 'these things evening themselves out over a season', as callers to BBC Radio Derby's *Sportscene Talk-in* cosily parroted on the following Monday evening. Refereeing standards are falling. Is something going to be done about it? That is the essential question. The answer lies in the recruiting and promoting procedures.

Ever since I can remember, Chelsea have been blessed with 'personality' players. Roy Bentley, Jimmy Greaves, Terry Venables, Peter Osgood, Alan Hudson, Charlie Cooke, Ron 'Chopper' Harris, David Webb, Ray Wilkins and a host of entertainers have glittered and sparkled over the years at Stamford Bridge. The club was founded as a full professional outfit in 1905, yet a solitary League championship title in 1955, a League Cup win in 1965 and a single FA Cup triumph in 1970 (2-1 v Leeds in a replay at Old Trafford) was the sum total of domestic honours they had won when the Rams visited them on this Saturday, 92 years later. Chelsea did win the European Cup-winners' Cup in 1971, beating a fading Real Madrid team 2-1 in a replay in Athens, but for a club which has always attracted the glitterati of showbusiness and politics and sits close to the centre of London, Chelsea Football Club has promised more than it has achieved in the hard currency of football honours. To their credit, Chelsea teams have always played with style, but in comparison to the aristocrats of Highbury and White Hart Lane, the faithful at Stamford Bridge, too often, have been left empty handed. Chelsea have always been full of promises and promisers.

This current Chelsea team follows easily in the footsteps of its predecessors. The names are somewhat more evocative, as Gianfranco Zola, Gianluca Vialli, Roberto di Matteo, Frank Leboeuf, Dan Petrescu, Dmitri Kharine, Erland Johnsen and Frode Grodas make up Ruud Gullit's band of soldiers of fortune — some say mercenaries — whose sharply-cut designer suits occupy the pegs in the home team dressing-room, which lies deep in the vast East Stand. The names are different, but the style is the same and the label of the 'nearly men' looked likely to fit once again. This Chelsea outfit looks eye-catching in attack, more eye-closing in defence.

In the second half, the introduction of Christian Dailly in place of Carbon, after an hour, did spark a spell of Rams pressure which promised an equaliser. Unfortunately, Mr Poll had his beady eye on the Scotsman. In quick succession, Dailly was harshly booked for a mild challenge near the touchline and was then sent off for an obstruction he could hardly avoid. The match was effectively over after 83 minutes and the third Chelsea goal was irrelevant.

What is not irrelevant is the amount of shirt pulling, holding and physically pulling back which referees have allowed to become an integral part of modern football. For a player, this is particular irritating. Skill is completely negated, frustration is often the result. Then comes the flare-up and in comes the referee, only to punish the wrong man. Reactive policing, rather than preventative medicine. There is little doubt that there has been a considerable increase of holding and shirt pulling in the past two or three years, yet most referees choose to ignore it. Shortly before he left the field for his early bath, Dailly nearly left the field without his shirt, as Johnsen almost dragged him into the East Stand Lower Deck — all seats £20, but everyone standing, just to get a reasonable view! True to form, the free-kick, incredibly, went against Dailly. Unbelievable. It was enough to make grown men weep.

"I expected something as soon as I saw the referee's name," said Jim Smith. "The sending off was a joke, but he's top of the cards, isn't he?" For the first time this season, I sensed an air of despondency about the manager as the Rams slipped to 15th in the table. One win in nine matches, two wins in 15. They are relegation statistics, no mistake.

Despite all the fine talk about Chelsea in the media, Stamford Bridge is a mess. It has always been a mess. The problem is that the land is the most valuable piece of real estate of any football ground in England and for more than 100 years various individuals have tried to get their hands on it for development purposes. The idea that making big money out of football is a fairly recent phenomenon is certainly not true at Stamford Bridge. Sport in general, and football in particular, has always taken second place as political, financial, legal and every other sort of battle has been fought over the site.

The man at the centre of the battles of Stamford Bridge for the past 14 years, has been Chelsea's flamboyant chairman, Ken Bates. A former chairman of Oldham Athletic, Bates has had a varied career during which he has trod on many toes, but even his enemies would have to admit that, without his determination, the chances of Chelsea still playing football at Stamford Bridge would be nil. Harold Godwinson himself, at the original battle of Stamford Bridge, where he defeated the Viking invader Harald Hardraada, near York, before marching back to Hastings to confront William the Conqueror, would have been hard put to defend his claimed inheritance — the throne of England — more stubbornly than Bates has defended his acquired land in London SW6. It is said that Bates paid £1 for the club in 1982 and then put in another £200,000 towards running costs. He was a brave man then and a fortune could be his reward now.

Since he assumed control, property developers like Marler Estates and Cabra Estates, both of whom acquired the lease of Stamford Bridge at different times, have had to give second best as Bates used every legal device to delay what appeared to be inevitable development of the ground. The Chelsea alternative to Bates was a stark future of ground sharing, with either Fulham or Queen's Park Rangers. Eventually, when the property market collapsed, Cabra went into liquidation and the Royal Bank of Scotland, the chief creditors, took over as landlords. In 1992 the bank granted the club a 20-year lease, with an option to buy the freehold of Stamford Bridge at any time in that period, for £16.5 million. Bates was hailed as a hero by some, as a 'lucky devil' by others. As soon as the

From the gantry… our commentary position at Elland Road before the Rams and Leeds fought out a drab goalless draw.

Soccer in the '90s. No, it's not Debenhams… the souvenir shop at Elland Road.

Ready for action at Filbert Street… Graham Richards, the author and Colin Gibson.

Looking out over Leicester… the Main Stand at Filbert Street looking towards the Fosse Restaurant and Executive Boxes.

The unique entrance to the East Stand at Filbert Street, set in a row of terrace houses.

The Riverside Stadium at Middlesbrough ...a model for the Rams' new ground at Pride Park.

About to kick-off at the Riverside on a night when the Rams were hammered.

Not quite like B Stand ...the light and airy concourse behind one of the stands at the Riverside.

Fabrizio Ravanelli and admirers at the Baseball Ground.

"Will anyone speak to me?" Colin Gibson waits patiently before the Middlesbrough Cup game at Derby.

He's there somewhere …Bryan Robson speaks to the press at the Baseball Ground after 'Boro defeated the Rams in the FA Cup.

The last FA Cup-tie at the Baseball Ground. The Middlesbrough team coach prepares to leave.

On the way to Goodison to see the visit of the Rams.

The church of St Luke the Evangelist pushes into the Gwladys Street Stand at Goodison Park. To compensate for loss of light, Everton provides two floodlights to shine through the stained-glass windows. Like several of today's clubs, Everton was formed from a Sunday School attached to a church, St Domingo's FC.

Where some great players have started. Practising behind the Park End Stand at Goodison.

Guests are still filing back from their half-time refreshments in the Goodison Park boardroom as the Rams and Everton return to the action.

BBC Radio Derby arrives at Old Trafford – at 11.30am!

The Derby County team coach arrive at Old Trafford, the so-called 'Theatre of Dreams'.

Noon at Old Trafford and the crowds are already gathering. Despite its futuristic appearance, the outside of the stadium still retains an old-time big-match atmosphere with vendors operating from carts and makeshift stalls.

The new North Stand at Old Trafford is so vast that a road goes under it – and tickets warn people suffering from vertigo to think again!

The Munich Clock at Old Trafford, the first memorial to those who died in the tragedy which stunned football in 1958.

Wining and dining in style before the Rams game at Old Trafford – for some at least!

The newer Munich memorial, and the statue to Sir Matt Busby.

Old Trafford, looking towards the scoreboard end with Derby County winning 2-0. It ended up 3-2 – a great day!

It looks more like Grand Central Station, but it's St James' Park, home of Newcastle United on the day the Rams came to visit.

"It's the only way to travel to away games!" Graham Richards at St James' Park.

"All right, lads?" Rams manager Jim Smith arrives at St James' Park.

Checking arrangements. Derby County's Ernie Hallam, veteran of hundreds of away trips, on the steps of St James' Park.

ink was dry on the agreement, Bates announced a scheme to develop the whole site, under the name of a holding company called Chelsea Village, the first development to be a North Stand to seat 10,700. Unfortunately, Chelsea could not raise the money and that is where Matthew Harding came in. He responded to a newspaper advertisement for investors, placed by Bates in the *Financial Times* in 1993, which is an unusual method of attracting investment. Harding cleverly agreed to put in £5 million in the form of loan stock — not a gift — to enable the North Stand to be completed. That is the stand that now bears his name.

Claiming to be a Chelsea supporter since childhood, it seemed a bit odd that the 40-year-old Harding, reckoned to be one of Britain's 100 richest individuals with a reputed salary in 1995 of £3.25 million, should wait so long to become involved with his beloved Chelsea. After all, the club had been nearly insolvent for some time. Harding also had another surprise up his sleeve for Ken Bates. In April 1995, Harding suddenly and very surprisingly, paid £16.5 million to buy the ground's freehold from the Royal Bank of Scotland, thus becoming Chelsea's fifth landlord since Bates arrived in 1982. Not only that, but Chelsea still had to pay Harding the £1.5 million rent they had been paying the bank. On the other hand, Chelsea still retained the option to purchase Stamford Bridge for the said £16.5 million.

The immediate consequence of Harding's action was a public fall out with Ken Bates, who was not used to sharing the spotlight at Stamford Bridge. It was a classic disagreement. Should money be spent on the team, or on the ground? Harding wanted to spend on the team, Bates wanted to press ahead with the Chelsea Village scheme. Plenty of dirty linen was washed in public. Interesting questions floated to the surface. Who were the mysterious overseas investors in Chelsea Village? Why had Harding not bought any shares in the company? Why was the altruistic Harding happy to receive £1.5 million rent from Chelsea? Would Bates' perimeter building in the Chelsea Village plan, squeeze the stadium below its potential capacity? Even the size of the pitch was reduced to a minimum until Harding sided with Glen Hoddle to force Bates to agree to reduce the South Stand scheme to enable football to be played on a decent-sized pitch. As the melodrama unfolded, with a plot fit to grace the West End stage, the media had a field day and the gossip columnists prospered. Chelsea supporters watched incredulously from the sidelines, as football was pushed to the background. Then, suddenly and dramatically, Harding was killed in a helicopter crash when he and some friends were returning from a Chelsea match at Burnden Park in October 1996. His death left Bates alone, again.

The Chelsea Village development is now going ahead. Stamford Bridge looks like a building site, with huge cranes dominating the skyline towards the King's Road. What used to be known as The Shed End will be replaced by a new South Stand, behind which is being constructed a 160-room hotel. The underground car-park has already been built, which is where Bates parks his Rolls-Royce. His office window in the three-tier East Stand overlooks the hotel development and also the entrance to the ground. Ken Bates is watching. He likes to keep an eye on things.

The 'new' Stamford Bridge owes a lot to Ken Bates. The old ground once held a crowd of 82,905 for a First Division match against Arsenal in 1935. That is the second-highest club record, after the 84,569 that attended at Maine Road in 1934, for Manchester City v Stoke City in the FA Cup. Before the FA Cup Final was moved to Wembley in 1923, Stamford Bridge hosted the three previous Finals, all of which finished with a 1-0 score line. Until 1967, a greyhound track surrounded the pitch, which meant that when playing at Stamford Bridge one felt remote and isolated, a long way away from the crowd. Then the ground was vast and made up of bits and bobs, with the old North Stand in the corner standing on stilts and the view from The Shed extremely distant. The plans for the new ground show a capacity of about 42,000. The new Stamford Bridge should be much more compact and have better acoustics. At present, its a long way from being complete, but perhaps after all, that is the story of Chelsea.

After the match, there was no hot water for the showers, the Derby County players had to make do with cold. I said that Stamford Bridge was always a mess — and it still is.

Team: Hoult; Laursen, C.Powell, Rowett, McGrath, Carbon (sub Dailly), Carsley, Asanovic, D.Powell, Sturridge, Ward (sub Willems).
Scorer: Asanovic
Attendance: 28,293

Saturday, 25th January 1997: FA Cup Fourth Round
Derby County 3 Aston Villa 1
What a boost for confidence. Goals by Van der Laan, Sturridge and Willems and a disappointing Villa side sunk without trace. The old Baseball Ground really came alive for this one and supporters went home with a warm glow. Can this be the year for Wembley?

Yorkshire Grit

Elland Road — Wednesday, 29th January 1997

WHEN the fixtures for the season were first published, the visit to Elland Road was scheduled for Easter Saturday. Because of international requirements it was then switched to the end of January. That means no Premiership matches at Easter in 1997. No wonder football fans are becoming completely disorientated. Not content with starting matches at unearthly times and playing on a variety of days, the authorities are now decimating the season itself. Is nothing sacred? Is this a further step towards summer football? It looks inevitable.

One of the problems is the increase in international matches. An unforeseen consequence of the influx of foreign players into our game, has been the increased disruption of teams, due to international commitments. County cricket clubs are finding this out when they try to engage overseas players and football is becoming similarly affected. Already, Martin O'Neill, the Leicester City manager, has had various discussions during the season with the American authorities about his goalkeeper, Kasey Keller, who was absent on international duty when the teams met at the Baseball Ground in November. The problem is likely to increase.

The passing of football at Easter means that another bench mark, which forms a structure for the football season, has disappeared. It's as though part of the vocabulary of the game has been destroyed. As winter gives way to spring each year, it was part of the language of the game that some of the promotion and relegation issues would be 'settled at Easter'. That was assuming that two and some-times three matches were played over a short period of time. No longer, not now. Relegation from the Premiership is going to be decided less swiftly. Relegation will be decided by a slower, more painful process — like drawing teeth. This season, every club has at least half a dozen matches left to play after Easter.

At least players will be spared the agony of blistered feet at Easter. Hard, bare surfaces belong to the past, as improved grass growing techniques and sophisticated watering systems have transformed most pitches in the last five years. If the ball, too, has changed, so have football boots. Wolves used to employ a 'cobbler' to look after the boots in the days of knock-in leather studs. He had his own business, but used to come into the ground at Molineux on three or four mornings a week. His main task was to add small layers of leather to studs that were wearing down. He also used to manu-facture excellent boots for players who liked to have them individually made and he travelled to all away matches with the first team, just in case ground conditions altered. With the advent of the low-cut 'continental' boots with screw-in studs and rubber-studded boots for hard and dry grounds, the football club 'cobbler' even-tually became redundant by the middle 1960s. No longer were three nails left protruding through the tops of the studs, to get a better grip on icy grounds.

Neither were those nails able to force themselves the other way through the sole of the boot, to produce the 'hot coals effect', when the bare diamond appeared on pitches towards the end of the season. No wonder many promotion and relegation issues were resolved at Easter. After three matches in four days, some players could hardly hobble. Hardening feet beforehand, by means of surgical spirit, or permanganate of potash, was a precaution adopted by the very wise.

Talking of pain, going to Elland Road to play Leeds United has never been a comfortable experience. Once Don Revie took over the manager's chair in 1961, Leeds quickly established a reputation appropriate more to *Mean Streets* than *The Sound of Music*. Revie was player-manager to begin with and used every trick, in and out of the book, to gain advantage for his team and himself. On one occasion I found myself marking him from a corner in the South Stand penalty-area. Revie stood well over 6ft tall and had a height advantage of more than six inches over me, but that wasn't sufficient for him. As the ball came over, Revie simply stood on my toes. He was 'Footballer of the Year' in 1955 and three times 'Manager of the Year', but he left English football in July 1977, searching for Arab gold.

There is no doubt that as Revie's team matured, the wonderful skill of players like John Giles, Billy Bremner, Peter Lorimer, Eddie Gray, Alan Clarke, Terry Cooper and the rest flourished and Leeds became arguably one of the best six teams since World War Two. Other nominations would be Arthur Rowe's 'push and run' team at Tottenham around 1950, the Busby Babes in the mid-1950s, the Manchester United team of Best, Law and Charlton in the 'Swinging Sixties' and Liverpool's ruthlessly efficient machines of 1978–80 and 1987–88. Would Leeds United have beaten the present Manchester United team? Yes, I think they would, but despite all their ability and protestations about been wrongly accused, Revie's Leeds United were always more hated than loved. The dark cloak of cynicism and menace, built up systematically in the early days, simply refused to fall away.

In contrast to the feelings aroused by the Revie team, a Leeds hero of earlier vintage was universally loved. John Charles was one of the three best British players I have seen play. George Best and Duncan Edwards were the others. I first saw Charles playing at centre-half for Leeds United at Hillsborough, when he was 18 years old. For some reason, my father and I stood on the paddock terrace in front of the Main Stand — the only time I can ever recall standing there — and Leeds played in their original colours of amber shirts with blue sleeves (they were known as the Peacocks in those days). Even at 18, Charles was of massive stature and already people were talking of greatness. Some years later, I saw Charles play again. This time he was at centre-forward and I was in my usual place, behind the goal on the Leppings Lane End terrace. It was a wet day and Charles scored a hat-trick. All the goals were headers and one went into the roof of the net from a distance of about 15 yards. No loop, just straight and powerful. Before lightweight, white, nylon goal nets became the norm, the old-fashioned, creosoted rope nets used to get heavy with rainwater which fell off them like water from a dripping tap. As Charles' header hit the net, the spray flew in all directions and you could hear the sound of the old leather ball, swishing around in the back netting. A few weeks later, Charles was transferred to Juventus in Italy. The Leeds manager was Raich Carter.

John Charles became a legend in Italy. When Derby County played Juventus in the European Cup in 1973, Brian Clough invited Charles to join the party for the trip to Italy, to act as a goodwill ambassador. Alan Durban, a fellow Welshman, never forgets how he and one or two other members of the Rams party accompanied Charles on a stroll down one of the streets of Turin. Many people sitting at cafe tables on the tree-lined boulevards recognised their former idol of more than a dozen years previously. As recognition slowly dawned on several faces, little groups of people spontaneously arose and applauded as John Charles passed by. Apparently it was rather like being with royalty. Amazing.

After the FA Cup wins against Gillingham and the thriller against Aston Villa, the Rams went to Elland Road with renewed confidence, despite having only won once on the ground in over 50 years. That sort of statistic has little relevance to players. It has much more significance for media people, who are always on the lookout for portents of fate. More relevant was the fact that Leeds had kept ten clean sheets during the season, most of which had come about since George Graham took over as manager from Howard Wilkinson. Before the game started, a 0-0 scoreline looked to be a good bet. Afterwards, Graham summed it up succinctly. "Three instantly forgettable performances, from two teams and the officials," he said. That was hard on the officials. Referee Keith Burge from Tonypandy did at least keep 'good order', as one would expect from a man coming from the same town as a former Speaker of the House of Commons, George Thomas, who was later made Lord Tonypandy. Darryl Powell nearly won the match for the Rams, coming on as substitute for Ron Willems and hitting the bar with four minutes left, but a Rams win would have been an unjust result for Leeds.

Once again, Aljosa Asanovic played well forward in the second half. After being involved effectively in a deeper role before the interval, he hardly figured in the game after that. Another ingredient noticeably missing at Elland Road, but very prominent in the Aston Villa game, was the accurate delivery of corners by Paul Simpson. The idea that Asanovic has a good left foot from dead-ball situations is false, notwithstanding his goal against Chelsea at Stamford Bridge. Simpson is far better. He demonstrated the difference in the match against Aston Villa and it is the absence of such quality which is a reason why the Rams still haven't scored from a corner in the Premiership all season. That, and not enough determination in the air in opposing penalty-areas. More than 230 corners have come and gone without reward. When margins are so tight and the line between success and failure so fine, on such details can promotion and relegation issues be settled.

Marco Gabbiadini made his 200th appearance for the Rams, in place of the injured Dean Sturridge. Gabbiadini was the first of Arthur Cox's big-money signings after Lionel Pickering decided to press the manager's palm with silver and invest millions of pounds in the club. Cox's message to Pickering was that the money was safe with him and would be recouped if Derby County ever needed to sell those players. Like much of the talk that emanated from the club at the time — and from many supporters who were beguiled by seductive promises — it was mostly 'pie in the sky'. A lot of money was wasted getting nowhere, before Cox left for Newcastle to rest his injured back on Kevin Keegan's bench. It is no secret that the inflated wages paid to Cox's purchases put the club — and Jim Smith — in a difficult position. The Rams manager has had to try to sell, in order to raise the money to buy, as the purse strings have tightened with the new ground in the offing. Persuading players to go elsewhere for less wages is not an easy task and a lot of stock at the Baseball Ground is past its sell by date. Free transfers look to be the consequence. The policy of loaning out players has helped to offset wages, but it is only a temporary and an unsatisfactory measure.

Gabbiadini did not improve his prospects of a transfer by his performance at Elland Road. On a surprisingly wet pitch, he tried hard, but was totally ineffectual and was replaced by Simpson after 76 minutes. A total of only two goals in the whole of 1996 — one of those coming on New Year's Day — is a sad decline for someone who earned the nickname 'Marco Goalo' in his spell at Sunderland.

'Rams Happy with a Draw' was the headline in the *Evening Telegraph* the following day and quite right too. "It was not a great game and I have to accept that, but in our position, we're there to get a result," said Smith. His words of praise for Jacob Laursen struck a chord: "He's a throwback to the old days. Jacob will play even when he has some pain. He suffered a bad cut near the end and needed six stitches, but he has already shown that he can recover quickly." George Curtis, who made a record 534 appearances for Coventry City, used to recover quickly. He once broke his nose each week for three successive weeks. His nose was nearer his ear by the time the surgeon finally operated. A piece of plastic was inserted to replace part of the centre bone, but George didn't miss a match. Now that really is — hard.

Unlike most grounds, Elland Road has always been on the outskirts of town. In that respect it is already in a similar environment to where the new grounds of Southampton, Sunderland, Bolton Wanderers and Derby County are being built. The M1 and M621 motorways run close by and there is a lot of land around, which is used for parking. The 13.5 acre site is owned by Leeds City Council and the club pays a stiff rent to its landlords. The Council bought the land off the club in 1985, for £2.5 million, when Leeds United were struggling in the old Second Division, but they returned to the top level in 1989-90, under the managership of Howard Wilkinson and went on to win the Football League title in 1991-92. That means that Leeds United are the last champions of the oldest professional competition, founded by 12 original member clubs in 1888, of which Derby County were one. Four years later, the Football League expanded to two divisions. One hundred years later, in 1992-93, the year following Leeds United's third championship triumph, the Football Association formed the Premier League, with only three original members of the Football League — Aston Villa, Blackburn Rovers and Everton, founder members of the new elite. As a result, the Football League has now become a second, many would say a secondary organisation, struggling to live off the financial scraps, grudgingly allowed to fall from the greedy Premiership table.

Having sold the ground back to the City Council in times of financial trouble in the 1980s, the upsurge in Leeds United's fortunes in the early 1990s meant that the 125-year lease negotiated with the City Council in 1985, became inappropriate. Under that agreement, the club paid the City Council a rent of £160,000 per year, *plus* 20 per cent of gate receipts and commercial income, above a certain figure. That figure had risen to over £1 milllion in 1990-91, so a new contract was negotiated. The terms of that mean that a higher base rate is paid and the receipts payment is limited. Even so, the club must feel that compared to most other Premiership clubs, there is a leak in their financial bucket.

Whatever the background politics, Elland Road has become a much more welcoming place than previously. Opposite the Main Stand, the ground is dominated by the massive East Stand, which is 40 metre high, 110 metres long and did have the largest spanning cantilevered roof roof in the world (51 metres), until the new construction at Old Trafford eclipsed it by eight metres. In 1995, Graham Richards and I sat at the rear of the Lower Tier in the East Stand to watch Australia beat Great Britain at Rugby League. We had a splendid view of a superb match and at half-time were able to take advantage of the wonderful facilities in the main concourse. The concourse has a central dining area to seat 400, is wide and airy has many food outlets and even a boutique. The intention was to open it as a shopping mall during the week, but that has not happened. It is an interesting idea, which reinforces the view that football has now become such an integral part of the leisure industry, that all football grounds will eventually become glorified shopping malls.

If Elland Road is dominated by the East Stand, the rest of the ground has been reconstructed extremely well. The corners between the stands have been filled in and the feeling is one of compactness that was not present before. The capacity is now fractionally under 40,000 and one can see why some of the Euro 96 matches were played there. Remarkably, the match between England and Sweden was the first home international England had played away from Wembley since 1966. People forget that the first international England played at Wembley, other than against Scotland, didn't take place until 1952. That was against Austria. Isn't it about time that more internationals were taken back to the provinces, like in Italy and Spain? Back to places like Anfield, Old Trafford, Villa Park and, perhaps, to Elland Road? What is more, at Elland Road the half-time refreshments provided for the media are the best in the Premiership. As Jim Smith and Steve MaClaren were going through their half-time routine to rouse the players, there was plenty of Lancashire hot pot being consumed upstairs, by the critics.

Team: Hoult; Carsley, C.Powell, Laursen, McGrath, Dailly, Trollope, Van der Laan, Asanovic, Gabbiadini (sub Simpson), Willems (sub D.Powell). *Attendance: 27,549.*

Friday, 31st January: News that Marco Gabbiadini is going on loan to Oxford United, having turned down a move to Ipswich Town. He was, apparently, 'unable to agree personal terms'.

Saturday, 1st February: Derby County 0 Liverpool 1

On a firm, dry and difficult surface, this match hinged on the sending off of Darryl Powell, shortly after the interval. The challenge was late and reckless, as the Liverpool defender Bjorntone Kvarme volleyed the ball clear at just below waist height. He undoubtedly suffered a painful crack on the ankle, as Powell arrived with foot aloft, but the contrasting reactions of the crowd, the professionals and the press, was interesting and revealing.

The crowd felt that Bjorntone Kvarme over reacted. The professionals on the field did not react particularly sharply. Afterwards, Mark Wright of Liverpool said he thought Powell was unlucky. Jim Smith thought 'intent' was not a part of Powell's action and a yellow card was an appropriate punishment. The national press was united, hysterical and sometimes inaccurate in its condemnation. Why? Why should the national press be so out of touch with most of the other reaction that was apparent in people who were there at the time.

"There should be no quibbling with this particular red card. Powell had already been booked, and his tackle on Bjorn Kvarme was not so much late as posthumous." — Joe Lovejoy in *The Sunday Times* (2.3.97). Actually, Powell hadn't been booked previously!

"Darryl Powell was punished for a challenge on Bjorn Tone Kvarme that was reckless in the extreme — the anger of the home supporters, loud and lingering, beggared belief …Although it appeared to most neutrals, and certainly this one, that dismissal was the least Powell deserved, Smith kept harping on about the incident, claiming that the foul merited no more than a yellow card." — Patrick Barclay, *Sunday Telegraph* (2.3.97).

"There is something still not quite right, something which doesn't gel about Liverpool. It is a pass too many, an over-elaboration, a quirky self-importance, all of which almost played into the hands of a side racked by injury and let down when Powell went crazily over the top on Bjorntone Kvarme …Those ignoramuses on the terraces spitting venom at the Norwegian — who they seemed to think took a dive when struck by a potential leg breaker — should be ashamed of themselves. Their reaction was one of the most spiteful I've seen for sometime." — Neil Harman, *Daily Mail* (3.3.97).

"…the sending-off of Darryl Powell, for one of the worst challenges of the season …He realised he had left Bjorntone Kvarme unmarked from Jason McAteer's throw-in and, from a distance of 15 yards, launched himself into a challenge of such recklessness it was a surprise that Kvarme's right ankle was only bruised. It was the type of tackle that spawns court cases like Elliott v Saunders. Worse was to follow. As Kvarme hobbled uncertainly along the touchline, he was greeted by cups of scalding tea raining down from the stands as Derby supporters vented their misguided wrath." — Martin Smith, *Daily Telegraph* (3.3.79). Remarkably, this particular reporter went on to chastise Jim Smith for 'lack of knowledge of the game's basic tenets'. It also turned out that a couple of supporters had chucked the dregs from their polystyrene cups in

Kvarme's general direction. Most of it probably went down the necks of the people in front. Hardly 'cups of scalding tea raining down ...'

Some people changed their minds about the incident after watching highlights on *Match of the Day*. They forget that television is entertainment and is not the truth. Television makes use of only two of our senses — vision and sound — and then only by courtesy of the cameraman, editor, producer, sound engineer, commentator etc. Television distorts speed, angle and time. It should be treated with caution. Just remind yourselves how easy it is to bat against fast bowlers like Curtly Ambrose and Alan Donald — on television. The judge in the Elliott v Saunders case allowed evidence only from witnesses on the spot. He refused to allow video evidence.

Alan Hansen said that some referees would have sent Powell off, others would not. Hardly a decisive view. He also pointed out that Powell ran a long way. Does that matter? Talk of an 'over the top' tackle, by Harman, himself a qualified referee, indicates his facility with a piece of football jargon, but lack of knowledge of the nuts and bolts of the game. Had Kvarme cleared the ball from off the floor, or with a low volley, Harman might have had a point, but not at the height the clearance was made. Barclay harped on about Jim Smith and 'intent' being irrelevant. From a player's point of view, intent is a crucial factor when boots are flying, whatever the technical wording of the rules. As in life, laws and rules are necessary for sports to function, but there are also certain conventions. It is a convention that every motorist who travels at 31mph in a built-up area is not arrested on the spot. The country would grind to a halt. Likewise with football. People assume that referees know the rules, but the criticism within the game is that too many referees do not understand the conventions.

Martin Smith on Jim Smith was simply insulting. I agreed with the Derby County manager. Powell deserved a yellow card. The national press deserved red.

Collecting Thoughts

Jim Smith

THE Rams had a fortnight's break between playing Liverpool and the fixture against West Ham United, because England were playing Italy at Wembley on Wednesday, 12th February, in a World Cup qualifying match. The build-up to this match was grossly over-hyped in the media. I thought it was the right time for collecting a few thoughts of a more sensible sort, from the Rams manager, Jim Smith.

Wednesday, 5th February 1997
The manager's office at the Baseball Ground is along the corridor which leads from the dressing-rooms. It is neat and bright and is, itself, shaped rather like a corridor; a widish one. Jim Smith's desk is at one end and a door at the other end leads to another office. The visitor sits in a rather old, but comfortable armchair in front of the desk. The desk is impressively tidy. On the shelves alongside the desk are numerous videos, and a television overlooks the room from a bracket on the opposite wall. Looking down the office reminded me of the long narrow cinema that used to be on London Road, the Cosy Cinema which later became the Cameo and is now an Italian restaurant. On a side wall, hangs a large picture of Sammy

Crooks. I thought that was rather appropriate. It happens to be the wall of the corridor along which Sammy used to bring the teamsheet on Friday mornings.

The manager's office was moved from its former position, next to the boardroom, during Arthur Cox's time and it signifies the change in managerial style that has evolved over the years. Just as managers now seem obliged to sit, or stand, or jump around near what used to be called the trainer's bench, rather than sit in the stand throughout the game, so, too, they make contact with players on a day-to-day basis, much more than used to be the case. At Wolves, Stan Cullis appeared infrequently. We always knew when he was around. Suddenly, the tempo of the practices would change. "He's here. He's here," the message would flash around the training ground and everyone knew what was meant. There was no dawdling then. After he'd gone, of course, things went back to normal. Slightly slower. Slightly more relaxed.

At the Baseball Ground, it was not too different. Sometimes it was possible to go a whole week without seeing Harry Storer at all, until he appeared just before kick-off, on Saturday. Training was left in the hands of Ralph Hann. What Storer did specialise in, was the word in the ear. I think sports psychologists now call it the 'one-to-one' approach. Sometimes it took place in the office. Occasionally, some wretched individual was summoned back to the Baseball Ground from Sinfin Lane, where we used to train. The message from Storer was always very clear. Often it was not repeatable.

Raich Carter was different. He used to come into the dressing-room, after training, for a good argument. In Raich's office at Mansfield, hung a life-sized oil portrait of himself, dressed in his England strip and an England cap on his head. Raich knew his own worth. The great players do. It's the ones below that level who are a pain in the backside. They're always trying to prove something. Great players don't have too.

Raich liked a good argument. About football, of course. It was at a time when Real Madrid were dominating Europe and Alfredo di

Stefano and Ferenc Puskas were playing sublimely. "Puskas? Puskas?" Raich would say. "Give me Peter Doherty, any time." That sort of talk always got the ball rolling and Raich would then sit back and let it roll. He did like a good argument, did Raich, but he could use an iron fist in an iron glove, if necessary. Most of all, he had great personal authority. Charisma is the word. Charisma is certainly not a word to be used lightly, but it is what Raich Carter had. He also transferred John Charles to Italy.

Brian Clough, too, was not noted for spending much time around his players, unless he meant it! Despite being more remote from players, the presence of such managers always seemed to be around, even when they weren't. So much of being a football manager is about individual personality and it takes all sorts. Those people from business backgrounds, who think that football managers should conform to some agreed conference formula, are way off target. The successful managers I have known operated in many different ways, but all have had, in simple terms, 'something about them'.

Joe Mercer had 'something about him'. He had humour, a quick wit and didn't take himself too seriously. He also had a favourite saying, when anyone got a bit too full of themselves. "Show us your medals," he'd say, which usually had the desired effect. Joe, of course, won every playing medal imaginable and every managerial medal, too, before he finished. Later, he became a director at Coventry City and it was there I briefly got to know him. On one occasion, four of us shared a taxi cab after a football function in London. The cabbie, who was an Arsenal supporter, recognised Joe immediately and mentioned that he had seen a particular match in which Joe had played. That was it. For the whole of the half-hour journey back to the hotel, Joe and the cabbie were locked in detailed discussion about a football match that happened long ago. Two hours later, Joe was still talking football, in the hotel bar, with total strangers. By then, it was well into the early hours of the morning. What Joe Mercer had was great respect for the game — and as much enthusiasm for football as it is possible to have.

Mercer was the first manager Jim Smith knew as a junior at Sheffield United. Some of the Mercer qualities probably rubbed off on Smith; a belief in good football, not too serious a face, and boundless enthusiasm. Underneath all the bonhomie, however, Mercer had a steely determination and Jim Smith has not survived as a football manager for 28 years without having bags of that. His early successes as a schoolboy boxing champion — he was runner-up in the Yorkshire championships — have stood him in good stead. Much of boxing is about survival. 'He survived' would be an appropriate epitaph for a successful football manager.

I first asked Jim Smith what had surprised him about this first season in the Premiership:

Jim: The major thing that has surprised me is the stadiums. That is one of the biggest changes since my days in the old First Division. How huge the stadiums are now, not that the crowds are bigger because then, so many people stood up. Now with the seats, they are bigger. The dressing-rooms and the corporate areas are bigger as well. They're so much different.

I.H. *Do the size of the stadiums and the presentation of the matches make each match a bigger 'event' than previously?*

Jim: The Premiership has become, because of the media attention and particularly the Sky attention, the only league that the 'big' reporters, if you like for want of a better word, from the majors, will report on, or seem to report on. It all makes it a bit showbiz.

I suggested that the intensity of each game was something different, too.

Jim: That is true. Again, it is because of the money and the extra finance that is going to happen and become available in some way, shape, or form next year, because of the new deal. It has made it *[the Premiership]* even more intense than before.

COLLECTING THOUGHTS

I.H. *What about the individual matches themselves? Am I right in thinking that the games played so far this season, had a greater intensity about them.*

Jim: Well. I look at Manchester United at home and Liverpool at home last Saturday, and Newcastle. The games, the majority of the games, actually, have been played at 100 miles per hour. Why that is, other than maybe the management pass on the importance of being in the Premiership, I don't know, but it seems to be about three time quicker than when I was last in it

I wondered if the gap between teams is less? In other words, there are very few matches in which you can have a relaxed game, or even a relaxed period within a game?

Jim: I think any team, be it Manchester United at the top of the league, or Middlesbrough and ourselves and everybody else with us, can set others problems. Take Liverpool on Saturday, here. Top of the league, or needing a win to go top, they ended up having one shot a goal, which is most unusual for a Liverpool side. One shot that mattered, anyway, that the 'keeper had to do anything about. And they scored. They would have expected more in the past, I'm sure. In fact, last time Derby went down, they came here and won 7-1. I think it would be fair to say that the level now is at the fitness level of it all and technically, we have to do it, if we are going to compete at this level. One thing we have to do, is work very hard. I suppose that is the way of nullifying their ability. Maybe it shouldn't be, but it is. Manchester United play quicker, but Liverpool like to play at their own pace and if you don't allow them, they find it more difficult. In the main, it's a rule of the thumb, that applies to them all. But you look at games now on the box and nearly every game is end to end.

Jim Smith's last point about most games being end-to-end, was interesting. I hadn't really thought of it like that before and I suggested to him that the hallmark of the great Liverpool sides of the past was their ability to control long periods of games and apply sustained pressure. Was it not possible to do that so much these days?

Jim: No. I mean you do get periods when teams are on top. But you don't so often now, and we haven't had an occasion, and we are rookies in the business, in all the away games, a team that has taken control of the game and said that's it, we're 2-1, or 2-0 up and you're finished. We've always had a chance and have come back late in games and got goals.

I.H. *So the intensity we spoke of is continuous. Last season, with all due respect to certain sides, it was possible to play, particularly at home, without the same degree of intensity as is needed this season?*

Jim: Yes. And I think we have said that concentration levels and fitness levels, skill levels, will have to go up considerably. Certainly myself and Steve and the staff have been surprised at how much intensity there is. We knew it was going to be the case, to some degree, but is a higher degree than we thought.

I.H. *What is the reason? Are defenders quicker?*

Jim: Oh yes. The defenders are quicker and better defenders now, this season. I think it would be fair to say that for ourselves, we lack genuine goalscoring forwards. At least goalscoring forwards who can get 20-25 goals a season, or, like Shearer, 35 goals a season. We miss that. We do lack a bit of that extra quality in midfield, so we have to double our workrate on that, but defensively, having played against them all now and except for Chelsea for a period, we've looked reasonably comfortable defensively in all our games. It's obviously easier to organise a defence than an attack. Attackers are more natural animals than coaching animals. You can't coach some of 'em, whatever you do. You might think you can, but you can't.

I.H. *A third of the season to go. I know players and management are only concerned with the next match in the short term and so they should be, but have you any view on how many points we need? My own view is 40 or 41. What's yours?*

Jim: History tells us 39. Historically that is basically right, but there's always going to be a year when it may be a little bit more than 39 and I think this year is going to be that year. It won't be 45, it'll be nearer 40. I mean, it may stay 39, but at this stage, we're looking ourselves at 42 points.

I asked the manager, if he had an open chequebook and, other than Alan Shearer, who would he buy? The answer was interesting and a name appeared that indicated the level at which Jim Smith was thinking. Were Derby County seriously interested in him?

Jim: Well, I mean, it would have to be a recognised goalscorer like Robbie Fowler, for one. Or Ferdinand, the other. They are opposites. Ferdinand gives you more in the air, but Fowler will get more goals than him. Patrik Kluivert probably answers them all. If we could get him, Kluivert, I think he would be quite useful.

But I think to be successful, you need a scorer. Manchester United do prove my point a bit wrong, as they've got six, seven, eight, nine goalscorers. I mean Shearer has almost got 30 goals now. Fowler is a 30 goals a season man. I mean, we could have won against Leeds, or Liverpool and many other games, by, as we have said, maximising our chances and minimising our mistakes. Ferdinand on Saturday, in the box, scores. Similar chance earlier, Robbie van der Laan, just misses. That's the difference. If I couldn't have Shearer, Ferdinand would do me.

I.H. *Of course, strikers need chances. Were we making enough chances?*

Jim: No. We won't do, but a striker of that quality would allow us to take a bigger percentage of chances we do make. I know we've got to get better, but nobody against us has created hundreds of chances either. Not like in the First Division. Actually, we've got the lowest amount of corners against , as low anyway, as the best in the Premiership. And we've got the most for. But we don't score at one end and let them in at the other. We're low on chances. We're third bottom, Wimbledon are bottom, but top on goals. Their percentage of goals is far higher than anybody, but shots at goals are less than anybody. Their finishing is good. Very interesting.

I.H. *Interesting in that, before this season, Ekoku hadn't got a great scoring record.*

Jim: No. And neither had Gayle. Something has certainly happened there, that's for sure.

I.H. *Finances are tight. Supporters recognise that fact, but, assuming we stay up, where do we go from there?*

Jim: I think, by staying up, there is £5 million more from Sky. Then we shall not be playing Liverpool with 18,000 maximum, we'll be playing Liverpool with 30,000, so we will be looking to generate, on average, 8,000 more people per game at home. Then you've got your boxes, your corporate stuff. I'm not really the man to talk to on that, but I do know there will be a major difference to out financial situation, next season.

I think what supporters will be saying is that if we do stay up, we need to improve.

We've got to improve each year, but it's like everything else, we don't actually need too much more. What we do need is better, much better quality. We've got the workers. We've got the defenders. We need a quality midfield player and a quality striker. To be fair, you're talking £6 million, I should imagine, unless you're very lucky, and we ain't got that kind of money this year. Possibly next year.

I suggested to Jim Smith that in the Premiership there were eight teams in the bottom zone, being what could be called 'towns' clubs: Middlesbrough, Coventry, Sunderland, Southampton, Leicester, Forest, Derby County, plus West Ham United. In the top zone are Manchester United, Liverpool, Arsenal, Tottenham, Chelsea, Newcastle, Aston Villa, who are 'big city' clubs. The exception this year being Wimbledon.

Jim: That's been the situation for a long time. Yes, Derby County won the League, Forest won the League, but they haven't been able to sustain what the bigger cities can sustain.

I.H. *Does this mean that as finance becomes more important, is the 'big city' club syndrome going to rule out Forest, or ourselves in future? In the middle of the table are clubs like Sheffield Wednesday, Leeds and Blackburn. Is our aim to move out of the bottom group into that middle group? Their target must be try to get into the top group and either qualify for Europe, or pick up a cup.*

Jim: You can't do that in the way that used to be the case. Then, gates of 40,000 were possible, but they were mostly standing and the difference to the big clubs wasn't so great financially. When attendances go down to 16,000, or 17,000 you can't compete. If they go back to 30,000, or 35,000, then you've got a chance of competing again, in the middle bracket. And compete well in the middle bracket.

Finally, I asked Jim Smith how Derby County compared with all the other clubs, he'd been at?

Jim: Well, what I must say is that I've felt at home here as much as anywhere I've been and I've only been here a year, if you know what I mean. I've felt that from day one. It's something I feel very much. The fans and everyone around the club here mean there is a warm feeling. I'm excited about the new stadium, because I think it will give a new impetus to the club. Other than that, it's similar to every other club — except Newcastle. Newcastle is a 'one off'. Everything there is about Newcastle. Here, I've just had a really good feeling about the place, since I walked in.

Saturday, 15th February: Derby County 1 West Ham United 0. A scruffy, scrambling match, but the Rams took three vital points — if only from a penalty — from a team who, during the week, had invested more than £7 million in signing Paul Kitson from Newcastle United (£2.3 million) and John Hartson from Arsenal (£5 million). The figures make the head spin. Is it brave, foolish or desperate? Kitson, the former Rams player, has played about a dozen games in two seasons at Newcastle, Hartson has been no more than a squad player at Highbury. Harry Storer's words come floating to the forefront of the mind "Yes, yes, I know that, but can he PLAY?"

Aljosa Asanovic can — and did. He was the difference between the sides, despite the theatricals that he and Igor Stimac have been practising. "I felt I was watching the Olympic diving competition," said Jim Smith. Asanovic and Stimac are tremendous players. They should stick to playing and forget acting. The club should make sure they do.

FA Cup fifth round: Blackburn Rovers 1 Coventry City 2. A surprise result. Derby County v Coventry City in the FA Cup sixth round. Wembley is creeping ever closer.

In Conversation With....

Tuesday, 18th February

...Paul McGrath

I.H. *Paul, you made your debut in 1982 and a lot of football has been played since then. How has football changed?*

Paul: I think training has probably changed quite a lot. Not for me, obviously. I don't do too much training these days, but I think the players today, the younger players, are a lot fitter than maybe they were when I first started. I mean, I got a shock when I came over here from Dublin, with the training regime, even then, but I think now they're a lot fitter.

I.H. *What about the play itself, on the field. The matches for example, are they any different?*

Paul: No, not really. I mean, obviously from team to team there are, some teams that have the long-ball system, for example. I suppose I played that with Ireland for quite a while, but there are a lot of teams getting the ball down and playing it around, so it varies from week to week and you have to cope with all sorts, really.

I.H. *Over the period of time, since you started, is the game faster, is there more physical contact? I get the impression there is a lot more holding of shirts, for example.*

Paul: Yes. There is. What I think is that it is for the reason that it is much quicker. There are more athletes. I think back to when I started, there were probably more footballers, really good footballers, you know, lads on the ball and that stuff. Now there's a lot of speed merchants in the game. That's why there's a lot of shirt holding and such, from me anyway. I've got to get hold of these people somehow, you know. They're a few things you have to bring into your game to — you know — slow people down. Basically, you need to get any sort of edge that you can.

I.H. *Do you think pitches have had an effect? Pitches being better means people can get about better?*

Paul: Yes. I mean they definitely are a lot better now. You still get a few that, because of the weather, get in a bad state, but overall, I think they're a hell of a lot better.

I.H. When you started with United, could you say sometimes, that you were going to such and such a place and it would be a heavy pitch?

Paul: Yes, you could.

I.H. *Can you do that now?*

Paul: No. Not now. Not really. Now it's basically turn up on the day and judge for yourself, they're pretty much the same. Most pitches are good.

I.H. *Over your career, you've played with the best and against the best. Who are the best? British players, I mean.*

Paul: Hmm. Well. I think they're quite a few. I've been lucky enough in my career to play against some of the best players in the world. I would think one of the most difficult opponents I've had, and I've played with him as well, is Mark Hughes. He just had strength, skill, you know. He had a lot going for him. Obviously, Alan Shearer has got to be up there. He's somebody you can't leave alone. If you give him a second, it can be game over. Ian Wright is another one, you know, he's given me difficult times.

I.H. *Interesting that they are three different styles of player.*

Paul: Yes, but each in their own way. That's why they've been so successful. They've got their own styles and no matter how you try to cope with them, they'll just get that half yard somewhere. That's the mark of the quality they are and, you know, back awhile, I think Kerry Dixon was a player I always found difficult to handle. He had great spring. That used to be my strength, heading the ball. He used to annoy me when he beat me, but he was quick on the deck as well.

I.H. *I happened to be looking at his record the other day. 193 League goals, he got. It's a lot of goals. isn't it?*

Paul: It is. I know a lot of people are surprised when I say that, but he was one of the toughest opponents I ever had.

I.H. *What about teams? The Liverpool team of the 80s must have been a good team.*

Paul: They were. They were. I mean, they were very difficult to beat. Funnily enough, if I remember back over my records — not that I do these days — but when I played with Man United, we always did fairly well against Liverpool. I mean , we didn't do so well against everyone else, but against Liverpool we seemed to step it up and we had some great battles with them. And also when I was at Villa. Liverpool were always a team that I enjoyed playing against.

I. H. *Liverpool sort of set the standard for everyone else, didn't they?*

Paul: Yes. They did. I mean, everyone wanted to aspire to what they were.

I.H. *Do you think the best Liverpool side of that period would have beaten the present Manchester United team?*

Paul: Ah, well. It would have been a great game, that's for sure. I don't know whether they'd have beaten them or not, but I think Man United have come on since then and now they're the ream that everyone is wanting to beat, because they have shown consistency over four or five seasons.

I.H. *The Premiership is very tight this season, more so than before. Why do you think that is?*

Paul: I don't really know. More teams are bringing in foreign players and getting more stability in the sides. Sides are going to Anfield and Man United and are probably not really as afraid as they would have been, perhaps, when I first started. The lesser teams — I shouldn't really say that — but they were almost beaten before they got there. Now teams realise they can go to such places and get a result.

I.H. *Do you think that is back to fitness, because they feel they can smother them.*

Paul: Yes, that's really what I'm saying. You have to be really fit to keep going. I mean, if you close people down, as a few teams have shown this season, stop them playing the sort of game they want, you can get a result. You run yourself into the ground for 90 minutes and sometimes it will come off. A lot of times it won't, but sometimes it will.

I.H. *Ireland. You've got back into the Ireland side and that, in a way, is justification for coming to Derby, isn't it. Why Derby? What did Jim Smith say to persuade you?*

Paul: He didn't have to say a lot, really. I've met him before, through Ron and I've utmost respect for him. I mean, we sat down for quarter of an hour, or so, and I was wanting to sign. He's got that sort of magnetism, really. There's a few managers that do have, that make players want to play for them and it was very, very simple.

I.H. *Dodgy knees. What's the dodginess?*

Paul: Nothing. Not since I left Man United. I've had no operations, nothing. Everyone's kept talking about my knees, but ...

I.H. *Have you had cartilages out?*

Paul: Oh yes, I have.

I.H. *All of them?*

Paul: In my right knee, yes. In my left there's still a bit there, somewhere, I'm sure. No, I haven't really had a problem since I left Man United.

I.H. *Do they ache after a game?*

Paul: They do, but that's probably old age, as much as anything.

I.H. *Don't tell me!*

Paul: No, really, I've no complaints about me knees. I'm thrilled that I've last this long.

I.H. *Taking about that, it's strange that we are saying footballers are fitter and able to close people down, but you do less training and are lasting longer. The two things are opposites, aren't they?*

Paul: Well, I mean, if someone was to say to me what way would you do things, to be honest, I don't know whether you need as much pushing in training, you know.

I.H. *I once remember a great Brazilian centre-half in the 1970s period and he said the most important thing for footballers was rest. I know they live in a different climate and look at things a different way, but ...*

Paul: When I first played games in United first team, I suffered because I hadn't got the fitness, but once you've got the games under your belt, 15 to 20 games or something, that takes care of itself. I think games get you fit. Then again ...

I.H. *Some players do need more, though, don't they?*

Paul: Yes, there are players who come up to me and say, "I don't know how you do that 'cause I would be knackered." They couldn't literally, walk on to a football pitch without putting in a really good week's training and some people are like that. I'm lucky, I'm not.

I.H. *Especially, younger players, perhaps, who feel they have to, otherwise they are missing out.*

Paul: Well, that's true as well. I've been blessed, I think, that I'm able to sit around all week and then, on Saturday, try and play, so ...I'm really lucky.

I.H. *Have you set yourself targets in the past, for length of career? At 30, to play to 35 and then at 35 to play to 40? I remember John Giles saying that people write footballers off at 30, but if you can last until you're 32, then you become accepted again and they never write you of again.*

Paul: Yes, well, I mean, people were saying, at 32, he can't push it much further. 33 came and then, 34, 35, 36, now 37 so who knows? I'm really enjoying my football, so.

I.H. *Stanley Matthews played at 50, you know.*

Paul: Ah well, but he really was a one off. I'm enjoying it. I just see every game as a bonus. I really don't look beyond, you know, next month.

I.H. *Can we stay up?*

Paul: Yes we can, without a doubt. I've seen the spirit the lads have shown in a lot of the games. A lot of the games we've been beaten in, we haven't got the points on the board, but we've shown great fighting spirit and we've gone to places like Wimbledon and Arsenal, Leeds and got results. Obviously there's been one or two places where we've let ourselves down, probably, but, overall, the football the lads have played in every way, has been fantastic. And so I think we can easily stay up.

...and Igor Stimac

I.H. *Igor. Let's go back 18 months, to the match at Tranmere. When that* *was happening and the goals were flying in, what were your thoughts then and after the game?*

Igor: It was a shock to me.

I.H. *I can imagine.*

Igor: I wasn't frustrated so much after the game. I was thinking about the next game. The next one was a first game, my first game, in front of Derby crowd. It's home pitch. So it was most important game for me. Tranmere game was a really big shock, because we lost 5-1. It was biggest defeat of the season and it was my debut, so ...but hopefully, I scored the goal and I didn't play so badly, no?

I.H. *No, but you must have felt a bit like, "What have I let myself in for?"*

Igor: I mean, it depends on the character of the player. I think that I have strong character and and am always confident enough to keep going.

I.H. *Why Derby? Why come to Derby County?*

Igor: Why? Lots of people ask me why, why, why? It just happened. It was a good idea at the time.
I was playing in Croatia and in that time I wanted to go abroad to play football. My agent contacted a couple of clubs. Derby was one of the clubs who was in a hurry to sign a new player. I came here.

I.H. *The Premiership. What are your thoughts about the Premiership? The style of play and so on.*

Igor: Yes. It's very exciting. You can really enjoy playing Premier, much more different than last season, when we played First

Division football. I mean the pitches are okay, but the quality of the football is not so good as in Premiership. You can't even compare it.

I.H. *Quicker?*

Igor: It's much quicker. It's much more quality. It's much more touches on the ball. There is not a lot of clubs who just kick the ball high, you know, all around the pitch. It is a big difference.

I.H. *You've played in Spain and other countries. Is there any difference between Premiership football and in Europe?*

Igor: Yes. It's much more different football.

I.H. *In what way?*

Igor: I think that the biggest difference is in the refereeing, because all about football in England is to make crowds content with the football. To make crowds happy and that's good. It's why your grounds are so full and why, wherever you go, people like football, people talk about football. Eat football, sleep football, drink football. Everything is football here. It is not the same in continental Europe and, I think, that is a bad side for you, because that kind of refereeing is where you lose when you play continental football matches. It's not the same, you know. I mean, you are protecting here some body to body contact. You can't hear whistles too often in one game. I mean, everything is okay, you can do whatever you want. You know what I mean? There is not too many bookings. In continental Europe, each contact can make you get booked. It's a big difference.

I.H. *What are your thoughts about the England versus Italy game? I presume you saw it on television. What did you think?*

Igor: I was hoping England will win, but with the starting line-up, when I saw the players who would start the game, I knew that England can't win that game. It was impossible with that starting line-up.

I.H. *In what respect?*

Igor: In the respect that you have to play with very skilful players against Italians. Hard workers, like Paul Ince and I think without Tony Adams and players like him, with the character, with the strong character within the team, you can't win.

I.H. *Do you think the problem was not that we didn't score a goal, but that we conceded a goal so early?*

Igor: I think it was a problem that they scored so early, but I didn't see from the beginning of that game that there was any possibility that England could score. You know what I mean, with Shearer up there on his own, it was impossible to score against Italians. You have to play with three strikers against Italians, if you want to score. But people talk now about Italians being well organised, tactically. No. England was bad. Italians didn't play good game for last 18 months. so, we don't need to talk about good Italian game. It was England's bad game.

I.H. *What about the stadiums in England?*

Igor: Great. The best stadiums in the world.

I.H. *Which one is the best?*

Igor: I mean, Old Trafford. I have played there, not the team. Anfield, Highbury. All the games. Atmosphere is very good.

IN CONVERSATION WITH...

I.H. *Which are the best dressing-rooms?*

Igor: The best dressing-room?

I.H. *At Highbury, they used to have the dressing-room floors heated and the floors were warm under your feet.*

Igor: Yes. I mean, the dressing-rooms at Man United are so big, a lot of space in there. You can really feel good.

I.H. *As you know, in the First Division, the away dressing-rooms can be poor.*

Igor: Terrible, terrible.

I.H. *On a cold day, you don't feel like it.*

Igor: You have to go in two groups, to get changed.

I.H. *You must be pleased with Al Asanovic's performances this season, because, presumably, you recommended him.*

Igor: Yes. We used to play six, of seven years together. Yes. I knew we needed a player like him to play in the Premier League, if we wanted to survive. So I told Jim and Stevie that I have a friend who can come and at the price to bring him over here was really exceptional.

I.H. *It was a gift, wasn't it?*

Igor: It was a gift, yes. I mean, you can't even think of one, If you see West Ham paid £5 million for Hartson, what you can think how much Al Asanovic, £55 million? You can't compare them.

I.H. *There's a third of the season to go. What are the qualities we need to stay up? What are the main ingredients? Spirit? Togetherness? Or what?*

Igor: Yes, spirit is a most important thing, but you can't have spirit if you don't work hard enough. That is the most important thing. I mean Steve McClaren is here. He is really good. Fantastic man, strong character. He's a good worker. He knows how to work with the players. That's most important thing. Then there's 'Gaffer'. He knows all the players in the Premier League. What's the right way, you know, to play them. its all very important.

I.H. *How do you think, as a player, you can improve? What are your strengths and weaknesses?*

Igor: My strengths?

I.H. *And weaknesses. How are you going to get better as a player?*

Igor: Explain me that.

I.H. *What do you need to do to improve, as a player, yourself?*

Igor: Myself?

I.H. *Yes.*

Igor: I mean. I'm not trying to improve myself, I'm just trying to do my job, because I know that I am a good player. I know that I can play well.

I.H. *I know that, I know that.*

Igor: I know that I can play very good, so I'm just trying to stay in side until conclusion, no? I don't want to go out of it so I don't want to make players in Derby County's team jealous. I don't want ...you know what I mean.

I.H. *I know what you mean.*

Igor: I just want to stay inside the team.

I.H. *What I mean, is that I've seen quite a lot of players, having lived quite a long time, you know.*

Igor: Yes, yes.

I.H. *I've seen some great players. Great players. Bobby Moore, people like that. Roy McFarland, here, who was manager before Jim Smith, he was a great player, a great player, one of the best three central defenders I've seen. They all had certain qualities. If you were to become a great player of that calibre, what would you have to do to improve sufficiently, to be in that bracket?*

Igor: *(laughing)* Maybe I. ...maybe I. ...no, I mean.

I.H. *It's an interesting question.*

Igor: Yes it's interesting question. The improvement I would like is I would like to challenge next season for the Premier League. It is a question I am going to talk with the people at the club at the end of this season, because I am very ambitious. I used to play in Croatia club that was always winning League, or Cup, or both. We won promotion last season. It's something. I'm not used to playing for survival. I want to go with Derby County and Premier League. That is what I want for myself, because I know that I can form one part of a team that can win the championship. That's all I want.

I.H. *I can remember, of course, when Derby County did win the champ-*

ionship — what would be the Premiership now.

Igor: '72? '73?

I.H. *Yes '72 and '75. As you get older like me, you forget that there are a lot of Derby County supporters who cannot remember that long ago. Some of them weren't even born, a lot of our supporters, so when I'm critical on the radio, sometimes, and I say we don't do this, or we don't do that and people complain and say he is too harsh, or whatever, what I'm doing, really, is comparing what we are doing now against that standard, you see?*

Igor: Yes, but it's not easy from 25 years ago.

I.H. *Of course it isn't, but I agree with you that you need always to be looking upwards.*

Igor: Yes, yes. I always want to go up, up the ladder. When I see that there is no more, I'm going.

I.H. *Finally, Igor, how is the family settled in Derby?*

Igor: You know, when results are okay, family is okay, everything is okay. I'm not the kind of man who came here to see the sun, or sea, or the weather. I came here to do my job. If I'm happy, my family is happy.

I.H. *Let's hope a goal, another goal is along the way.*

Igor: Yes. That would be nice.

Wednesday, 19th February: Derby County 2 Sheffield Wednesday 2
A wild, wet and windy night, heavy, sticky pitch and an excellent match. The referee, Paul Alcock, of Gillingham notoriety, did well

to get it played. Igor Stimac scored his second ever goal for the Rams!

"Derby showed a lot of spirit. They are in no way a relegation team," said Wednesday manager David Pleat. Let's hope so, but one was left with feeling that the Rams had again let two points slip. Leading 2-1 with ten minutes to go, they conceded an equaliser that owed as much to a slip in concentration, as it did to a possible offside decision that never came.

Collecting More Thoughts

Lionel Pickering

Sir Matt Busby believed that football was a game to be enjoyed. If you weren't enjoying it, there was no much use in being involved. Bearing in mind the Rams' precarious position in the League table at the time, I asked Lionel Pickering if he was enjoying this season in the Premiership.

Lionel: Yes. To be honest, I'm enjoying the Premiership better than the First Division. Although there's a lot a stake and we don't want to get relegated, the fact that we committed ourselves to a stadium that season, at a minimum cost of £16 million to £18 million, meant it was so vitally important to get promotion — and nobody could guarantee it. I must admit, when we committed ourselves to the Premiership in January last year, we were top of the League, but of course, there was a mini-slide, if you can call it that, and it was quite stressful at times. Having got there, I think there was a big sense of relief.

I think that Jim has really built a team that will cope with the Premiership and possibly we'll need one or two players, we know that, we can always see where there is needed refinements, but there is a basis for a good Premiership side. The feeling is one, really, of relief that we've made a fairly good start to the first half of the season and, with a bit of luck, we *will just about survive.*

I.H. *You've been to a number of the away matches. What has struck you about the stadiums we've been to? Which have impressed you, for example?*

Lionel: Well, first of all, I've been to all the away matches, except when I had 'flu at Christmas and didn't go to Sunderland. Obviously, the big grounds are quite impressive, but, I mean, Chelsea for instance, they're rebuilding and no doubt the stand I sat in, the Main Stand, is impressive, but looking at the rest of it, it looked like a tip to me. You saw it yourself. For instance, sitting near to us, down on the left there and getting into trouble with the stewards, were the Derby County supporters. They were getting into trouble with the stewards because they were being told to sit down and when they sat down, they couldn't see over the level of the ridge there. Obviously the people on the front couldn't see properly and they stood up, so everyone had to stand up. That is quite a bad design fault. I've heard a lot of criticism of the Baseball Ground, but by and large, unless you are behind a post, you can see and I just feel that people critics it, but I feel once it's gone all-seater, I think it's looked a damn good ground. It looks a bit quaint, with the roofs and things, as you'd expect when it's as old as it is, but I think Leicester is not a lot to shout about and a few other grounds, West Ham for example, is nothing to shout about. Southampton, I didn't think was any great shakes either, was it?

I.H. *It must have been an advantage, with our stadium being built, to have gone to these grounds this season, to put into practice some of the things we've been seeing?*

Lionel: Oh it was. We've been looking, actually, over the years.

We've been to Wolves four or five times when there's not been a match on. Forest, Arsenal, Spurs and Blackburn, for instance, were particularly helpful, as were Middlesbrough. They were very helpful and I have to say, there hasn't been a club really, that hasn't been very helpful, which is nice. Arsenal, by the way, were one of the most helpful. I'd been invited to Arsenal two or three years ago, when we first started thinking about a stadium and they gave me a tour and I told them about it — our new stadium — and they said, "Oh we've changed one or two things since then," and they got one of the commissionaires to take me round again.

Obviously we've been picking brains. We've had our chief executive, Keith Loring and Andrew McKenzie, the chief executive of Derbyshire Enterprises and one or two other people, have all gone up to Blackburn and places like that, to study their accounting systems, how they take the phone calls or whatever, you know, and everyone has been so helpful.

I.H. *When a new stadium is being built, people think of the view of the pitch, car-parking, access etc, but tend not to be aware of the logistical problems of running the stadium. The infrastructure.*

Lionel: By building our own new stadium, it's given us a big advantage to see how other clubs have fared. Whereas Wolves completed theirs two or three years ago, we now know the mistakes they have made. They're quite open about it — 'I wish we'd have made this room, or we've got all these corridors, or whatever' — and it really does help. We have, actually made, I think it is 27, alterations on the Middlesbrough design.

I suppose it's a bit like moving to a new house. You try to get everything right, but in the end, you'll forget one or two things, but it's encouraging that we've been in the Premiership and been able to take advantage of that.

We discussed the possibilities, assuming the Rams stay up. I suggested to Lionel that improvement was necessary, we didn't want to be scuffling around the relegation places again.

Lionel: Well. Jim is well aware of that and I'm sure he has talked to you about that. There are two, or three positions he probably feels could be improved upon. On the other hand, we've got to say there are one or two players coming through that ought to improve. I mean, I don't know how you rate people like Carsley and Flynn. I think they've both improved this season, haven't they?

I.H. *Well, I think they have. I think they can do a job, but I don't think they're Premiership players.*

Lionel: They have actually played a big part in the middle part of the season, when others have got injured, and have come in and they've not let the club down. Neither has Van der Laan when he's come back.

I.H. *No. I personally think that Van der Laan has been a big addition now he's come back. I think his leadership qualities, apart from anything else, have been very valuable.*

Lionel: Dailly, for instance. He made a bright start and then we thought, 'Hang on, he's not ready yet, he's young.' Now he came back, as you know, against Villa, and he's obviously going to be a permanent player. I think that, in the last couple of weeks, you've got Van der Laan, Dailly, back in the side and that's like having two new players in. When you think of Jim's thinking, letting Van der Laan out on loan and then he dropped Dailly, or he was injured, and now he's back in again.

I.H. *Yes, obviously Jim is talking, quite rightly, about raising the quality in the side. In the short term, that means we are going to have to purchase some players and, presumably, the close season is going to be that time —*

assuming we stay up. Now then. Supposing we go down. What happens then?'

Lionel: Well, I suppose some of these players we've got will want to leave. I think, possibly, the Croatians would want to leave. Anybody wanting to play international football would want to move on. But we don't talk about tthat while there's a fighting chance of staying up.

I.H. *We'll, quite. But it doesn't harm to be realistic and face the fact that we could go down. I mean, that's what the name of the game is. I think we'll stay up, but I think it will be very close.*

Lionel: On the other hand, I'm not saying Jim will go around willing to sell these people. I'm just saying it's like, if Newcastle wanted him, he'd go like a shot. So would these players, because I think both these players, particularly, have impressed.

I.H. *Now then, Lionel, you can remember the last Cup Final, can't you?*

Lionel: I can. I didn't see it, by the way. I listened to it on 'the wireless', as we called it.

I.H. *Really? Well, we're three wins from the Cup Final this season, aren't we?*

Lionel: I'll tell you what. It's a very, very good opportunity. We've got to win two home games and get drawn against Chesterfield, or Wrexham and we're in the Final.

I.H. *Exactly. That would be something, wouldn't it? Chesterfield, at Hills-borough. Then if we won the Final, we'd be in Europe again. It's terrific to look forward to these things and when you think of, what, a year ago, 18 months ago, when we were going to various places we won't mention, to be in the position we are in now is terrific progress, isn't it?*

Lionel: Yes, it is. Three from Wembley and four, possibly, from Europe. But, on the other hand, that's pie in the sky and I'd like to say that we are more interested in staying in the Premier League, than winning the Final.

I.H. *Let's get back to reality. When you put your money into Derby County, Lionel, there was no way in which you could make a profit on it, at that time. Now, of course, things have changed. Various clubs are making profits on their investments, through flotations and that sort of thing. How do you stand on that?*

Lionel: Hmm. Well. First of all, the money I put into the club was interest free and I believe the losses since then have been about £7 million to £8 million. There's only one bloke been paying the wages over about five years. So, first of all, despite what Mr Fearn tried to imply for a long time, that I was getting interest on the money, it was a load of rubbish. That was totally uncalled for.

I.H. *I think most sensible people understand that.*

Lionel: Apart from the losses, well. I mean, you're saying, 'What happens if we float?' Well, there's no decision to float. If we do float, and the club makes any money ...I say 'the club', as currently, at this minute, we're about £8 million in debt, and that's to pay for the stadium. We want one or two more things, it will be even more in debt and it we do float, I should think that one of the things will be to clear the debts. It will not be to line my pockets. If at some future date, in five years time, it can afford to pay me back some of the money I've lent it, I will be delighted to accept it. It will only be when Jim Smith has got his players and the debts of the club have been paid off.

I.H. *Yes. I personally think that when you put your money in and risked it in the way that you did, because the situation has changed, I think —*

and I think I'd have a lot of support — that you ought to get your money back, as a minimum.

Lionel: On the one hand, it is a loan. It is a long-standing loan. It is one of those loans that you may never ever get back, if Derby County had gone bust. It's not a question of 'I should get the money back'. It's a loan and it will not be with interest either, it will be straightforward money back. But there's no doubt, if there is some profit at all, I've got various companies that have been running on loans and if we can put the odd 'mill' back into a company, we will do.

I.H. *Yes, I mean, it is a situation that has changed, dramatically in football, in this last 18 months, or so.*

Lionel: If you stay in the Premier League, the rest of them are still with the pack. If we can possibly stay in the Premier League and stay there for two, or three years, or four years, then we should be okay.

I.H. *Anything then is possible?*

Lionel: I think we've got the right manager. I think he's bought very wisely and I believe that if you give him some money, I don't think he is going to run around like a kid in a sweet shop. He'll be very shrewd and also, you know, you may not have to buy anybody, because of the Bosman thing.

I.H. *Well, that's a different thing. Yes, of course, that's altered the situation again, hasn't it?*

Lionel: I'm sure he'll *[Jim Smith]* be looking around at players who are going to be available at the end of the season, who are going for free. Okay, of course you're going to have to pay through the nose in wages aren't you, but there is a benefit there?

I.H. *What Kenny Dalglish says in his book, is that football management is all about making correct decisions. I think Jim Smith has shown the difference and the whole outlook of a club is transformed, if you have someone who is making the proper decisions.*

Lionel: Yes. Well, I mean, he wasn't frightened to sign on foreigners. Without naming names, a manager who would never sign a foreigner because he wouldn't know how to handle them. I mean, although Jim was only with a minor club as a player, he is well respected and he is tougher than he looks. If players, either through loss of form, or injury, drop out, the player who comes in and plays well, he stays in. It's what I think is quite a ruthless streak, but it is a very fair streak as well and it doesn't matter what your name is, if he thinks that somebody is doing a good job, in they come. I mean, at the moment, Darryl Powell isn't in the side. Trollope is and Van der Laan and Dailly.

I.H. *So much about building teams is about fitting things together, a bit like a jigsaw puzzle and balance and that sort of thing is important. At the moment, I think we will stay up. Let's put it this way. I think we've got the capability to stay up, which is always the first thing, but I think it's going to be pretty tight.*

Lionel: I think you have got to bear in mind that this is the toughest season of all in the Premier League's history, with all these foreign players coming in.

I.H. *That's true.*

Lionel: There's no team running away with it and, I think it was Dalglish who said recently, that there's not a great deal of difference between the top team and the bottom and there's a lot of truth in that. The only difference between Newcastle and Derby was one shot from Shearer, wasn't it? We played Chelsea, when they played like they did against Liverpool in both halves and we were only 2-1 down, despite a disputed penalty and then they only beat us when we had ten men.

I.H. *Well. Without the penalty just before half-time, we'd have gone in level and I think the sending off was the thing that changed the game. We were actually in the game at that stage. Chelsea, actually, didn't impress me as much as they impressed many other people. I thought they were quite nice going forward, but I thought they were open in defence.*

Lionel: I know, but they are a very attractive side going forward. I thought they did what they did against Leicester, they went off the boil and it was only when we had a man sent off, they were able to make it 3-1. That's where they are probably lacking. There's no doubt about it, going forward, there isn't a better team in Britain.

I.H. *No, but on the other hand, Lionel, you've seen Chelsea teams of the past, thinking back to the 60s and 70s, and they were an attractive side then, but they never won a great deal. They won an odd thing or two, but compared to the other big London clubs, they didn't.*

Lionel: No, they've always been on the outside.

I.H. *That's right, they've always been the 'nearly' men'. Very attractive.*

Lionel: Nothing like Arsenal, or Spurs.

Just finally, Lionel, I think we're agreed on most things. That we'll just stay up this season and then next year we have to build on that, but you can't go forward unless you build on firm foundations and they seem to be there.

Lionel: The foundations are solid. Arthur Cox spent a lot of money, you know. I would have said that was a pretty strong team.

I.H. *No. I wouldn't.*

Lionel: Well, perhaps you hadn't got the right manager, had you? He didn't believe in himself. I mean, look at Pembridge, he played all right last night. He wouldn't play for Arthur, or Roy, would he? There was something wrong somewhere.

I.H. *If you look at all the players who have gone from Derby — Kitson, Short, Johnson — they're all marginal players at other clubs. They're not regulars.*

Lionel: They are at Premier League clubs. They're not scrap heaps.

I.H. *No, I'm not saying they were, but if you spend that amount of money…*

Lionel: Kitson hasn't had a proper chance at Newcastle. I rated him quite highly.

I.H. *Did you?*

Lionel: Oh yes. On the field I did.

I.H. *I think he's a 'nearly' man.*

Lionel: If you say that to Everton about Shorty, they'll jump at you. I said to them I understand Shorty hasn't done too well. They said, 'Who's told you that?' I said 'Well you read it in the papers.' They said, 'Oh, no, no. He's a good solid player, part of the squad.'

I.H. *Well, they'll defend their own, don't worry about that. They'll not admit they've made a mistake, will they, even if they have? I think Craig Short was quite a reasonable player, but I just think the players that Arthur bought weren't going to gel into a good side, because of the style of player they were. They were individual types of players and there were too many* *runners with the ball and you can't build a good pattern in a side with too many of that sort. If you buy inconsistent players, you get an inconsistent team.*

Lionel: He should have got his midfield sorted out shouldn't he?

I.H. *Yes, of course he should.*

Lionel: I mean, it's all right having all these people, having everybody back for corners, all behind the ball. Oh dear. I mean, we should have paralysed that First Division.

Well, I think so! Spending that amount of money in that division, it should have been spent better and if it had have been, then we'd have been up earlier than we have been, but that's water under the bridge now. You learn from experience.

If we'd have gone up under Arthur, or Roy, we might have come straight down again, whereas Jim was able to flog 'em all, get rid of them. Again, like we've said, about [what might happen] with the Croatians [if we get relegated], it wasn't a question that he got rid of them, they wanted to go and as far as he's concerned, if you want to go, go. Obviously he had sufficient experience to pluck players out of the hat, he knew the players he wanted and, fortunately, he did it at the first shot, which is great credit to Jim and I won't take anything away from him.

I.H. *Good judgment. That's what you need.*

Lionel: I think he's got that. He's not a bad bloke either. You can at least talk to him, anyway.

The Foxes

Saturday, 22nd February — Filbert Street

WHAT a disaster. Leicester City 4 Derby County 2. Sometimes a scoreline can tell a false story. This one didn't. It hardly scratched the surface of a dreadful performance, which brought all the fears of relegation simmering to the surface again. Such a dismal defensive display, left players and supporters looking dispirited and sad, long before the end, as an injury-hit Leicester City team gave the Rams a lesson in the basic requirements of defence and attack.

"All generalisations are dangerous, even this one," said Alexandre Dumas, but as supporters bemoaned the display with phrases like 'lack of commitment' and 'wrong attitude' it was up to the Rams management to make a more specific analysis of what went wrong.

As the final whistle went, with Filbert Street gleeful and Leicester supporters celebrating uproariously, the Rams players straggled off the pitch like the bedraggled crew of ship run aground in rough seas. In contrast, the Foxes' dishevelled scoring duo of Ian Marshall and Steve Claridge danced with delight. The looked for all the world like urchins in a playground, but they had given the Rams' back three defenders, Gary Rowett, Paul McGrath and Igor Stimac, a torrid time. At the other end, Leicester's three central defenders,

Spencer Prior, Julian Watts and Steve Walsh, hardly big names in comparison, allowed Dean Sturridge and Ashley Ward no room at all. Whatever happens in midfield, it is what happens in each penalty-area that decides the result of football matches.

The crux of the matter at Filbert Street was that individual defensive mistakes set the Rams on a downward spiral and boosted the confidence of a make-shift Leicester City team. Whichever way you look at it, this performance wasn't good enough. The respect, so desperately sought and gained in the early weeks of the season, when Premiership football was an exciting, new adventure, will disappear as surely as the sands of time — if we have more of this. Does such a defeat signal the beginning of the end for the Rams?

They couldn't have wished for a better start. Within two minutes, a shot by Paul Trollope, deflected inadvertently by Sturridge, spun crazily into the Leicester City net. Were the Rams lulled into false sense of security, especially after all the pre-match talk of Leicester's problems due to injury and suspension? Did the team collectively think that it would be only a matter of time before three points landed safely in the bag? It is very easy to attribute motive to such feelings, but what about the evidence?

Leicester's first goal came, initially, because of Sturridge's inability to control a pass out of defence. From the resulting throw-in, Leicester gained possession and a mis-hit centre followed. Then came the second mistake. Rowett allowed Marshall far too much room on the edge of the penalty-area and the Leicester striker swivelled to hit a superb volley past goalkeeper Russell Hoult. A good shot, but from a defensive point of view, a poor goal.

Leicester's second goal was laughable — unless you happened to be a Rams fan. A long pass back by Chris Powell saw Hoult adjust to get into position to kick it first time with his right foot. Then he stumbled. Like a man whose bootlaces had been tied together, Hoult staggered forwards. The ball bounced off his shins and trickled, almost apologetically, towards an astonished Marshall. He walked it into an unguarded goal. Around the ground, Rams supporters were stunned. Hopes and great expectations whisked away in the blink of an eye — and from a position of strength. No wonder emotions are stirred by fatuous phrases like 'it's only a game'. So it is, but this is Filbert Street, remember? This game was against Leicester City.

Uncannily like the match at Southampton, an early 1-0 lead was transformed, so swiftly, into a 2-1 deficit. Once more, away from the cosy confines of the Baseball Ground environment, the Rams' goal-keeper was culpable. How strange that all Hoult's mistakes, that have led to goals, have come in away matches. Is it coincidence? The psychologists, that growing band of consultants who have invaded the sporting scene, will undoubtedly have an explanation, of sorts. When sports psychologists are around, I am reminded of an anec-dote attributed to the philosopher Bertrand Russell about what went on in the minds of primitive people and the bland interp-retation of many people concerning the problem. Russell said: "Professor Verrall, a great classical scholar, was asked what an ancient Mycenean was like. He replied, 'No-one knows, but Miss Harrison will tell you'."

There are many stories involving managers of teams who have been unable to win at home, taking their players on a coach ride before home matches in an attempt to recreate an away match atmosphere. Successful? I don't know, but it was called 'psychology' at the time.

In a tight match, a goal has two immediate effects. It deflates the team that concedes it and it boosts the team that scores it. In the scoring team, actions become sharper, players are more alert and react more quickly than the opposition. In other words, the team becomes more confident. Confidence is a word much used in professional sport and if it could be bottled and sold, there would be no need for sports psychologists.

Another claim, sometimes made by disappointed fans, concerns fitness, because a side that is winning usually looks fitter than a side that is losing. It is usually an illusion. At Premiership level, the difference in fitness levels between teams is very slight. Again, it is a matter of confidence. What really happens is that there is an increase in confidence, in a team's collective mind, about its ability to win the match. When Leicester made it 3-1, four minutes later, thanks to some more dreadful defending, the Rams' brittle and already badly battered confidence disappeared on the wind.

The third goal was the result of two bad mistakes, again. Stimac got too far under a routine lob 30 yards out and when the ball was swept across the penalty-area, Rowett should have kicked it into the spectators behind the goal. Instead, he let it run and Marshall, lurking behind, scored easily. His hat-trick had taken just 19 minutes. For the rest of the first half, the Rams continued to look unsteady at the back and couldn't hold the ball at the front. The tactic of playing Lee Carsley in midfield, presumably to mark Leicester's Garry Parker, meant Christian Dailly played as a right wing-back. It smacked of tactics gone mad. It didn't work. In such a situation, leadership qualities are valuable and those of 'flu victim Robin van der Laan were badly missed. The Rams drifted onwards, like a ship without a rudder. The half-time whistle was a blessed relief.

Whatever was said at the interval, the Rams began the second half with more purpose. Again the ideal start was achieved, when Sturridge turned Stimac's shot into the net after two minutes and, at 3-2 down, the Rams were back in the game. Twelve minutes later they were out of it, completely. A high, inswinging corner from Parker was allowed to drop to the edge of the goal-area. A goal-keeper's ball? Absolutely. Disappointingly, Hoult stayed at home, the ball dropped loose and Claridge helped himself. This time there was no comeback and the Rams faded away.

Later in the evening, it was a sombre group that arrived at David Brunning's house, to sample excellent cooking and rare wines. David is a Leicester supporter and a friend of Graham Richards since student days. He is now a circuit judge, who specialises in fraud cases. He keeps a marvellous wine cellar and is a superb cook. When the Rams visit Leicester, he invites us to his lovely home to chew the fat, in a manner of speaking. At the moment, he is having a new house built, but his temporary rented accommodation was welcoming indeed. This time the victorious Leicester manager was due to join us, but, somehow, in the euphoria of victory, Martin O'Neill got sidetracked and missed a most congenial evening. It's impossible to remain despondent in the face of David Brunning's hospitality and once an excellent meal had been consumed and the glow of a 1973 vintage red wine had taken effect, the events of the afternoon faded gently into the background.

If the disappointment felt by Rams supporters about such a performance was keenly discussed on the short trip back to Derby, it is nothing to the frustration felt by players and management. Even then, there is a difference. Players have the advantage of playing and the physical exertion has the effect of relieving the in-built tension. Managers and coaches have no such release. Long gone are the days when managers used to sit in the stand throughout a game, dressed in crombie overcoats and wearing trilby hats. Some looked like bank clerks, some more like gangsters from a 1940s movie. Did they get a better overall picture of the game than that available from the bench? I wonder.

Nowadays, most managers give passable imitations of cats on a hot tin roof, from their positions on the touchline. None is more active than O'Neill. It must be the Irish blood boiling that makes him leap and dance with every incident throughout a match, but his judgement in buying players from the lower divisions is of the ice cool variety. Purchases like Claridge from Birmingham, Marshall from Ipswich, Neil Lennon from Crewe, Spencer Prior from Norwich, Matt Elliott from Oxford and Muzzy Izzet, a reserve at Chelsea, are testimony to his knowledge and faith in his own ability to get the best from his players. Against the Rams, Leicester City were certainly not at their strongest, but they were most definitely at their best. Was it a 'one off' by the Rams? Let's hope so, but the performances at Aston Villa, Luton, Southampton and Sunderland leave a niggle at the back of the mind. Has this team got enough players prepared to take responsibility when the going gets tougher — as it surely will?

From the Main Stand commentary position at Filbert Street, is one of the best views in the whole of the Premiership, both for viewing the match and seeing beyond the ground itself. The stands on the opposite side and behind the goal to the left are low structures and above them, it is possible to see right across the city of Leicester. Some people actually get a reasonable view of the match from some of the higher buildings that lie just beyond the Burnmoor Road Stand opposite. It is also possible to catch a glimpse of a corner of Leicester Tigers' rugby stadium on Welford Road. When darkness descends, a kaleidoscope of light shines out from the shops, factories and high-rise flats. It is very much an an industrial landscape, but no less interesting for that and the streets of the terraced houses which crowd in on Filbert Street have, over the years, echoed the sound of millions of pairs of feet, marching 't' match'.

There is also at Filbert Street, one of the most remarkable entrances to any football ground in England. In Burnmoor Road, the entrance to the East Stand is between terraced houses, just about level with the halfway line. Indeed, the entrance is so tight between houses, that there are bedrooms actually above the turn-stiles. It symbolises the tightness of the ground, hemmed in by ter-raced housing and factory walls and it demonstrates the difficulty that the club has in increasing the 22,500 capacity. Any attempt to build upwards has always been thwarted by planning objections and it is somewhat unrealistic to expect Leicester City to buy up the whole street, as Liverpool did with Kemlyn Road, so that they were able to extend the Centenary Stand at Anfield — despite the Mason sisters. Thus Filbert Street looks destined to remain a rather odd-shaped stadium, with two low stands and two high ones and limited gate potential. Other ways of raising income have had to be explored.

If building upwards on Burnmoor Road is not possible, around the corner in Filbert Street, the problem is equally pressing. At least the existing stand roof was raised a little in 1975, to allow a row of executive boxes to be constructed above the terrace below. The narrowness of the area available means that the inhabitants of the boxes are almost perched on top of the crossbar and they get a wonderful view of corner-kicks at that end of the ground. Spectators also get a good view from the South Stand, at the opposite end of the ground, from which a long shadow is cast over a third of the pitch, when the sun is low in the sky in autumn. After a touch of frost, it used to be possible to play at Filbert Street under two sets of conditions at the same time. Hard and frosty to a point about 30 yards from the goal at the South Stand end, wet and muddy over the rest of the ground. Quite difficult.

To solve the problem of frost in the 1970s, Leicester hired a plastic cover from a firm at Ibstock that specialised in making such things for market gardens. Hot air was blown under the cover, which rose like a balloon to form a tent. Players were able to train on the pitch underneath the cover, provided they could stand the heat. Eventually the experiment was abandoned because of cost, although Leicester, like West Ham United, still use plastic sheeting to cover the pitch. It seems a bit at odds with the all-singing, all-dancing, all-modern Premiership.

If Leicester City is limited financially, because of ground size, the club has long been at the forefront of commercial activity. Glossy brochures abound in the reception area, aggressive marketing is encouraged. The Foxes are about football, but Leicester City is, very much, about business. There is a marketing director, a public relations officer, a head of publicity, a conference and banqueting manager, a corporate sales manager and a marketing manager, all concerned with promoting what they call the 'City Business Stadium'. Between 1990-95, commercial income has risen from £900,000 to £4.5 million. No doubt it will rise higher as the full benefits of the splendidly equipped Main Stand, opened in 1993, are realised. Three conference and exhibition suites feature in the stand, two of which are named after Gordon Banks and Gary Lineker, while above the club shop at the corner of Filbert Street is the top-class Fosse Restaurant. The brochures refer to Filbert Street as 'a business centre', claiming it to be 'a five-star hotel without rooms'. Certainly the fixtures and fittings behind the scenes are comparable with hotels of four-star quality and above and it is all very impressive and very, very businesslike, but someone must pay the price. Is there significance in the fact that in the corporate hospitality boxes and executive suites, match day programmes are provided free of charge, but in the streets around the ground, they cost £2?

Team: Hoult; Dailly (sub Rahmberg), C.Powell (sub Laursen), Rowett, McGrath (sub Simpson), Stimac, Carsley, Trollop, Asanovic, Sturridge, Ward.
Scorer: Sturridge 2.
Attendance: 20,323.
"To say I'm not pleased with the defence, is an understatement," said Jim Smith in the *Derby Evening Telegraph*.

Wednesday, 26th February 1997: FA Cup Fifth Round
Derby County 3 Coventry City 2.
Another marvellous cup night under the floodlights. All the ingredients were there. A full house, television cameras, a sticky pitch and Coventry City two goals ahead in ten minutes, as Russell Hoult and Christian Dailly collided for the first goal and Hoult could only half-stop a low cross shot, which resulted in the second. Ashley Ward and Robin van der Laan brought things level at half-time and Dean Sturridge won it in the last minute, as the Baseball Ground erupted and supporters went wild. Wembley, perhaps?

Saturday, 1st March 1997
Derby County 3 Chelsea 2
Another thriller as the Rams, again came from behind to win. On

a firm, uneven pitch and with a stiff breeze, some of Chelsea's foreign imports were not too happy. Gianfranco Zola sat on the bench and Roberto Di Matteo was first off the pitch at the end — by a country mile. Frank Leboeuf was the exception. He held Chelsea's defence together, but was sent off midway through he second half, for handling on the goal-line. Aljosa Asanovic equalised form the penalty spot; Ashley Ward turned in the winner. At 2-1 to Chelsea, Jacob Laursen drove the ball against his own goal post at the Osmaston End. It's amazing how people forget incidents like that in the euphoria afterwards. It was a vital moment in the season. This was an incredibly important result for the Rams. ten matches to go.

Tuesday, 4th March 1997: Premiership table (bottom):

	P	W	D	L	F	A	Pts
Leicester City	26	9	6	11	32	38	33
Everton	27	8	8	11	34	40	32
Derby County	**28**	**7**	**11**	**10**	**30**	**38**	**32**
Tottenham Hotspur	27	9	5	13	30	38	32
Blackburn Rovers	26	7	10	9	27	25	31
Sunderland	27	7	8	12	23	34	29
Coventry City	29	6	11	12	26	39	29
Nottingham Forest	27	6	9	12	24	40	27
West Ham United	26	6	7	14	24	37	25
Southampton	26	6	6	14	35	44	24
Middlesbrough	26	5	7	14	31	48	19

(Middlesbrough deducted 3 points)

At the turn of the year, Andy Gray, speaking on Sky Sports television, said that 46 points would be needed to avoid relegation. He had forgotten to do his homework. Since 1990, 42 matches have been played in four seasons and 38 matches in three seasons. The team that finished fourth-from-bottom of the table gained an average of 1.07 points per match over the 42-match seasons and 1.06 points per match over the 38-match seasons. Gray was thinking only of the 42-match seasons when 45 points was the target. At 1.06 points per match for 38 games, teams need 40-41 points.

After 19 matches — the halfway stage — the Rams had 22 points. Ahead of schedule. Since then, nine matches have produced ten points, so productivity is declining. Remember, Jim Smith won Manager of the Month in December. It is all 'ifs' and 'buts', but it is the weft and warp of what football is about and the subject of much conversation at The White Lion. One other simpler statistic. The teams that stay up win ten matches in a season.

A Foreign Legion

The Cellnet Riverside Stadium — Wednesday, 5th March 1997

BRIAN CLOUGH played centre-forward for Middlesbrough in the second half of the 1950s. When Clough's name is mentioned, it is inevitable that people think of Clough the manager, but it is unlikely that the man himself would think that way. Like all ex-players, Clough believes that, whatever happens afterwards, the best thing about the game is playing it. People who have never played professional football find it hard to understand that statement, especially when former players go on to make names for themselves in other fields, as Clough and many others have done. What is so easily forgotten is that the fundamental reason why players become players in the first place, is that they have a simple, but very deep desire to play the game.

Football is a simple game, but not easy to play. Despite that, someone somewhere will always be telling his mates how he could have been a professional footballer — if only he had got the chance; if luck hadn't turned against him; if he hadn't got injured; if it hadn't been for the war; if only, if only, if only; if only, when he had a trial for Arsenal, the youth team manager hadn't been too busy looking at someone else. Then, perhaps, another individual will chime in to say that he did have the chance to turn professional with Chelsea, but decided to take up accountancy instead. 'More money' used to be the usual reason given then, if not now. It's all absolute rubbish. Desire is the thing. To be a professional footballer means you have to have the desire. To be a great player, you need great desire. The desire to play. It never goes.

Clough the player, was a formidable presence. He had a great desire to score goals. Not spectacular goals, just goals. He wasn't especially quick, nor anything special in the air, neither had he a particularly good left foot, but he had great balance and a wonderfully developed sense of timing for arriving in the penalty-area at the same time as the ball. In 213 League games for Middlesbrough, between 1955-60, he scored 197 goals, the highest goals-per-game ratio of any goalscorer since World War Two. Then he was transferred to Sunderland and scored 53 goals in 58 appearances, before a knee injury, sustained on Boxing Day 1962, virtually ended his career. Describing the collision with Bury goalkeeper Chris Harker, Clough said, "I sensed an opportunity to score …Suddenly it was as if someone had just turned out the lights."

Two years later, Clough attempted a comeback, in which he played three games and scored one goal. They were the only appearances and the only goal he scored in the First Division. Some critics voiced doubts about his ability to score as freely in the top flight, others are sure he would have succeeded. I go with them. Anyone backing against Brian Clough in football matters, has always needed a large bank balance.

These days, large bank balances are what Middlesbrough Football Club and its legion of foreign players, is all about. Nowhere have the changes that have occurred in football over the past five years, let alone the previous 35 years, been more vividly illustrated than at Middlesbrough. When Brian Clough was scoring goals, Middlesbrough played at traditional Ayresome Park and the maximum wage for footballers was £20 per week. Now, Middlesbrough play at the newly-constructed Cellnet Riverside Stadium and it is reported that the current centre-forward, Italian Fabrizio Ravanelli, receives £42,000 per week for his efforts. The transfer fee was £7 million to Juventus. Despite that and the presence of other foreign imports, noteably the Brazilian pair Juninho and Emerson, the team were bottom of the Premiership table, as the Rams made the midweek journey north. Unfortunately, it become a very wet Wednesday in Middlesbrough.

It must be difficult for international football cognoscenti to visualise a town, with a population of 145,000, situated on the sometimes bleak coast of North-East England, as being a place where Copacobana Beach, the warm Algarve and the glamourous Italian Rivera are juxtaposed. It is rumoured that Ravanelli had no idea where Middlesbrough was before he was attracted to Teesside to ply his trade. Attracted, no doubt, by the huge salary, rather than the biting wind that can whistle through the streets of Middlesbrough on a January evening. The Brazilian, Emerson, transferred from Sporting Lisbon, was even less enamoured. His agent, of which there seems to be several, had worked overtime to try to engineer a release from his contract. So far, Steve Gibson, the young Middlesbrough chairman, has stood firm. "These players came here with open eyes and signed contracts. It's been their performances that put us at the bottom of the table and they have to accept responsibility," he told the *Sunday Times* a few days after the Rams visit.

The football world waits with interest to see what happens if Middlesbrough are relegated.

Whatever happens, Middlesbrough represent a new influence creeping into English football. Since 1980, the big city clubs, with their huge population bases, have increased their grip on the destiny of the Premiership title. Arsenal, Tottenham, Liverpool, Everton, Manchester United and Aston Villa, having great corporate financial power and prestige, are the traditional strongholds of the game. They have captured 31 out of 46 championship titles since the war and 15 out of 17 since 1980. In the modern financial climate, their position is thought to remain unchallenged. Or is it?

The arrival of wealthy entrepreneurial owners at football clubs, like Jack Walker at Blackburn and Sir John Hall at Newcastle, has witnessed a new dimension introduced into English football. Lionel Pickering at Derby County and Sir Jack Hayward at Wolves, are individuals who are identified with their local clubs, having been supporters for several years, as indeed has Walker at Blackburn. In 1995, Blackburn Rovers won the Premiership title, in 1996, New-castle United had it within their grasp and faltered, but Jack Walker and Sir John Hall have sent a few ripples into the upper echelons of the football pool. At Middlesbrough, Steve Gibson, is intent on sending more.

The Middlesbrough chairman, is younger than his manager, Bryan Robson. At 20, he was Middlesbrough's youngest Labour councillor. During the 1980s, he built up a chemical distribution company, after borrowing £1,000 from his father, a welder. He amassed a fortune, estimated at more than £70 million, which put him into the *Sunday Times* list of Britain's Richest 500 people. At Middlesbrough, Gibson followed Walker's example. He appointed a star name to be manager when the club were in the Football League Division One. Like Blackburn, Middlesbrough soon achieved promotion, but further success has not followed immediately, like it did for Rovers. Now, both clubs are finding the going tough.

Three things added extra spice to the trip. First, the Rams have only ten matches left to decide their destiny in the Premiership. Thanks to the exciting 3-2 victory over Chelsea, supporters are now more optimistic about the chances of survival and with 32 points in the bag, it was thought that three more wins would achieve safety. Second, the FA Cup draw, by one of those strange quirks of fortune, had paired Derby County and Middlesbrough in the quarter-final, the tie to be played at the Baseball Ground, three days after the trip to Middlesbrough. It would be last-ever FA Cup-tie on the ground. Third, the new Derby County stadium, now beginning to dominate the skyline on Pride Park, will be almost a

Colin Gibson points something out at Newcastle United's new-look stadium. Graham Richards observes from the trainer's 'dug-out'.

Surely they can do better than this at Newcastle?

Preparing for commentary on Newcastle v Derby County.

Looking across St James' Park as the teams run out.

The VIP and players' entrance to Coventry City's Highfield Road. Security is tight and the fans can't exactly pat their favourites on the back as they go into the ground. Rams chief executive, Keith Loring, converses.

Referee Roger Dilkes arrives for what will be his last game in charge, at Highfield Road.

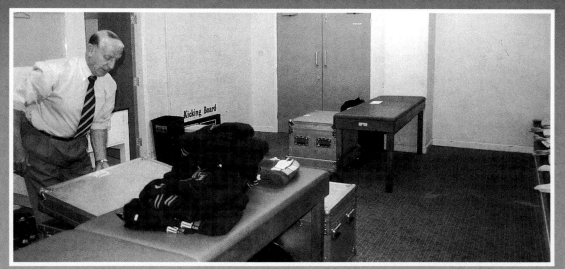

Gordon Guthrie lays out the Rams' kit in the Highfield Road dressing-room.

Pam Steele acts as Colin Gibson's 'voice' at Highfield Road, and (right) Kelly Smith sets things up at Highfield Road before being asked to leave – with escort! Those Coventry officials are a bit too officious.

Looking across to the massed ranks of Rams supporters at Highfield Road. Derby County always take good support away but on this day it was bordering on the spectacular.

End of the journey. Rams players with wives and friends relax in the Main Stand after the last away game of the season, at Highfield Road.

Taking shape. The Rams' new stadium at Pride Park under construction in January 1997. Once the site had been cleared, the stadium took shape with astonishing speed.

The Baseball Ground floodlights dominate the skyline in the Pear Tree area of the city. They blazed away on nights when the might of Benfica and Real Madrid were sent packing from the tight terraced streets which once wrapped themselves around the famous old stadium.

"Let's have a pint first." Supporters gather outside the Windmill pub, formerly the Cambridge Hotel, before the last-ever League game at the Baseball Ground.

"Get your programmes here." There'll be no street corners for programme sellers at the Rams' new stadium.

Will there be a Hector Suite at the new ground?

For the last time ...the main entrance at the Baseball Ground is less grand than St James's Park – but it's more homely.

Looking over 'B' Stand on the last day. Those spectators at the rear of the Osmaston Upper Stand had a good view over the skyline towards Normanton and Littleover.

The view from Cambridge Street. That fish and chip shop will miss match-days.

Eric Steele trying to make the best of the commentary position at the Baseball Ground before the last match, against Arsenal.

Dave Mackay acknowledges the full house as the pre-match ceremony continues.

Derby County and Arsenal players observe a minute's silence before the last game. Rams fans cast their minds back over the great games and the great players they'd seen at the Baseball Ground.

The Rams players went on a 'lap of honour' afterwards. Unfortunately, so did the ground stewards. What did they think was going to happen?

After the club's attempts at pomp and ceremony, finally it's the fans' time. On to the Baseball Ground they spilled, in orderly fashion, to have their moment on the pitch which has seen so many famous occasions. Some are cheering for the manager, some are chatting, some are standing alone …thinking.

It's all over. Darkness falls on the Baseball Ground, the breeze whips up the litter …it's just a time for ghosts now.

replica image of the new Middlesbrough stadium, albeit with modifications to improve the original design. It was, therefore, a buoyant BBC Radio Derby ensemble that prepared for the journey north — until we saw the car.

For a number of years, BBC Radio Derby Sport was the proud recipient of a car sponsored by Auto Windscreens. The last model was a Ford Mondeo, which achieved notoriety when it was overturned in the car-park at The New Den after the First Division Play-off semi-final against Millwall in 1994. That night, four of us accompanied the wrecked vehicle back to the East Midlands, travelling in the cab of a breakdown truck which moved at about 20m.p.h. As we skirted the backstreets of London, to avoid the trouble spots lingering around The New Den, the driver was astounded to hear Colin Gibson filing live reports on his mobile phone into news bulletins on national radio, BBC World Service and television. The story of the violence on that evening made news around the country and beyond. Having done the commentary and then kept the programme going long after schedule, describing the scenes at the ground, Graham Richards and I were fast asleep when we eventually arrived back in Derby at about 5.00am the following morning.

Needless to say, the BBC Radio Derby car became something of a celebrity, having being photographed on its back with its wheels in the air. Unfortunately, that celebrity status didn't save it from the dead hand of BBC regulations. The Corporation was unhappy that advertising guidelines were apparently being flouted and so the sponsored car was withdrawn. Now, probably at greater expense, we travel by hire car, usually a Vauxhall Vectra, but not this time. One look at the car provided for this trip and Graham decided to take the Mercedes. Colin and Pam Steele, who was making her first trip to an away match, to complement her Saturday afternoon *Sportscene* experience in the studio, travelled in the small Volkswagen. I went with Graham.

Just up the North-East coast from Whitby and Robin Hood's

Bay, lies the town of Saltburn. Historically, Saltburn was a port of call for smugglers and The Ship Inn, which nestles in the bay alongside the beach, dates back to the 15th century. In Victorian times Saltburn was a seaside resort, mainly for inhabitants of towns around North Yorkshire and Durham and it still retains the funicular railway, which in summer transports people from the promenade up to the cliff top. There is also a pier, but Saltburn, like so many small seaside towns, looks rather tatty and run down and living on past glories. It was worth a walk on the pier, though, for a breath of sea air and marvel at half a dozen surfers sweeping in on the North Sea tide. Great balance, but too cold.

Around 6.15pm, we finally approached Middlesbrough from the direction of the A19. Unlike at Pride Park, where vast wastelands mean that the stadium skeleton rises like a Hollywood film set in the distance, The Riverside Stadium appears quite suddenly, on the right, just over the iron bridge that crosses the River Tees. Later, an accident on that very road meant that kick-off was delayed until 8.00pm. Delayed kick-offs are catching on.

First impressions of what the new Derby County stadium will look like, were mildly encouraging, but access and exit seemed problematical. With the River Tees and the North Sea preventing movement eastwards and a working dock lying tight behind the North Stand, space at The Riverside is at a premium. No doubt, as the area develops — and there are plans for a marina and heritage centre — it is possible that approach roads and footpaths will provide a network of thoroughfares that have been standard requirements for football stadiums in this country. If so, the signs that at present proclaim 'No Matchday Parking' may also be removed.

It was dusk when we arrived. The lights on and around the place gave the stadium a futuristic appearance and the huge vessel, moored in the dock behind the North Stand, cast giant shafts of light on the glistening surface of wet tarmac. Warm though the evening was, the stadium felt cold inside and it lacked charm. It was rather like a new housing estate, before the trees have grown to soften the sharp edges. As construction materials for new stands in the post-Taylor stadiums, concrete and plastic, though necessary, are poor replacements for wood. Older main stands, like at Highbury, Villa Park, Upton Park and Anfield, still wrap themselves around their occupants in a warmer and more welcoming manner. The Cellnet Riverside Stadium felt harsh and impersonal. In a difficult-to-define sort of way, it was rather disappointing.

It wasn't half as disappointing as the result. Middlesbrough won 6-1 and in the second half, the Rams were reduced to a shambles. Echoes of away performances at Luton, Southampton and Sunderland came drifting back as the Rams became devoid of determination, discipline and leadership. "It was schoolyard stuff," said the Rams manager, afterwards. "We were like amateurs at 2-0 down, thinking we could show them by running through and scoring."

The most annoying part of all was that it started so well. In the first 20 minutes, the Rams played as well as at any match away from home this season and Middlesbrough looked a desperately poor outfit, lacking in confidence. Dean Sturridge especially, created several excellent positions in and around the Middlesbrough penalty-area, but he didn't make anything of them. Mark Schwarzer, Middlesbrough's new £1 million Australian goalkeeper from Bradford City, was tested only once and Derby County's lack of power in the air in attack was again apparent.

Schwarzer is the fourth goalkeeper Middlesbrough have tried this season, which highlights one reason why they are at the bottom of the table. It is axiomatic that a team cannot win championships without a good goalkeeper and had Peter Schmeichel and Pavel Srnicek swapped jerseys last season, Newcastle, not Manchester United, would probably have been Premiership champions. Likewise, relegation can hinge on which goalkeeper makes most errors in the scuffling at the bottom of the table.

In his *The Soccer Syndrome*, John Moynihan wrote: 'A goalkeeper is a man on his own, based in an open box with a net, and alone with his problems.' It is a schizophrenic business, goalkeeping. Huge applause for a spectacular save, downright degredation for the blunder that costs a goal. Some goalkeepers are luckier than others. Mistakes can be covered up by last-ditch scrapes off the line, or the desperate clearance of a loose ball that has slithered through the fingers like wet fish. Not all mistakes lead to losing scorelines, but although the conventional wisdom states that all goalkeepers make mistakes, which is undeniably true, some mistakes matter more than others. What matters, ultimately, is 'how many'? Peter Taylor always claimed that Peter Shilton was worth ten points a season to Nottingham Forest. What Taylor, himself a former Middlesbrough goalkeeper, meant was not that Shilton would make more good saves than his rivals, but would make fewer mistakes.

Schwarzer isn't the first foreign goalkeeper that Middlesbrough have had. Long before Ravanelli, Middlesbrough's Italian connection was supplied by Rolando Ugolini, whose family came to Glasgow when he was a baby and who spoke with a pronounced Scottish accent despite being born in an area famous for its olive groves. Ugolini used to delight the Ayresome Park regulars with some prodigious acrobatics between the posts. He was only 5ft 9ins tall, but it was said that he was so agile that, from a standing position in the centre of the goal, he could spring to touch the angle of post and crossbar at either side. Whether he could or not, he played 320 League games for Middlesbrough, before moving to Wrexham, about the time that Brian Clough was breaking into the first team.

This Premiership season, Russell Hoult has certainly not been as reliable as he was last season in Division One. I wonder why? The goals are still the same size and the job, technically, must be pretty much the same. Last season it was hard to remember a Hoult mistake, this season there have been too many for comfort, especially in matches away from the Baseball Ground. Unfortunately, at The Riverside, he was guilty of two more, which left the Rams 1-0 down at half-time and 2-0 adrift early in the second half.

In between, Sturridge missed an excellent chance to level the scores and then Ashley Ward threw away the chance to reduce the deficit to 2-1. Were Hoult's errors worse than Sturridge's and Ward's? It's not a relevant comparison. "If you can't pay the price, don't roll the dice," is a gambler's expression. Perhaps goalkeepers are gamblers at heart and sometimes they pay the price. Brian Glanville wrote an interesting novel about them. It is called *Goalkeepers are Crazy*.

After Middlesbrough's third goal went in after 70 minutes, the Rams collapsed completely. It wasn't pretty. It augers badly for the FA Cup match in three days time. At least the drive back was smooth.

Team: Hoult; Carsley (sub Simpson), Rowett, Laursen (sub McGrath), Stimac, Dailly, Van der Laan, D.Powell, Asanovic (sub Willems), Sturridge, Ward.
Scorer: Simpson
Attendance: 29,739

Saturday, 8th March 1997: FA Cup Quarter-Final

Any thoughts that Rams supporters might have had of walking down Wembley Way, were shattered in the last-ever FA Cup-tie at the Baseball Ground. On a firm, bobbly surface, Juninho ran the Rams ragged in the first half and scored a delightful goal to put Middlesbrough ahead. Ravanelli made it 2-0 in the last minute, but the Rams were well beaten long before the end. It was a strangely muted game.

In the semi-final draw, three teams wanted to be drawn against the heroes of Chesterfield. Middlesbrough drew out the plum, to be played at Old Trafford on Sunday, 13th April. The Crooked Spire will be lonely on that day. Chelsea versus Wimbledon, at Highbury, is the other match. The Rams can only look back at what might have been. An FA Cup semi-final against Chesterfield? It would have been nice. Almost exactly 40 years ago — on Easter Monday 1957 — the Rams beat the Spireites 7-1 at the Baseball Ground to all but clinch the Third Division North championship.

The Toffees

Goodison Park — Saturday, 15th March 1997

TWO days before we went to Goodison Park, the news broke that the Rams had made a £2 million offer to Aston Villa to bring Tommy Johnson back to the Baseball Ground. Two million was just the starting point. Wages, bonuses and further payments would take the fee considerably higher. Has the world gone mad? Johnson is a scallywag of a player, who attracts sympathy from old ladies and manic supporters because of his tearaway enthusiasm and lively humour. Not by accident was 'Tommies' the name given to British private soldiers in World War One, of which nearly half a million lost their lives at the Battle of The Somme alone. 'Your Country needs You,' was the famous poster, with the accusing finger, pointing. Derby County's situation maybe serious, but surely not desperate enough for the finger to be pointing at such a loose cannon as Tommy Johnson.

Everton, themselves, were having problems, with only one win in the previous 12 games. When they beat the Rams 1-0 at the Baseball Ground, back in early December, the Toffees stood sixth in the table. Now they sat one point and two places above the Rams and the Everton fans were becoming less than happy with their former striking hero and present manager, Joe Royle. Such matches are often called six-pointers. They're not really. What the Rams need to do at Goodison Park, is avoid defeat.

Goodison Park was the first major ground in English football. Everton moved there in 1892, having previously played at Anfield Road for eight seasons, before falling out with the landlord, John Houlding. He went on form his own club. He called it — Liverpool!

Everton developed Goodison Park very quickly. Three stands were built and a large bank constructed on the fourth side of the ground. The FA were sufficiently impressed that the 1894 Cup Final, between Notts County and Bolton Wanderers (4-1), was staged there before a crowd of 37,000. The following year, the first international on the ground was played, when England beat Scotland 3-0. Everton were soon the richest club in the country. Other internationals, particularly against Ireland, were played on a regular basis at Goodison Park, until Wembley began to be used more frequently for international matches from the end of the 1950s.

In the 1966 World Cup tournament, there were some memorable moments at Goodison Park. One unsavoury moment was when Pele was savagely tackled by Portuguese defender Morais. Tackled? Hardly. In this case 'tackled' is a euphamism for 'kicked' — and kicked very hard at that. Down went Pele, just outside the penalty-area, but, like a cork, he bobbed up again. Marais wasn't finished. He had a job to do. Not many players managed to kick Pele twice in such quick succession, but Marais succeeded and he caught Pele again. This time, the Brazilian twisted as he went down and in so doing aggravated a knee injury, which had already made him doubtful for the tournament. As the heavily limping Pele was assisted off the field and out of the competition, Brazil's hopes died with him. All neutral spectators in the crowd of 62,204, were saddened.

There were brighter moments at Goodison Park. 'Little Bird'

Garrincha, a legendary right winger, now long past his best, curved a sublime free-kick with the outside of his right foot into the top corner of the Bulgarian goal, to remind us of former glories. Garrincha, from the slums of Rio, was born with one leg an inch or two shorter than the other. It didn't prevent him having explosive pace in the previous two World Cups, but not this time. "You have nothing to fear from Brazil," said Alf Ramsey, in those peculiar clipped tones, when he addressed the England players soon after having watched the Brazilians in a pre-tournament warm-up match in Sweden. "We couldn't believe it," said George Cohen, the right back.

Ramsey was right. Even with Pele, Brazil were a shadow of the previous two World Cup winning sides. Without Pele, they were lost.

Also at Goodison Park, Lev Yashin, the giant, gaunt, 'man in black' captained his country from between the posts, as the Russians were beaten 2-1 by Germany in the semi-final. Yashin was left flat-footed by a free-kick from Franz Beckenbauer and incurred the wrath of his team manager, but with Sabo injured and Chislenko sent off, the Russians had other problems, too. Some years later, Yashin had thrombosis and was forced to have a leg amputated. He died of cancer at only 60 years of age. As if to remind the Goodison faithful of the long list of outstanding number-nines to have played for Everton, Florian Albert floated through the middle like a ghost for Hungary, and Bene, with a corkscrew dribble, scored a marvellous goal against Gilmar of Brazil, as the Magyars won 3-1, but they then proved too fragile to combat the Russians in the quarter-final at Old Trafford.

To cap it all, along came the North Koreans. Having produced one of the shocks of all time in international football, by beating Italy 1-0 at Ayresome Park, the smiling Koreans with the difficult names had the effrontery to take a 3-0 lead against the well-fancied, but startled Portuguese. Then in stepped Eusebio, to restore order. Known as 'the Black Pearl', the man born in Mozambique with the ferocious right foot and electric speed off the mark, overwhelmed the Koreans and Portugal won 5-3. Still smiling, Pak Doo Ik, Li Chan Myung, Pak Seung-zin, Ha Yung Kyoo and friends, left Goodison Park to an ovation seldom heard for losers, as 51,780 roared their approval. Although the black and white television images were grainy then and look grainier now, especially in an age of digital technology, the magic lingers on. The Everton ground, with the big 'D' behind each goal, never looked better for World Cup 66 and football in the 'Swinging Sixties' at Goodison Park, really did reflect the style and the times.

These times at Goodison are different. Those Evertonions, who remember the style and grace of Alex Young, known as 'the Golden Vision', the midfield of Kendall, Ball and Harvey, and Everton's reputation of being a 'School of Soccer Science' are depressed by the scuffling, long-ball, biff and bang type of football that Everton are currently playing. The end results are not justifying the means either, as Everton have won only one of 12 matches played since they, rather fortunately, beat the Rams 1-0 at the Baseball Ground, back in early December. In addition, the proposals of chairman Peter Johnson, for Everton to abandon Goodison Park and move to a new stadium on the outskirts of town has caused controversy and a 'Goodison for Everton' campaign has already started. The mood, on at least half of Merseyside, is grim. The other half of Merseyside is probably chuckling gleefully.

As a spectacle, the match was dire. With Dean Sturridge suspended, the Rams fielded Ashley Ward as a lone striker and played for a draw. They came within 11 minutes of obtaining it, until Dave Watson, Everton's veteran centre-half, secured the points with a left-foot shot from 15 yards, after the umpeenth knock down from beanpole Scottish centre-forward Duncan Ferguson, coupled with a loss of concentration in the Rams defence. It meant, for the Rams, both a third defeat in a row and a third away defeat in a row. Joe Royle was vastly relieved. "That should relieve the pressure a little,," he said. "It's really been hissing out of here recently."

Ferguson follows a long line of inspiring Everton centre-forwards. After the match at the Baseball Ground, Royle suggested that Ferguson could be the best of all. Sometimes it is difficult to know how much tongue this genial Joe has in his cheek, when he addresses the media, but it is hard to imagine that he seriously thinks that the current holder of the number-nine shirt at Goodison Park is, or will ever become, a more potent force than any one of Dixie Dean (60 League goals in 1927-28 alone), Tommy Lawton, Jock Dodds, Dave Hickson, Alex Young, Fred Pickering, Joe Royle himself, (Everton's youngest-ever debutant at 16 years of age), Bob Latchford, Andy Gray, Graeme Sharp and Gary Lineker. Part of being a good player is being fit to play and Ferguson misses too many matches and scores too few goals to warrant eulogies such as that. What he does do is condition the style of Everton's play, which mainly consists of heaving the ball high in his direction from all parts of the pitch. It is not proving to be successful. Not according to Everton's position in the Premiership and not according to the fans outside the ground before the match. Only Royle's long-standing love affair with Everton Football Club, which the fans respect, is stifling outright condemnation of their manager's record and, significantly, playing style and tactics. Next season could be a tough one for affable Joe.

For Jim Smith, there were signs at Goodison Park from which the Rams could gain encouragement. Despite the reservations about Ferguson, who is undeniably a difficult customer to play against, the Rams competed well in the air and smothered most of the scraps that fell around, until the fateful one. That is always the danger when playing to a defensive plan, and some supporters and reporters were critical of the Rams not making more attacking forays. Hindsight is always remarkably accurate and of all the teams in the Premiership to play for a draw against, Everton perhaps carry the greatest threat, when Ferguson plays. But on the credit side, the collectivity, so badly missing at Leicester and Middlesbrough, seemed to be returning at Goodison Park. On the debit side, simply having a lot of bodies in midfield does not necessarily mean that midfield functions effectively. The Rams' passing in the first half was poor and possession was conceded far too often, as it was when Everton hoisted the centre from which they scored. It was all a long way from World Cup 66 and the 'School of Soccer Science'.

It's interesting to speculate that Goodison Park could have changed its name to the Baseball Ground earlier this century. Grounds in this country get their names from geographical circumstances, such as streets, roads, or areas of towns. The Baseball Ground is an exception in being named after an activity that took place on it, namely baseball. Chicago White Sox and the New York Yankees played a baseball match at Goodison Park shortly after World War One, and Dixie Dean won medals for his local baseball club, Caledonia.

Everton say they will hold a referendum among supporters about the proposed move from Goodison Park.

Team: Taylor; Carsley (sub Simpson), C.Powell, Laursen, McGrath (sub Carbon), Rowett, Dailly, Trollope, D.Powell, Asanovic, Ward. *Attendance: 32,140*

Monday, 17th March 1997: Marino Rahmberg went back to Sweden. Leonart Johansen, president of UEFA, recommended him. Perhaps he is better at committee meetings.

Saturday, 22nd March 1997: Derby County 4 Tottenham Hotspur 2
What a relief. The first of five home and three away matches, from which eight points are needed to reach a points target of 40. Before the match, Jim Smith thought nine points were needed for safety. The three obtained here were crucial. Two early goals from Robin van der Laan and Paul Trollope calmed the nerves. Then Spurs scored twice. "Oh dear," said someone sitting near me. Others put it more strongly. A deflected shot from Dean Sturridge — who says

we haven't had any luck this season? — and a short-range effort from Ashley Ward had Smith bubbling in the press conference afterwards. Is he feeling the pressure? I hope so. If not, pigs are flying. The selection of Matt Carbon at centre-forward smacked of desperation. Is someone suggesting Carbon will play centre-forward for the last eight matches? If not, why in this one? Van der Laan was the real difference in the second half, with Trollope not far behind. They provided the leadership and the foundation for Aljosa Asanovic to catch the eye, significantly, in a more withdrawn, central and influential position.

Middlesbrough, with four wins out of five, and West Ham United have suddenly sprung to life. "In a photo finish, always back the fastest finishing horse," say the gambling fraternity. Southampton looked doomed, Coventry City are fading. We need one other team. Forest? Sunderland? They drew 1-1 at Roker Park. Smith now thinks 39 points will be sufficient. They still need getting. Lincoln City won six in a row in 1958, having won only five out of 36 previously. They beat Cardiff City 3-1 in the last match. It was a replay of a match abandoned earlier in the season because of snow — when Cardiff were leading 3-0! In the end, Lincoln avoided the drop by one point. It shows that anything can happen. Manchester United at Old Trafford looms next. Promotion and relegation won't be sorted out at Easter this time. There are no matches!

Wednesday, 25th March 1997: Costa Rican internationals Maurico Solis and Paulo Wanchope fly in tomorrow to sign for the Rams in a £1.25 million deal. Solis is a midfielder and Wanchope is a striker with, according to Jim Smith: "Terrific pace and great spring." Smith suggests he can jump as high as Duncan Ferguson and has 'rubber legs, like Faustino Asprilla'. Interesting. Wanchope has certainly excited the Rams manager and those who are a little sceptical should remember that very few people knew of Igor Stimac, or Aljosa Asanovic, before they arrived at the Baseball Ground. Few people will know of Costa Rica either! On the other hand, Smith also signed Alberto Tarantini from Boca Juniors to play for Birmingham City and probably wished he hadn't. Tarantini followed Osvaldo Ardiles and Ricardo Villa to England in 1978. He was an Argentinian World Cup winner, too, but didn't get on with opponents and referees and was often in trouble. He was sold to Cordoba after a season.

Smith was also appointed manager of Newcastle United when that club had the first Brazilian to play in England on their books. Mirandinha was his name, inconsistency was his game. Brilliant one minute, abject and disinterested the next, Mirandinha's two years on Tyneside epitomised the spectacular ups and downs that are inherent in the Newcastle story. Geordie and Latin temperaments can be volatile, even separately. Taken together, they make a heady cocktail. It wasn't too long before Mirandinha went back to Palmeiras and the sunshine of Brazil.

Thursday, 26th March 1997 — Transfer Deadline Day

Jim Smith sprang a surprise. The Costa Ricans came, as expected. What was not expected was the arrival of a goalkeeper from Estonia. His name, Mart Poom — at a cost of £500,000. From apparently not having any money, the Rams have suddenly splashed out £1.75 million in quick time. Presumably the decision to sell next season's season tickets so early, had this in mind.

It is the second time Smith has signed Poom. He brought him to Portsmouth in 1994, but the move didn't work out. He must value him highly. The next match is Manchester United (away) and Smith says that Poom is number one. "We need a goalkeeper of top quality," he said.

Professional sport can be a cruel business. Having waited in the shadows as deputy to Peter Shilton and then Steve Sutton, Martin Taylor seized his chance to establish himself as Derby County's goalkeeper, only to suffer a dreadful broken leg, which threatened his career. A year and a half later and with much hard work, worry and personal anguish behind him, he finally displaced Russell

Hoult. He then played three matches without serious blemish, only to find himself on the Rams' unwanted list, again. Perhaps a silver lining dawns. Wycombe Wanderers do want Taylor, at least on loan to the end of the season.

Meanwhile, Middlesbrough lost their appeal against the three-point penalty for failing to turn up at Blackburn earlier in the season. Even Sir George Carman QC couldn't save them. Most of football was pleased, anarchy looked to be the alternative. The other main story is that Joe Royle has left Everton.

I wonder how many transfers, which are hurried through to beat the deadline are successful? How many clubs actually achieve the desired result of gaining promotion, or avoiding relegation? It can have can the reverse effect. The classic case is when Malcolm Allison purchased Rodney Marsh and Manchester City's five-point grip on the League championship title was washed away. Marsh, jokingly, always blames goalkeeper Joe Corrigan for the catastrophe. I wonder whether the purchase of Pierre van Hooijdonk for £4 million will save Forest? Darren Wassell, to Birmingham City (loan), Sean Flynn, to Stoke City (loan), and Kevin Cooper to Stockport County (loan) are the Rams other outgoings before the deadline.

The Coach

TALKED with Steve McClaren, appropriately enough, at The Ramarena, Raynesway, which is the Rams' training ground. McClaren began his playing career at Hull City in the later 1970s. He signed for the Rams in 1985, but was injured in a match against Rotherham United and by the time he regained fitness, Arthur Cox had signed John Gregory. A good passer of the ball, McClaren made 30 appearances for the Rams, before moving to Bristol City in 1987. He turned to coaching as injury increasingly threatened his career and he was reserve-team coach at Oxford when Jim Smith recruited him for Derby County. It was a shrewd move by the manager, as it headed off accusations at the time that Smith was too old, too outdated and past his sell-by date. More significantly, it brought a sharp new brain to the Baseball Ground. The Smith-McClaren partnership is now well established and the results, so far, show that it works. How and why, only the players know. On the other hand, perhaps they don't. I asked McClaren about the changes in training methods since he began his career at Hull:

Steve: You're asking me to go back a long way. Well, what I remember about the training when I was a young lad was a lot of running, more fitness involved. Weights. And just generally playing on a Saturday. I just found it was very hard work, pre-season was a long slog. Er, for two years, it was very, very hard. There was a lot of running, 'cos I think they believed then that youngsters, coming from school, needed building up to get them fitter. I think now, the difference is more of a scientific approach. We're realising the growth spurts of youngsters and knowing that at 16 to 18 they're growing up, developing bones and muscle, but everybody's different. I tended to find, we used to get a lot of injuries, as a youngster. I blame one of the things — it might not be so much that — but I had a lot of back trouble in my mid-20s and I think I relate that back to the heavy workload I did when I was 16, 17 and 18. So I think now what we tend to do is to take a more scientific approach, realise how the lads are developing and which ways they are developing and modifying training towards that. So I don't think it is as heavy, it's monitored more stringently. Fitness tests, all kinds of tests we do now with youngsters, with everyone, that we never had when we were young lads. There was never a gauge.

I.H. *When people talk about players being fitter now, they're not actually fitter, because they are doing more work. What they're doing is better work?*

Steve: That's right. It's more beneficial. Shorter time, more quality. I know clubs, one spoke to me about it last week — I won't mention the club — but this club had a lot of good young kids that never went on to develop at 19, 20, 21, to develop their potential. It was found out that they were working them very, very hard when they came in and giving them heavy weights and building them up that injuries and burn-out appeared far earlier than if it had been monitored — a little less work and more quality. I think what we're developing now is that down from 16 and doing it with the schoolboys and educating the schoolboys, making sure they don't overplay. Another bad thing when I was young was youngsters who were playing two, three games, over the weekend. And cross-training with tennis, squash, cricket, sometimes rugby and so you were forever playing sport, every day, every night and then running, keeping fit. We were training too much and not being monitored as to the effect of it. Now, with all the equipment and all the science coming into it, we can monitor everyone. We know what is happening to a person's body at any given time.

THE COACH

I.H. *How do you do that?*

Steve: We have various tests. We can test stamina, speed, flexibility. There are so many different tests we use here.

I.H. *Do you use machinery?*

Steve: We can do.

I.H. *Or measurement devices?*

Steve: Yes, measurement devices. I mean, we have fitness tests here. We went to Lilleshall and had them tested there pre-season. Got the records back from there. That was stamina, body fat, flexibility, speed and strength. All the main ingredients of fitness, we had them tested. On machinery, plus field tests. Since then, we've bought the machinery ourselves and at regular intervals, we test our players. Now that goes all the way through from youngsters through to the first team. They're regularly tested. We know we're a little hit and miss with a player's form, or he's coming back from injury, as to what level of fitness he's at a certain stage. We can test that at any day. So we know that he's, say 80 per cent of what he normally is, he's fit to play. Or he's 100 per cent, or only 70 per cent. He could play, but you might get trouble in the last 20 minutes because of that 30 per cent that's lacking from being 100 per cent.

I.H. *I suppose that's invaluable in the substitution business.*

Steve: Of course, of course. We can monitor if a player's been out injured for three weeks and it's his first game back, we know he'll tire in 20 minutes, but we have more information at hand to make a decision and say, well he should be okay, because he's 100 per cent when he came back to us … It's just more information and more control.

I.H. *What strikes me about that, is that if all Premiership clubs are on to that, then the likelihood is that the levels of fitness are going to be very close. Whereby it might be said that when you first started, or when I played, the levels of fitness, one club to another, could be quite a lot different.*

Steve: I think you could be right and also I think you could be wrong in the fact that you're working at different levels. What information you had 20 years ago, all football clubs had that inform-ation, or could use that information. You know what I mean. Now, 20 years on, we're a bit more scientific, we've got more information, but it's there and available to all clubs. So I think it's all relative. The same information was available 20 years ago to everybody, and the same information is available to everybody the same today. They were not as fit as the modern game, but relatively the same, all the way through.

I.H. *I just wonder whether 20 years ago, the information was available to everybody, but because it's more scientific now, more measurable if you like, then it was more past down from one generation to another and the old rule of thumb.*

Steve: Yes. That's right

I.H. *Not that I'm knocking that, because there were some very fit teams about, but the range, if you like, from one team to another, within a league, might have been considerable.*

Steve: I think now, what you're saying, is there's a narrowing of the gap, because more teams are the same.

I.H. *The thing that's struck me this season about watching the Premiership is that all the teams to me, anyway, seem very similar in fitness levels. The only team I would pick, and it may because of their style of play, who seemed to have the edge, were Wimbledon.*

Steve: Hmmm.

I.H. *Apparently, they came back a fortnight earlier than anyone else for pre-season. Whether these things are coincidental, I think they probably are. They may make something of it for that sort of reason.*

Steve: I agree. But you look at that and Wimbledon lost their first three games.

I.H. *Exactly. Exactly.*

Steve: Our pre-season was a little bit jumbled and mixed-up, but we had a good start. It's all about peaking at the right time and the more information you've got , the better. The season is a long season. You're going to have highs, you're going to have lows. Individual players are going to peak at individual times and so having this information and the ability to test players …you will know, for instance, Gary Rowett, is having a bit of a bad time. Let's test him. And you might find that on his stamina he's down and then you've got to look into that problem, rather than assume, as you would 15 years ago, 'He's having a bad time, let's leave him out.' Now we want to know the reasons why he's having a bad time and the information is available to us and we use that information to say. 'Gary Rowett's having a bad time, because… and we need to do so and so to get him back.'

I.H. *Malcolm Allison once wrote a book called* Soccer for Thinkers *in which he relates all his points to players at that time. For example, if he was talking about 'awareness' , he'd mention a particular player so you could visualise what he was talking about. One of the things he said was, 'If a letter drops through your letterbox, to say that you're playing against Liverpool at Anfield today, what's the first thing that goes through your mind?' He says the first thought that would go through most people's minds is, 'I shall be knackered.' Allison claims that the thought that doesn't go through* *the mind is, 'I lack the ability' or 'I'm not talented enough,' it's 'I'll be knackered.' The first thing they think of is lack of fitness. He says that if you turn that round, fitness is the key to confidence. The thing that you doubt is your fitness, not your ability.*

Steve: ...I fully agree with that, but I think that is more of a total thing, whereas preparation gives players confidence. Preparing. If we have a week, from Saturday to Saturday, ...we do the work in preparation so that in that week we will do fitness work, technique work, team work and anything else. Within that week, we've prepared on them ...I feel so much more confident going into the game. So I think fitness is one of the ingredients.

I.H. *I know from playing squash that the thing that worries people is lack of fitness. They don't worry about lack of skill. It backs up what Allison says.*

Steve: It does. What is the main ingredient in that sport? You've got various things. In football, fitness is high up, as is technique, without one you can't produce the other. Awareness, you've got to have that. It's different for other sports, for example a golfer. You've got to have priorities, but the biggest thing that breeds confidence is preparation. As a player, I felt that and now I do as well.

I.H. *What about the extrovert player, who is full of himself and believes he can do it easily?*

Steve: In what respect?

I.H. *Well, we've both met players who are very self-confident and they can perform and they do perform with less preparation, if you like, than what would be appropriate for another player not of that temperament?*

Steve: I agree. And I go back again, to the individual. Everyone is different. What is good for you, might not be good for me. What we try to do is tailor everybody's needs, so we know, for instance, that Robbie van der Laan needs a good week's training before he plays and he needs to do extra on top of what he normally does.

I.H. *Is that physical, or mental, or both?*

Steve: It's both. He feels happy with doing that and if he doesn't do that, the doubts creep in: 'I've not done the preparation. Will I be right on Saturday?' Whereas you might have somebody like Asa, whose got tremendous technique and in the week, he comes in, does his work, doesn't do any extra. He works and then he goes home. He comes in Saturday and performs. Everybody is so different. You have to take that into account, with the approach to all players. I can't say to Asa what I might say to Robbie You can't say to Asa, 'You've had a bad game and you need to do extra in the week to be right for next Saturday.'

I.H. *Do you think smaller playing staffs have benefited that approach? I think back to days when staffs were so much bigger.*

Steve: I think it's going to get where the coach-player ratio will come down. Some days you can be taking 20 players. To benefit 20 players in a training session is very difficult. That is going to come down, it's as simple as that. It maybe one coach to every ten to 12 players. I believe in the future we're going to have a goalkeeping coach, a defensive coach, a midfield coach and an attacking coach, who work individually, like American football, and then the head coach brings them all together into the full picture. I think the sooner, the better.

Players today understand a lot more of the information available to them. They want to know that information. That's what I've found at this level. They want to know how fit they are and they want to know why. These players want to improve, they don't want to stand still. We have more information to give them, to give them individual attention.

I.H. *Do you think you can get too much information?*

Steve: I don't think you can. It depends on how much information the individual can take in, but I think too much is better than too little. Each individual has a job to do on Saturday. On a blank sheet of paper, he should be able to write out his job description. Everybody has a job description in business, it's no different to players. If they're playing right-back, they've got to know what they're job is at right-back, for next Saturday's game. The difficulty is getting players to understand the information.

I.H. *Everything in life is a balance. That's why I say, can too much information create anxiety?*

Steve: That is the key to coaching ...

We talked a lot more, into the afternoon. Interesting stuff. Steve McClaren, modern coach.

Theatre Of Dreams

Old Trafford — Saturday, 5th April 1997

JOHN Arlott once wrote: 'Football can be no more than a minor corner of any balanced life. Within the corner, however, it can be roundly satisfying.' Roundly satisfying? On a cold, grey day at the 'Theatre of Dreams' — a fantasy name created by the Manchester United publicity machine — life became very satisfying. The Reds 2, The Rams 3 — and didn't we enjoy it!

Even the most optimistic Derby County supporters, who made the journey over the northern hills of Derbyshire, through Buxton, via the Cat and Fiddle, up Long Hill, or along the A6, would have been hard pressed to make a logical case for victory at Old Trafford. The nagging worry of being dragged back into the relegation issue was still present, even though the win over Tottenham Hotspur was a giant step to safety. Thirty-five points with seven matches to go, including visits to Old Trafford, St James's Park and Highfield Road, means that the Rams are still vulnerable and could still fall off the high wire. Whatever else this Premiership football season has produced, it has produced tension. Now, it was about to give the Rams a taste of glory.

Strangely, as we gathered at our rendezvous, at the Little Chef at

Adlington, near Stockport, we hardly discussed the impending match. The odds seemed to be overwhelmingly in favour of the home team, bidding to become Premiership champions for a second successive season and for the fourth time in five years. United's impressive home record before the game was : P15 W11 D3 L1 F31 A11 and with Derby County possessing a mediocre away record of : P16 W1 D7 L8 F14 A35, it hardly looked to be a fair contest — on paper.

When nervousness creeps in, the age-old dressing-room cliches drift back. 'They may look good on paper, but they don't play on paper,' is a hoary old chestnut, but it's true. 'It's what happens on the day,' is another. As tension mounts before a big match occasion, such comforts are handed down from one generation of players to another. They will have heartened the Derby County players as they settled into their hotel on Thursday evening. Interesting move this, travelling to Manchester on Thursday and training in the area on Friday morning. Does it really matter? The management will claim so, if they win.

Whatever misgivings supporters might have about a particular match, professional players do not look at it the same way. Part of being a 'professional' player is about backing yourself against the opposition; being competitive. We are not talking about talent here. Talent is about being able to do things, technical things. Talent is about individual skills, attributes, tools to do the job, but that's not ability. Ability is the whole thing. Everyone has talent, greater or lesser. You don't get to be a professional player without it, but although talent is necessary, ability is what counts. Ability is being able to do your business — when it matters. Robbie van der Laan put it a simpler way: "There's always one or two teams who get something at Old Trafford and we feel it could be us." He's a good leader, this Dutchman with a Potteries accent.

The point was proved. United had the greater talent, but the Rams were more competitive on the day. They had the ability. As United increased the tempo in the second half, the Rams defended superbly. Paul McGrath, back on a pitch he knows so well, was a colossus, but everyone played a part. Even so, two goals were conceded to a United team beginning to threaten serious intent after half-time and the last ten minutes was played in a frenzy of excitement and passion. It was as thrilling a spectacle as you are likely to get and the most memorable match of the season.

What about 'Mr One Chop'? The tall, gangly Costa Rican international, who has several other names, including Watson, is the stuff of which heroes are made. He scored a goal which will be talked about for years. Talked about by Rams supporters. Talked about by United supporters, too, no doubt.

It all started so innocuously. Collecting the ball just inside his own half, Wanchope set off from a wide right midfield position and headed diagonally towards the Stretford End. A total of 4,088 United supporters, looking down from the third deck of the massive North Stand and a dizzy height of 35 metres, were reasonably relaxed as Wanchope began to move. The 7,352 spectators sitting in the second tier, with 32 hospitality boxes in the rear, felt fairly comfortable as he made ground through midfield, but 14,000 more committed fans, seated on two levels in the lower tier and nearer to the action and with 55 hospitality boxes behind, began to stir uneasily, sensing danger, as the penalty-area hove into sight.

Such a long, loping stride is devilishly deceptive. Phillip Neville's legs were working overtime, but he was making no impression, as Wanchope loped on ....and on. On he strode, to the edge of the United penalty-area, brushing aside two bemused defenders along the way, with Neville still snapping away like a terrier at the heels of a Great Dane. Talking of which, out rushed Peter Schmeichel. He needn't have bothered. Wanchope, leaning left, very calmly slid the ball with his right foot past the goalkeeper's left hand and watched it roll lazily into the back of the United net. The Stretfordenders were stunned, as the ball nestled there cosily, right in front of their astonished eyes. Amazing? I should say so. Disbelief floated around

Old Trafford. Wanchope celebrated like a Harlem Globetrotter. Then, he was engulfed by delighted teammates.

When Jim Smith signed Wanchope, the manager likened his legs to those of Faustino Asprilla — wobbly. "We haven't got any socks long enough to fit him," said Jim Fearn, the Rams press officer, in the United press room at half-time. Asprilla had a similar sensational impact on his debut, when he came on as a substitute for Newcastle United against Middlesbrough at The Riverside Stadium. So far, Asprilla has been an enigma Let's hope Wanchope survives.

In the euphoria, it was easy to forget that Estonian goalkeeper, Mart Poom, was also making his debut. Two early saves from headers by Eric Cantona and Ryan Giggs gave him — and the supporters — confidence. Soon the chants of 'Poooom …Pooooom …Pooooom,' rumbled around Old Trafford, like approaching thunder. Some chants are infectious. 'Pooooom …Pooooom,' could be one of them.

After it was all over, Jim Smith lit a cigar during the after-match press conference and was quietly reflective. Three unexpected points takes the Rams to a total of 38 and with six matches left, four of which are at the Baseball Ground, things look more comfortable now. The Premiership survival target of 40 to 41 points is within touching distance and the cloak of worry, so apparent on the manager's shoulders before the Tottenham match a fortnight ago, has fallen away. These are the moments managers live for, to savour and cherish. A stiff whisky and a good cigar.

Nearly everything about Old Trafford is impressive. Even as we arrived, just before noon, cleaners were hard at work throughout the stands on each side of the ground, giving the bright red seats a final dusting. It was a detail, but highly significant. Bill Shankly used to tell apprentices at Liverpool that whenever they were told to sweep the terraces at Anfield, they should 'sweep them well, eh?'.

From the press box, which is situated alongside the directors' box at Old Trafford, there is a perfect view of the pitch. That is important for us. In the hurly burly of goalmouth scramble, a good view of the action is essential for radio broadcasting, as radio commentary is instant, with little thinking time and no time at all for cool, reasoned consideration. There is no time, either, for action replays. First reactions dominate. Knowledge and experience counts. What is said, is said — and quickly. It needs to be right, first time. Sitting in a chair at home, the listener wants to feel part of the event, to be 'engaged in the occasion'. He, or she, needs to capture a flavour of the atmosphere, to be able to form in the mind's eye, with the help of the imagination, a picture of what is happening — and, of course, know the score.

Behind the press box in the Main Stand, is the press room. Leading off to the side, is an interview room which has aircraft cabin type seats and is arranged like a small cinema. There is also a room which is reserved for radio interviews and across the passage is the Radio Manchester United studio, which broadcasts throughout matchdays and at certain other times on a wavelength that can be received in a limited area around Manchester. The various press officers and stewards were helpful and considerate and the aim seems to be to assist the media perform its various tasks, particularly in what can sometimes be a hectic after-match period. Such an attitude contrasts strikingly with that at certain other clubs. I suppose if you want to be the best, you need to provide the best and whoever has been consulted about press and media arrangements at Old Trafford, knew his business.

Perhaps it was David Meek. Until his retirement last year, he was the *Manchester Evening News* reporter on Manchester United affairs since 1958. He is co-author of the official Manchester United history, published in 1988, and other United publications and is steeped in United affairs. For 14 years after he started, Meek travelled on the team coach, privy to juicy stories, club politics and football secrets. Then in 1972 he wrote an article under the heading 'Be Fair to Frank', suggesting that the club directors should share some of the responsibility with manager Frank O'Farrell for the problems United were having at the time, notably with George

Best. The *Manchester Evening News* quickly received a letter from club secretary, Les Olive, on behalf of the United board of directors, stating: 'Mr David Meek is no longer welcome to travel on the team coach.' Unbeknown to Meek, the club had already decided to sack O'Farrell, but Matt Busby believed that Meek did know and was supporting O'Farrell, thus defying the club.

Such is the problem for the local media. It has to preserve a delicate balance between conflicting interests: readers, or listeners and the club. Both need to be kept happy. Without access to the club, readers, or listeners may not get the information to which they are entitled, but football clubs are notorious for being sensitive to criticism, objective or otherwise. The danger is that local media people — radio and newspapers — get seduced into an easy life and fall into the habit of simply becoming a mouthpiece for the club. They stop telling it as they see it. As players, we always reckoned that Wilf Shaw's match reports in the *Derby Evening Telegraph* on Monday evenings, came straight from Harry Storer's office on Monday mornings.

It is impossible to visit Old Trafford, without being reminded of the Munich Air Disaster. The Munich memorial clock, the commemorative plaque denoting the names of those who died, the bronze statue of Sir Matt Busby, are all sited on the rear of the East Stand, as you approach the ground along Sir Matt Busby Way. They are poignant reminders of what happened on 6th February 1958, when a specially-chartered Elizabethan aircraft, Lord Burghley, bringing the Manchester United party back from a European Cup quarter-final against Red Star Belgrade, crashed in the snow at Munich airport. Twice the plane went down the runway to attempt a take off and twice it turned back. The third attempt was fatal. Eight players died as a result of the crash, three others never played again. Eight journalists died, including Frank Swift, the former Manchester City and England goalkeeper. Club secretary Walter Crickmer died, as did trainer Tom Curry and coach Bert Whalley. Four other passengers died and Matt Busby was left fighting for his life. The Busby Babes were destroyed and a legend arose from the ashes.

Although Matt Busby rebuilt United to win the European Cup ten years later, the story of Munich is embedded in football lore and within United's soul. How good was that team? How great would it have become? Perhaps the greatest? Who knows? For those of us who, briefly, saw the Busby Babes play, it was a footballing privilege.

Albert Scanlon was a Busby Babe. He was a flying left winger, who played against Red Star Belgrade and survived 'the Crash'. He didn't say too much about it, when he became a playing colleague of mine at Mansfield, but the frost bite scars that covered his body were reminders of the 20 minutes he lay in the snow at Munich, along with those who died. Rescuers thought that he, too, was dead. He didn't talk about it much.

Busby's 'new' United team of the 1960s, included stars like George Best, Bobby Charlton and Dennis Law, and Old Trafford hosted some marvellous European Cup nights against teams like Real Madrid and Benfica, featuring Alfredo di Stefano, Ferenc Puskas and Eusebio. Getting a ticket was virtually impossible, unless you knew Albert Scanlon. It is likely that Albert was wheeling and dealing in tickets when he was in his cradle. By the time we knew him, he probably spent more time on tickets than he did on football. Maybe, but without the name 'Albert Scanlon' as a passport, there's no way I would have seen those great teams and players play at Old Trafford in those wonderful years. "Just mention I sent you," he would say, as three or four of us set out, hopefully, on the journey over the Pennines and despite all the 'Sold Out' notices hanging from the selling hatches outside the ground, we were never disappointed when we enquired at the main ticket office. "Albert Scanlon? Certainly, sir. How many?" The aura and magic of a Busby Babe could move mountains, long after Munich.

The modern United is a great tribute to Alex Ferguson. Like him or loath him, the abrasive Glaswegian from Govan, a long way removed from the image created by the avuncular Busby, has taken

United to great heights. Until Ferguson landed his first Premiership title in 1993, United hadn't won the championship of the top flight for 26 years and the continued presence of Busby at the club was thought to be a debilitating factor hanging over the efforts of all the managers who followed him. Busby created the modern United and the club is always in his debt, but with Busby in the boardroom, successive managers like Wilf McGuinness, Frank O'Farrell, Tommy Docherty, Dave Sexton and Ron Atkinson found it impossible to shake off the Busby shadow, despite intermittent FA Cup success. 'The championship' became United's Holy Grail, until Ferguson succeeded. Now it is the European Cup.

"How will this result affect United's chances against Borussia Dortmund, next Wednesday?" was one of the questions Ferguson was asked after the Rams match. "We'll be ready," he said, but he was also generous in his praise for the Rams: "Hands up to Derby. They worked really hard for victory. They had a good game plan, almost as if they knew our team in advance." On the other hand, what United didn't know about, was Paulo Wanchope!

What I didn't know about, was Eric Cantona. It was my first view of him, live. Of course, I'd seen him play on television, but that's not the same. Best, Law, Charlton, Pat Crerand, Tommy Taylor, Liam (Billy) Whelan, Eddie Colman, Roger Byrne, I'd seen all those players in action. I'd also heard Charlton talk about Cantona and he puts him, Cantona, in their category. It wasn't until the second half that I appreciated what Charlton had been talking about. Cantona was superb. He is a big man, but his control and balance are sublime and his strength and poise, especially when he scored United's first goal immediately after the interval, is exceptional. Paul Trollope performed an excellent man-for-man marking role on the United captain and must have been thrilled at playing so well against him, but Cantona certainly goes into my list of great players — and I don't use the word lightly. Incidentally, Charlton puts Duncan Edwards into a category of his own.

If we didn't discuss the match much on the way up, we certainly talked about it plenty on the way back. Graham went to Blackpool, presumably to celebrate on the Big Dipper. The *Manchester Evening News — The Pink —* lasted me nearly all week. *Match of the Day* was a real treat.

Team: Poom; Laursen, McGrath, Dailly, C.Powell, Van der Laan, Trollope, D.Powell, Wanchope (sub Simpson) Ward, Sturridge.
Scorers: Ward, Wanchope, Sturridge.
Attendance: 55,243

Wednesday, 9th April 1997: Derby County 1 Southampton 1

From the top of the table to the bottom and if the management got the 'game plan' exactly right at Old Trafford, it went somewhat wrong against Southampton. Darryl Powell's own-goal in the last minute gave the Saints a point, but they dominated the second half, as any idea of Derby County passing the ball went out of the window. Wanchope was relegated to the substitute's bench and a midfield foursome of Van der Laan, Trollope, Darryl Powell, plus Asanovic seemed like one too many honest toiler for a game at home, following so soon after the joys of Old Trafford. The side had little shape and no balance. Admittedly, a point is a point, but the process was painful. The Saints were expecting a battering in the first 20 minutes and the Rams supporters were ready to give it to them. They didn't get the chance.

Saturday, 12th April 1997: Derby County 2 Aston Villa 1

I missed this match to attend my youngest son's wedding. The wedding date was arranged with the FA Cup semi-finals in mind, but Middlesbrough spoiled the best-laid plans. I hope they get relegated and Chesterfield win. Just think, it should have been Chesterfield versus Derby County, probably at Hillsborough, on the Sunday. Then I could have attended both events. Still, it was good to hear the result. 42 points and the Rams are safe. Forget cautious pessimists.

Geordie Fortress

St James' Park — Saturday, 19th April 1997

Friday, 18th April 1997: The BBC Radio party departed for 'Geordie Land' at 4pm. As mentioned before, Colin Gibson likes to get to matches early, but this time he was blameless. Graham Richards wanted to see Durham. We stayed at a new Travel Inn and went into Durham to an Italian restaurant. Ever since the Anglo-Italian tournament and a couple of trips to Italy, Colin and Graham favour a particular type of Italian wine. I can never remember the name, but am quite happy to drink it, especially as Graham is paying. Phil Mugford contributes to the evening by dragging us to a couple of low dives in downtown Durham where you can hardly hear yourself think, before we adjourn to the restaurant. It's quite a convivial evening. Kenny Dalglish is currently staying at the County Hotel in Durham, but Colin decided not to pay him a visit and request an interview.

Saturday, 19th April 1997:
We took a stroll on the beach at Whitley Bay on Saturday morning. Joe Harvey, who captained Newcastle to three Wembley FA Cup triumphs in five years, between 1951-55, later became chief scout and then manager of the club. Harvey discovered Paul Gascoigne

and he used to take the Newcastle players training at Whitley Bay. Quite what they did there is hard to imagine, because the wind whistles off the North Sea, even in mid–April, and the chances of a calm day in January must be quite remote. My word, it was cold. Even though he is a world traveller, Graham Richards has been fooled by the beautiful warm weather of the previous weekend and is taking the opportunity to introduce us to his spring wardrobe collection. He soon regretted it. It is said that a characteristic of the inhabitants of this part of the world is the many pink faces, brought about by the wind. We were fairly sure that Graham's was the result of the walk at Whitley Bay, rather than the visit to the restaurant the night before.

The upsurge in Newcastle United's fortunes in the 1990s has been remarkable. Back in 1992, the Rams played the Magpies at the Baseball Ground, on Easter Monday. The match was refereed by a certain Mr Coddington. Three Newcastle players, plus assistant manager, Terry McDermott , were sent off, as the Rams won 4-1, to send Newcastle United to the brink of the old Third Division. They averted that fate on the very last day of the season, by winning at Leicester, and since then, their fortunes have soared onwards and upwards. The catalysts for such an enormous explosion in football energy on Tyneside have been undoubtedly Sir John Hall and Kevin Keegan.

The North-East is often referred too as being a hotbed of football, where the passion for the game is greater than anywhere else. It is a myth. If it were true, clubs like Hartlepool, Darlington, Bishop Auckland, Whitley Bay and Spennymoor would get bigger attendances than they do and a famous club like North Shields would not have gone out of business. Ashington, Durham City and, more recently, Gateshead, have all been members of the Football League, but have not survived. The passion for football in the North-East is probably no more and no less than in any other area, but it makes for a good battle cry and public relations slogan. What is certainly true is that the North-East has produced some outstanding players, who have made their names elsewhere, while supporters of the big three clubs, Newcastle, Sunderland and Middlesbrough, have been starved of success for longer than most. Grandfathers' tales of how Newcastle won the FA Cup must have worn thin for more than 40 years in the North-East and erked younger followers. Then, with a tremendous impact, came Sir John Hall and Kevin Keegan.

To the outsider, the image of Sir John is that of a medieval baron, who rules his kingdom with a rod of iron like a latter day Duke of Northumberland. His early claim to fame was as the developer of the massive MetroCentre in Gateshead, but when he succeeded to his position as chairman of the board of directors of Newcastle United in 1992, after a boardroom battle for power with the McKeag family, the spotlight picked him out more brightly than, perhaps, even he ever imagined.

It's intriguing that in the 16th century, John Dudley, who did become the Duke of Northumberland, rose to prominence in the reign of Henry VIII. He gained much wealth and acquired much property. After Henry died, a ferocious power struggle took place, involving the Duke of Somerset, who was Lord Protector and ruled the country on behalf of the nine-year old Edward VI. As a result, Northumberland became the chief power in the state and took the title of Lord President. He then wanted more and attempted to put his daughter-in-law, Lady Jane Grey, on the throne of England, instead of Mary Tudor. Mary was a daughter of Henry VIII and the rightful heir. Battles were fought and blood was shed, before the Duke of Northumberland's ambition to control the whole of England was thwarted. He was defeated and sent to the Tower. Eventually, the 16th century Duke of Northumberland was executed.

Hall's inspired move was to appoint Kevin Keegan as manager of Newcastle United in February 1992. I have never been to the MetroCentre to shop, but I have seen Keegan play football. A 'bubble and squeak' type of player with immense energy and enthusiasm, Keegan was European Footballer of the Year in two successive years (1978 and 1979) when he played for SV Hamburg, which is an achievement far beyond the wildest dreams of any current Premiership player, including Alan Shearer. Yet acknowledgement of Keegan the player, was always grudging. 'Works hard, but lacks flair,' was a damning-with-faint-praise type of accolade. The same has been said of Jansher Khan, the great squash player, of Nick Faldo the golfer — 'too mechanical' — and Sir Donald Bradman, who rewrote all the cricket records. We do like our heroes to satisfy all criteria, and in addition, be easy on the eye. Keegan may have been short of greatness, but he must have been a great man to have had in your side.

We know less about Sir John Hall. We never saw him play. He never entertained Newcastle supporters in the way that Jackie Milburn did, or Len White, or Malcolm Macdonald, Alan Shearer, or all the other number-nines who graced St James's Park. Sir John arouses ambivalent emotions in the hearts and minds of football followers outside his self-styled 'Geordie Nation'. People who have grown up with the game feel that football is worthwhile for its own sake, a means in itself. For Sir John Hall, it is doubtful if football is a game to be enjoyed for its own sake. It is more a means to an end. What precisely that end is, we can only speculate. What is undeniably true, is that without Sir John Hall, Newcastle United would not be the power in football it is today. Power. Is that the real motivation for people like Sir John Hall and the Duke of Northumberland?

The number-nine at Newcastle has always carried a special aura. Perhaps the magic began with Hughie Gallacher, who captained the Geordies to the last of their four championship titles in 1927. Gallacher was only 5ft 6ins tall and a genius. He signed for Derby County in 1934 and scored within six minutes of his debut. His off-the-field drinking habits were well documented, but his death was tragic. He committed suicide by throwing himself under the wheels of the Edinburgh–York express, near the Tyne Bridge. Sam Weaver, a teammate of Gallacher's at Newcastle, once told me that the tragedy took place on the very spot where the train was always stopped to let Hughie alight, so that he could avoid the crowds that used to gather at the station, to welcome the team back from away trips.

If the arrival of the home players at Villa Park on match days is spectacular — described when the Rams played there back in August — that of the Newcastle players and the Derby County team at St James' Park was positively gladiatorial. Whereas the entrance to Old Trafford, Anfield, Goodison Park and even Highbury, is stylishly discreet, the frontage at St James' Park is like the entrance to a top hotel, all glitz and glass frontage. Wide steps lead up to the reception entrance and barriers are erected to keep the fans at a distance. As the players approach from the car-park behind the Sir John Hall Stand at the north end of the ground, or arrive by taxi and limousine, they are besieged by supporters. The whole affair is like the arrival of the celebrities, on film premier night, at the Empire Theatre in Leicester Square. Nowhere is football and showbusiness so graphically symbolised as when players stride up the steps, waving to the fans. Even more worrying is the waving by insignificant officials.

The match got off to a dramatic start. A kick down the field by Gary Rowett was missed by the Newcastle central defenders and Dean Sturridge scored in 32 seconds. He was away from the halfway line and never looked like missing as Shaka Hislop came out. Such situations are never as easy as they look. A lot of time can be difficult to handle, the sudden shot in a crowded goalmouth is far easier, but Sturridge scored his first-ever goal for the Rams with a similar chance, when he substituted for Paul Kitson against Millwall in August 1994. The Rams have come a long way since then and so has Sturridge. Earlier in the week he had been in the news for a different reason as his lawyer appealed on grounds of 'exceptional hardship' at Stafford Crown Court, against a six-month ban for speeding, his fourth offence in a year. 'Hardship plea by £3,000 footballer,' screamed the headlines in the *Daily Telegraph*, as various financial details were disclosed in court, including the revelation that Sturridge earns £3,000 per week, the Rams players receive £600 for a win and Sturridge receives money for 'scoring a fixed number of goals'. I wonder what the defenders think of that?

It's all a long way from when Tommy Docherty requested a rise in his basic wages at Preston North End, who were then one of the country's top teams. At that time, £14 in the season and £12 in the close season was the maximum wage, for all players. The manager decreed that Docherty should be paid £2 less than the great Tom Finney. "Why is that?" asked Docherty. "You're not as good a player as Tom Finney," was the answer. "I am in the summer," replied the 'Doc' — and he got his rise.

Waving to the fans while making a celebrity entrance before the game was not an option when Sturridge scored at the New Den, but the result was the same. Then, the home side won 4–1. This time it was 3–1 and could have been plenty more. "We were really up for it at Old Trafford," said Jim Smith. "This was a bit of a holiday." That may be, but the Rams' tactics were hard to understand. They seemed to confuse themselves more than the opposition and midfield was a disaster, with David Batty running the show. The decision to have Paul Trollope marking Faustino Asprilla backfired in a big way and removed the Rams midfielder from that central area of the pitch, as Asprilla led him a merry dance, mostly up and down the wings. Aljosa Asanovic started in the middle and was then stationed out wide on the left, while Robbie Van der Laan was left to handle Batty, Robert Lee and Robbie Elliott, until Chris Powell and Gary Rowett were pushed into midfield to try to help. The Rams were totally lopsided, ill-balanced and disorganised. Coach Steve McClaren spent the first ten minutes of the match rushing to the touchline to give instructions to players, who came to the sideline seemingly bemused by what was happening.

In Liverpool's successful years, many people wanted to know 'the secret' of Liverpool's greatness and how it came about. Tom Saunders, a member of the famous Anfield boot room from 1969–

93 and now a Liverpool director explained in *Three Sides of the Mersey*, a book co-authored by Andrew Ward, son of Tim Ward, the former Rams player and manager. Saunders said, "What it's been about is good players being allowed to express themselves. I can't recall a time here when players have been looking towards the bench for advice for what should happen next. Those kind of players have never been here. It's a decision-making game and you want men who can assume responsibility and make decisions on the pitch while the game's going on."

At Newcastle, the Rams were completely the opposite.

Once again, poor goalkeeping was a desperate handicap. Russell Hoult, back in the team because new-signing Mart Poom was injured, had a nightmare game. He palmed a corner into his own net to gift Newcastle an equaliser in the first half and then completely missed a 25-yard drive from Shearer, which made the score 3-1. When Asprilla was substituted late in the second half, the whole stadium rose as one to applauded. It was a marvellous moment. The sound was deafening. The Rams did well not to capitulate after that.

Kenny Dalglish gave his usual after- the- match press conference. Short, sharp, enigmatic. The consensus press view is that Dalglish will produce a more cautious team than Keegan, but it's interesting that Asprilla has figured more in recent matches than he did in Keegan's later period.

The talk around Newcastle at the moment is that Sir John Hall is anxious for the club to move to a new stadium a few hundred yards north of St James' Park. The rationale is that the present stadium, which holds 36,610, is not big enough and planning permission will not be granted to extend it. There has long been a problem between the club and the City Council about development, because the freehold of the ground is held by the City Council, not the club. Despite the fact that future season ticket holders will have to guarantee their ticket by buying a ten-year bond for £500, there is a waiting list of 12,000. On match days, pubs in Newcastle pay the club to screen the game and 1,000 fans watch at a cinema nearby. There's no doubting the current enthusiasm in 'Geordie Land'.

There used to be a time when football clubs played at 'football grounds'. Now they play at stadiums. Synonymous with 'stadium' are words like arena, amphitheatre, coliseum, bowl, dome and hippodrome. All have showbusiness connotations. Giles Smith wrote a warning article in the *Daily Telegraph* about AFC Ajax's new home, the Amsterdam Arena, which has a sliding roof and underground parking.

> Financed by the city of Amsterdam and a consortium *[that word again]* of shareholders including the club, the Arena was built with Tina Turner concerts and football equally in mind. So not for Ajax the tragic Tannoy of football ground legend, with its pre-war wiring and coffee-tin speakers, in whose random buzz you might quite legitimately be unable to distinguish between the fire alarm and the new single from the Spice Girls. The Arena's PA is made to shock and turned up to where the bass frequency pummel your chest.

> But above all, "the most advanced football stadium in the world" means a night out which is, for better or worse, only dimly recognisable as the experience of going to a football match. Odd to sit there on Wednesday in the Arena's strangely still air (even with the roof open) watching two teams who represent the cream of European football — and feeling as if one was in America.

> It wasn't just the hot dog and coke stalls holding an exclusive franchise on the concourse, although that helped. It was more the relentless packaging wrapped round every aspect of the night, and which in the end began to look like bad faith; as if you could not be trusted to find the game alone entertaining enough.

Smith goes on to say how many supporters of Ajax have reservations about all the shiny glitter and glitz. The old stadium, the De Meer has been pulled down, *but as a fan told me,* "it was personal. It had atmosphere and history". About the Arena, they were less convinced from a footballing point of view.

"The players feel nervous there," one said of the team, who have done all their best work away in Europe this season away from home. "It's beautiful, but it's cold, it's too big and there's too much money involved."

Ajax's lavish youth complex is called 'the Future'. Youngsters are coached from the age of eight, but Ajax have always had difficulty in holding on to players and with the Bosman ruling that will increase. Patrick Kluivert is on his way to Italy, the coach Louis van Gaal is moving too. Only eight players remain of the 17 who won the European Champions Cup in 1995.

The speculation which leads to football clubs playing in arenas is predicted on boom. Its response to downtime has yet to be adequately tested. That, one suspects, will become the football issue of our age, not just in Amsterdam, but all over. How can there be a transitional period when your roof costs £5,000 to switch on and the shareholders are watching from their boxes? And how long before football has to hand back the keys to Tina Turner?

Is Newcastle United about to travel that road?

Team: Hoult; Laursen, C.Powell (sub D. Powell), Rowett, Dailly, McGrath, Van der Laan (sub Solis), Trollope, Asanovic, Sturridge, Ward (sub Wanchope)
Scorer: Sturridge
Attendance: 36,553

Wednesday, 23rd April 1997:
Derby County 0 Nottingham Forest 0
Not a match to remember.

GEORDIE FORTRESS

Friday, 4th May 1997:

The announcement came that Paul McGrath is to leave Derby County in the summer. There have been rumblings for weeks about what might, or not happen and the signs were not promising for McGrath. Now the decision is taken.

"He was was as good a signing as I've ever made and did a fantastic job for Derby," said Jim Smith.

It has been a real pleasure to watch McGrath play this season. There's no substitute for class and McGrath had that in plenty. Without his contribution the Rams would certainly have not survived. He has played more matches than Igor Stimac.

"As I've said before, this decision has nothing to do with Paul's ability. He'll be 38 next season and his injuries will not improve," said Smith.

What has changed since McGrath came in October is the emergence of Christian Dailly as a promising central defender and the likelihood that Jacob Laursen will also play in central defence, a position he occupies for Denmark. Dean Yates, Gary Rowett, Matt Carbon and Stimac are the other central defensive candidates and all have more experience of Premiership football than they had when McGrath arrived to provide it. Furthermore, with McGrath's peculiar training regime, it must be difficult to involve him in certain collective training situations, upon which coaches and managers rely. Some players are difficult to assimilate into a team pattern, because they are loose cannons on the field. With McGrath, it could be the other way round. Then again, he is Irish.

Sky Blues Forever

Saturday, 3rd May 1997 — Highfield Road

I N THE WEEK of the General Election, the final journey of this eventful season sent us to Coventry. Winston Churchill once said of his political opponent: "Mr Attlee is a modest man, but then he has much to be modest about." That is unfair on Attlee, but the sentiment could apply to Coventry City. Going to Coventry is hardly a journey to one of the traditional hotbeds of English football, yet apart from Liverpool, Everton and Arsenal, Coventry City is a club that has stayed longer in the top flight of English football than any other. They were promoted in 1967 — and they've had their moments.

One came in 1987. Under joint managers John Sillett and George Curtis, they won the FA Cup, by beating Tottenham Hotspur 3-2 in extra-time and the celebrations seemed to last for years. It's the only time they have won the trophy. That year, 1987, is also the only time that Coventry City have been in the Final, or, indeed, the semi-final, while the limit of their League Cup success is two semi-final appearances and they have never finished higher than sixth in the top division of football. That position did qualify them to play in Europe, in the UEFA Cup, but they lost 6–1 in the second round to Bayern Munich (away) and although they won the home leg 2–1, it wasn't a campaign that set the country agog. No. To claim that the trophy cabinet at Highfield Road is full to overflowing, is being economical with the truth.

It's at the other end of the table that Coventry City have constantly caught the eye. Long-serving supporters of the Sky Blues must have either nerves of steel, or nerves with frayed endings, as they have witnessed many relegation battles. Whatever the system of relegation — one team, two teams, three teams, Play-offs — and whatever the size of the division, Coventry City invariably get involved. Modest the achievements of Coventry City may be, but supporters have had some exciting times.

Perhaps the most exciting times came in the mid-1960s when Coventry City were climbing from the old Third Division to the First, under the dynamic leadership of BBC pundit, Jimmy Hill. He was appointed manager of the club in 1961 and that's when the Sky Blues were born. Away went the old blue and white stripes, in came sky blue. Not only for the strip, but for the whole of the club. Sky Blue was Coventry City.

A new Sky Blue Stand was built on the Highfield Road ground that the club has occupied since 1899. It featured new plastic moulded seats — sky blue, of course. Radio Sky Blue took to the airwaves, Sky Blue Travel booked supporters' holidays and an executive Sky Blue Train transported them to away matches. There was pre-match razzamataz, half-time entertainment and the first electronic scoreboard installed on any football ground. In 1965, close-circuit television relayed pictures of a match at Ninian Park, Cardiff, back to Highfield Road, an innovation that nearly failed because of fog. Luckily Hill's magic touch didn't desert him and at kick-off time, there was a 'gate' of over 10,000 to watch the 'Sky Blues' go on to win 2–1. Does all this sound familiar? It does now, but more than 30 years ago, it was something special. In September 1964, incidentally, a crowd of 38,278 saw the Rams beat Coventry

2-0 at Highfield Road in the old Second Division with goals from Alan Durban and Eddie Thomas.

Of course, the Sky Blue revolution could not have succeeded without success on the field. There may have been plenty of frills off the field, but on it, Hill's teams were hard working and functional. George Curtis, Dietmar Bruck, George Hudson, Ernie Machin were not to be tangled with lightly and they did the job. The complete package added up to something that lit a spark in the football world, as 51,455 people crowded into Highfield Road to watch Coventry City play Wolves in the Second Division championship deciding match of 1967. The Sky Blues became champions and were promoted to the First Division, but the bubble was about to burst. Two days before the new season was scheduled to begin, Jimmy Hill resigned, to take up a job in television and the skies over Coventry City have never been quite so blue since. Now the shirts are striped — black and blue — and the Sky Blues are on the edge of relegation, once again. On 3rd May 1997, exactly 30 years since the Bantams, as they used to be known, reached the top division, the lower half of the Premiership table looked like this:.

	P	W	D	L	F	A	Pts
Derby County	**36**	**10**	**10**	**13**	**42**	**54**	**43**
Everton	36	10	12	14	43	52	42
Blackburn Rovers	35	9	14	12	40	37	41
Leicester City	35	10	10	15	39	50	40
Southampton	36	9	11	16	48	55	38
West Ham United	35	9	11	15	34	46	38
Coventry City	36	8	14	14	35	51	38
Sunderland	36	9	10	17	32	52	37
Middlesbrough	34	9	9	16	44	54	33
Nottingham Forest	36	6	15	15	30	53	33

If Coventry City had a problem, so had we. Election fever had overtaken Colin Gibson. He had lost his voice, which for a broadcaster is quite a handicap. On the morning of the match, he failed a late fitness test and it was decided that Pam Steele should travel to Highfield Road to act as Colin's 'voice'. Pam is in the second year of a communications degree course at Trent University and is learning the business. BBC Radio Derby has a very good record of encouraging young talent and Pam may well go on to scale the heights in the broadcasting world. Also on the trip is Kelly Smith, who is taking 'A' levels and hopes to go on to university to do a similar course. She has been on work experience assignments at the studios and has not been to an away match before, so this is a special event for her. Graham Richards is going direct to the ground.

Twenty years ago, I worked for a year at Coventry City. Jimmy Hill had returned to the club, as chairman, in 1975 and, after retiring from first-class cricket in 1972 and spending three years at Birmingham University and a year at Loughborough, I was looking for a job.

The advertisement was for 'A Coordinator of Enterprise Sky Blue, an experimental project involving the Duke of Edinburgh's Award Scheme and Coventry City Football Club'. The driving force behind the project was a remarkable man called Alick Dick, who among other things had been managing director of Standard Triumph, before that company became British Leyland. He was also a trustee of the Duke of Edinburgh's Award, a season ticket holder at Coventry City and had a connection with Sidney Stringer College, which was an inner-city comprehensive school near Highfield Road.

Alick Dick had the idea that perhaps some young people who would not normally be interested in the Duke of Edinburgh's Award, might become so if football was involved, particularly football at Coventry City. Hill and Eddie Plumley, the secretary at Coventry City, who later went to Watford to be chief executive in their spectacular rise up the football ladder, were very interested in any sort of community involvement, which had been the hallmark of the Sky Blue surge in the 1960s. After leaving full-time professional football in 1968, I had worked in the youth service for four years during the winter months, while still playing cricket in the summer and so when 'Enterprise Sky Blue' was launched, it had a committee of Coventry businessmen, a lot of support from Jimmy Hill, Eddie Plumley and Coventry City, a charismatic headmaster of Sidney Stringer College called Arfon Jones, a blank sheet of paper and me. After a year I left 'Enterprise Sky Blue' because it really needed someone to live nearer the action and Coventry was never going to be home for me. Later, David Moorcroft, the Olympic athlete, who was from Coventry, took the project on further.

What was a particularly feature of that period was the friendliness and understanding of the people at Coventry City, but when we arrived at Highfield Road this time, things had changed. The welcome was hard and impersonal. With Colin croaking away, we attempted to convince the Coventry administration that Pam Steele's presence was essential, if we were to do a five-hour *Sportscene* programme. We explained that if Colin had not lost his voice, Pam would not be there and, although Kelly should, perhaps, not have come in the circumstances, the problem was a genuine one. It was of no avail. We were informed that 16-year-old Kelly would be escorted from the ground by stewards, presumably in jack boots, if she was seen anywhere in the vicinity of the press box, or in the stadium. I wonder where all the goodwill went to?

Thanks to Derby County, Kelly did manage to get a ticket to sit with the Rams supporters on the other side of the ground, which defeated the purpose of her coming, but prevented her being banished to the streets outside. The following week I spoke to someone who was the recipient of complimentary hospitality in the Coventry City Executive Club. He had a fine lunch and watched the match from the comfort and spaciousness of a private box. Kelly Smith will not forget her visit to Highfield Road and I will try to remember better times at Coventry City.

If Coventry City were as unforgiving on the field as they are off it, they would not be in danger of going down to the First Division. The goals the Rams scored were gifts. The first from Gary Rowett was from a free-kick out near the left touchline that took a slight deflection off Gary McAllister's head on its way into the net: 1-0. The second was a kick down the field by Mart Poom that bounced through after a slight touch from Ashley Ward, and Dean Sturridge lobbed goalkeeper Steve Ogrizovic: 2-1. This is Sturridge's 11th goal of the season in the Premiership and, in the last month, he has begun to look more like a Premiership player. The hardest job in football is putting the ball in the net, which is why goalscorers are valued so highly. It's important, however, to distinguish between goals — and goals. Some goals have a higher value than others. League goals are the ones that really matter. No-one denies that Fabrizio Ravanelli scores goals, but many of them have been in cup ties and only three of his Premiership goals have been scored away from The Riverside. Several of those scored at home have been later goals, in matches that Middlesbrough have won handsomely. What is more important than the total number of goals an individual player scores, is having someone who scores in a high proportion of matches in which he plays. Coventry City's goal in this match came from a penalty, when Christian Dailly climbed on the back of Dion Dublin, but despite Coventry pressure in the second half, the Rams always looked to be in control.

Derby County's foreign contingent in this match was somewhat reduced. No Igor Stimac, no Paulo Wanchop, no Mauricio Solis, and Aljosa Asanovic 'rested'. The Rams line-up looked a little plain on the teamsheet, but the performance was encouraging. In fact the side looked better balanced on the field, with Ward having his best game for a considerable time and Dailly, Rowett and Jacob Laursen forming a solid unit at the back against the aerial power of Dublin. In the second half, Dean Yates returned to first-team football after his long lay-off since the Wimbledon match in early January. If only Yates could stay fit. He really is a good defender.

The Highfield Road ground has improved enormously. Now it

is a tidy, compact stadium and the open-end Kop has been replaced by a splendid East Stand. It is at that end where in 1964, Coventry City installed one of the first electronic scoreboards. Jimmy Hill took advantage of it in a season in the mid-1970s when the Sky Blues were engaged in their annual fight against relegation. Bristol City were also involved in avoiding the drop and in the final match of the season at Highfield Road, the evening kick-off between the two teams was delayed because of crowd congestion. Other relegation candidates were playing that night and their matches finished on time, but at Highfield Road there was still time to play. Hill ordered the results to be posted on the scoreboard, which showed that a draw would be sufficient to keep both teams in the First Division. The last five minutes saw the ball being played exclusively around the centre circle, as players were terrified of going near each other's penalty-area. Hill was reprimanded by the FA and now the authorities are meticulous in ensuring that the final round of matches take place on the same day and kick-off simultaneously, hence the Rams' final match of this season, against Arsenal at the Baseball Ground, begins at 4.00pm along with every one else's because a couple will be televised.

Once again, the Rams travelling support was tremendous. Throughout this season, people have spent hundred of pounds following Derby County away from home. During last season, a chap approached me at the County Ground, Northampton, where Derbyshire were playing the home side in a County Championship match. It was when negotiations were taking place between Derby County and BBC Radio Derby about the contract for commentary rights for the Rams in the Premiership. "Don't forget the fans on the motorway," he said. "We travel up and down the M1 every week. There are a lot of us who meet at the various services and discuss the match preview and after-the-match reactions and would miss the coverage dreadfully if it were not on the radio. It keeps us in touch with the Rams and makes us feel part of it."

From Southampton in the south to Newcastle in the north,

Rams travelling fans were there, making their presence felt. The pitch is sometimes a hostile place and there's nothing like having support in enemy territory.

This result is a grievous blow to Coventry City. They have spent around £20 million. in buying a lot of players, but they still haven't got a team. The other results have gone against them and chairman Bryan Richardson looked a forlorn figure afterwards, as he was interviewed in the directors' box by Tony Francis for Central Television. Further along in the Main Stand, the Rams players could afford to relax in the knowledge of a job well done. Now the Sky Blues have to win against Tottenham Hotspur at White Hart Lane next Saturday — and then hope. It's rather ironic that Coventry City may go out of the Premiership at the very ground where the Rams and this 'Journey through a Season' began.

Team: Poom; Carsley (sub Yates), C. Powell, Laursen, Rowett, Dailly, Van der Laan (sub Willems), Trollope, D. Powell: Sturridge, Ward.
Scorers: Rowett, Sturridge.
Attendance: 22,839

Moving On

14th September 1895 — The Baseball Ground
Derby County 2 Sunderland 0

IN many ways, the Baseball Ground is like old slippers. Well worn, a hole or two in the soles, tatty round the edges, but snug and reliable. You know where you are with old slippers. You are loath to change to new ones, but eventually, you have to. So it is with the Baseball Ground. In the image conscious world of the financially crazy Premiership, the traditional footballing values projected by the Baseball Ground are deemed to be no longer sufficient for the job. A new football ground, like new slippers, is needed.

Arsenal are today's visitors for the final senior competitive match to be staged at the Baseball Ground. Appropriate really, for historically, Arsenal are the most famous club in England and the 'old lady' deserves the best. She has done her best for the Rams this momentous season, for it is the home form that has enabled the team to survive in the Premiership. Since Christmas, Jim Smith and most supporters have put their faith in the home form in order to avoid relegation. Rightly, they believed that the old Baseball Ground would not let them down — and it didn't. Just when most needed, the home victories against Leicester City and Tottenham Hotspur revived flagging fortunes in the early and latter parts of the season. The Chelsea victory was vital. A home win against Aston Villa virtually sealed the issue. The Rams were safe, almost.

"Wait until we get you at our place," was a favoured remark to an opponent, when things weren't going too well in an away match a long way from home. It carried an extra threat when the Baseball Ground was the 'our place' in question. Millwall players were always happy to make that sort of remark when referring to The Den, but it probably doesn't carry the same discouraging implication now, despite the Rams Play-off experiences at The New Den.

The Rams will not be able to rely on the Baseball Ground for that little bit extra next season. In effect, the team will be playing 'away' in the Premiership every week, until the new ground and supporters get to know each other. They've had more than 100 years to get to know each other at the Baseball Ground, every nook and every cranny.

My first acquaintance with the Baseball Ground came via a cold shower down the back of the neck in 1954. We were inspecting the dressing-rooms, prior to playing a 'junior' (under-14) schoolboy international match against Northern Ireland the following day and had done some light training at the Royal School for the Deaf ground on Ashbourne Road. Our team manager insisted that we had a cold shower after a hot bath. "Closes the pores," he said. I was also intrigued by the notice high above the mirror in the dressing-room which said, 'The biggest crime in football is giving the ball to the opposition.' I wonder if it's still there.

What will not be there is the glass of water that used to stand on the ledge beside the door. The glass had a strip of Elastoplast stuck to the side and on it the word 'Les' was written. As we lined up to go out, with Harry Storer trying to see whether Barrie Hutchinson was wearing 'rubbers' when everyone else was in 'studs', the referee's bell would ring, at which signal, our big raw-boned centre-half, Les Moore, would yank the front teeth out of his mouth and deposit them in the glass. "Remember the wife and kids," he would announce and then he'd go and kick spots off the opposing centre-forward. Incidentally, the teeth were false.

There were some parts of the Baseball Ground that I never really knew, like the visitors' dressing-room. Juniors and apprentices changed there during the week and the heating was always turned off on Thursday lunch times. That was so that the visiting team didn't become too comfortable before kick-off time on Saturday. There were always profuse apologies from the administrative staff, about water shortages and the lack of decent plumbers, but in January it was like an ice box.

Memories, memories. Where the office is now, there used to be a small gymnasium. Upstairs was a snooker room where Albert Mays used to take on all-comers. He was one of the best snooker players in Derbyshire. On the mat, he wasn't so good. The mat was where he sat to guard the goal in the 'crab football' matches we played on Friday mornings after training. Goalkeepers weren't allowed to handle the ball if they came off the mat, but Albert always fancied himself as a sort of sweeper. The game was quite dangerous , especially for a Friday, and trainer Ralph Hann hated us playing. Harry Storer tried to ban it, unsuccessfully: an apprentice was always stationed at the bottom of the steps leading to the passage from the manager's office. One day, Albert got very bold, came off his mat and kicked the wall bars instead the ball. He didn't dare tell Storer, or Ralph. He played the next day. X-rays taken the following week showed that he had broken a bone in his foot. Laugh? Albert nearly cried.

When many older people think of the Baseball Ground, they think of the pitch. So they should. It's the most important part. Did it used to be heavy? Indeed it did, very heavy. In a League Cup tie against Norwich City, Matt Crowe took a penalty for the Canaries at the Normanton End. He struck the ball along the floor, which was a serious mistake. Terry Adlington, playing a rare game in goal because Ken Oxford was injured, walked out and picked it up. The ball pulled up as though it was on elastic. That was the end where Joe Corrigan 'lost' the penalty spot.

The mind's eye sees different things for different people: Real Madrid; 'King' Kevin; the Chelsea match; Steve Powell's debut; Sammy Crooks and dancing feet; Benfica and Juventus; Rotherham United; the Offilers' Ales sign; Tommy Powell; Boston United; Roy 'Mac' and that wonderful standing jump; smoke from Ley's chimney; Archie's scuttling run; Shilton clapping and nodding; Plymouth Argyle; 'Raich', 'Peter' and Jackie Stamps; mud, mud, mud; flat caps and overcoats; Hoppy's goal; Bobby Davison, darting in; the 'Tin Man'; two championship teams and floodlit nights; Albert Mays' back pass; Dave Mackay running out — you couldn't lose; Gentile; Eusebio; Crystal Palace; Brian Clough and more and more…

My personal preference has always been for the development of a 'new' Baseball Ground on the existing site, as outlined in the original plans. This journey through a season has confirmed that opinion. Most of the clubs in the Premiership have carried out the requirements of the Taylor Report in that way and in so doing have retained the familiarity of feeling for supporters of 'going to the match'. Part of going to the match is getting there. Now supporters will be getting somewhere else. To Pride Park. The die is cast and it is accepted, but it will all take time. A new football culture is developing in this country, controlled by commercialism and showbusiness packaging, and new stadiums will hurry that process, whatever happens, it will take a long time to create an atmosphere as unique as that at the Baseball Ground.

In time, the Baseball Ground will be only a memory, but memories are what dreams are made of. The new stadium awaits. The old ground may eventually be covered with housing, or industrial units, or, like at Leeds Road, Huddersfield, a supermarket, but whatever becomes of it, the Baseball Ground has a special niche in football history. For those who worked, watched and for some who played, the Baseball Ground, like old slippers, has given us great comfort.

Final Score: 11th May 1997 — The Baseball Ground: Derby County 1 Arsenal 3.

Reflections

"ANYTHING above relegation was regarded as a complete success, in August. To finish ninth, or tenth, was beyond the wildest dreams and a marvellous launching pad for a new season, on a new ground. It's far better than we expected. I think it's the best season of the 20 that I've commentated on, on BBC Radio Derby. The occasions have been more grand, the back-up staff and Colin, Ian, Eric, on top of their form and the matches hugely enjoyable, largely because of foreign imports and famous situations. Though we've had more successful seasons — I've seen two championships won and a promotion — I would put down the season just finishing, 1996-97, as the most enjoyable I've ever had on local radio." — *Graham Richards.*

"Job achieved. 40 points was the target. 46 gained. Delighted for squad, management and directors alike." — *Eric Steele.*

"Well. Certainly one of the most enjoyable since I've been watching Derby County and that's since 1977. Who'd have thought that three years ago, the end of the Cox and McFarland era, that we'd be playing at grounds like Old Trafford again and Anfield and holding our own in the majority of those games. That's probably the single most pleasurable moment this season, standing in front of all those Derby County fans at Old Trafford at quarter to five, with the scoreboard recording a 3-2 victory. Absolutely an incredible moment." — *Phil Mugford.*

"Denis Bergkamp ran past me, about a yard away, for the final match against Arsenal. Who would have thought that two years ago we would have seen him playing at the Baseball Ground. Also, great credit is due to the directors and staff, for the decisions to take Derby County forward to enable them to compete at the financial levels required in the Premiership. The high points? For me, the draw at Highbury and, of course, the win at Manchester United. Yes. We're all looking forward to next season and the new ground." — *Colin Gibson.*

There is no doubt that the glitz and glamour of the Premiership, aided and abetted by television, is very seductive. The colour within the grounds is something we haven't ever seen before. Huge blocks of black and white at St James's Park, bright red at Old Trafford, Anfield and Highbury, royal blue at Goodison Park, lit up the Premiership stadiums as brightly as the brilliant floodlights. Most of the pitches, too, are emerald green. The dull, sepia, brown and grey that dominated the terraces pre–Taylor Report is gone. Of course, standing on an open terrace in pouring rain was never an environment for wearing a frothy, stylishly cut fashion number in January. If all-seater stadiums have been a boon to replica shirt manufacturers and commercial income, they've sounded the death knell for flat caps and big boots.

When I began this journey through a season, I did so believing that football was about going to the match, watching the teams play, reading about it in the newspapers, listening to it on radio, or watching it on television. Football was about football. I felt that most people who went to football matches looked at in that way. Now I know different. 'Going to the match' has taken on a different meaning. It is a different experience for a 'new' audience. Premiership football exists for more than the game. The match has become 'an event', an amalgam of commercial opportunity and show-business, with ridiculous animals and painted faces and relentless disc jockey announcers, screaming absurdities and pounding the senses. Football is becoming a side issue to the main 'event', as marketing executives threaten to take over the sporting world.

Programmes are different, too. They used to show the teams in playing order and programme collectors knew who played when and where. The programme told us so. In future years, how will we know who played for Derby County in the 'Theatre of Dreams'? Now, the programme tells us everything and it tells us nothing. It should inform you of the team, instead it is about the sale of replica shorts. "Only £4.99 madam." Like many of the trappings of Premiership football, there is more and more about less and less.

What of the football? I once remember Raich Carter saying that it is possible to watch a good game of football at any level, providing the teams are well matched. All the experts agree that the Premiership is the tightest league around and all the teams can beat each other. It makes for exciting matches, but as Lester Piggott was fond of saying, when he got off the winner following a blanket photo finish: "They can't all be good horses." So it is in the much-hyped Premiership and much of the football reflected that. Once the package was opened, the goods were, too often, disappointing.

Yet, for Rams supporters it has been a memorable journey, this journey through a season. What measures of emotion have been experienced. We had hope, in the warm days of summer, when we set out to White Hart Lane in August. Relief in autumn, when the first win of the season was registered at Ewood Park and the early weeks were safely negotiated. Ironic, I suppose, that the first and the last wins of the season were recorded on the road. As the cold winds of winter began to bite, there was frustration in the result at Highbury and despair at the performances at The Dell and Roker Park.

Then came the FA Cup and not one, but two visits to the quaint Priestfield Stadium. Was that when the Rams reasserted themselves, gained confidence, restored Robbie van der Laan to the team, then Paul Trollope, against Villa — and prospered? There were frowns of anguish on the brows of supporters after Filbert Street, The Riverside and Goodison Park. Nerves were beginning to tingle as the shadow of relegation drifted close behind. "Don't look over your shoulder, young man," I hear a voice. "Have faith and confidence." But the prayer mats were out and it looked a bit dodgy. Yet magical moments were just around the corner. They came on a damp Saturday in spring, when the 'Theatre of Dreams' became a cacophony of black and white sound, swirling round the stands and provided enough stories to keep grandchildren entranced for years. "Were you really there, grandad, when Paulo Wanchope scored that marvellous goal?"

In the end, the Rams owed survival largely to what happened at home, at the much- loved Baseball Ground. The away results did matter, though, and for those intrepid Rams supporters, including the BBC Radio Derby commentary team, who travelled the roads of footballing England, the journey was wonderfully worthwhile.

FA PREMIER LEAGUE

	P	W	D	L	F	A	W	D	L	F	A	Pts
Manchester U	38	12	5	2	38	17	9	7	3	38	27	75
Newcastle U	38	13	3	3	54	20	6	8	5	19	20	68
Arsenal	38	10	5	4	36	18	9	6	4	26	14	68
Liverpool	38	10	6	3	38	19	9	5	5	24	18	68
Aston Villa	38	11	5	3	27	13	6	5	8	20	21	61
Chelsea	38	9	8	2	33	22	7	3	9	25	33	59
Sheffield W	38	8	10	1	25	16	6	5	8	25	35	57
Wimbledon	38	9	6	4	28	21	6	5	8	21	25	56
Leicester C	38	7	5	7	22	26	5	6	8	24	28	47
Tottenham H	38	8	4	7	19	17	5	3	11	25	34	46
Leeds U	38	7	7	5	15	13	4	6	9	13	25	46
Derby C	**38**	**8**	**6**	**5**	**25**	**22**	**3**	**7**	**9**	**20**	**36**	**46**
Blackburn R	38	8	4	7	28	23	1	11	7	14	20	42
West Ham U	38	7	6	6	27	25	3	6	10	12	23	42
Everton	38	7	4	8	24	22	3	8	8	20	35	42
Southampton	38	6	7	6	32	24	4	4	11	18	32	41
Coventry C	38	4	8	7	19	23	5	6	8	19	31	41
Sunderland	38	7	6	6	20	18	3	4	12	15	35	40
Middlesbrough	38	8	5	6	34	25	2	7	10	17	35	*39
Nottingham F	38	3	9	7	15	27	3	7	9	16	32	34

* Middlesbrough deducted 3 points

Bibliography

Dunphy, Eamon, *A Strange Kind of Glory*, Heinmann, 1991.

Inglis, S., *Football Grounds of Britain*, Collins Willow, Third Edition 1996.

Kelly, S. ed, *The Kingswood Book of Football*, Kingswood Press, 1992.

Mortimer, G, *Derby County A Compete Record 1884-1988*, Breedon Books, 1988.

Taylor, Rogan & Ward, Andrew, *Three Sides of the Mersey*, Robson Books, 1993.

Walvin, J., *The People's Game*, Mainstream Publishing, 1994.

Index